Gary
Rhodes
cookery year

spring into summer

To my family

Jennie, Samuel and George, who all
bring spring and summer thoughts
to my mind. With love.

This book is published to accompany the
television series entitled *Gary Rhodes
Cookery Year* first broadcast on BBC2
in 2002.

Executive producer: Nick Vaughan-Barratt
Series producer: Siobhan Mulholland

Published by BBC Worldwide Ltd,
Woodlands, 80 Wood Lane,
London W12 0TT

First published 2002
Reprinted 2002
First published in paperback 2005
Reprinted 2005
Text copyright © Gary Rhodes 2002
The moral right of the author has been
asserted

Photographs by Sîan Irvine copyright
© BBC Worldwide Ltd 2002

ISBN 0 563 52245 3

Commissioning Editor: Nicky Copeland
Project Editors: Charlotte Lochhead and
Khadija Manjlai
Copy Editor: Lewis Esson
Art Director: Lisa Pettibone
Designer: Andrew Barron @ Thextension
Food prepared for photography
by Gary Rhodes
Food Economists: Jo Pratt and
Wayne Tapsfield
Stylist: Bo Chapman

Typeset in Century ITC and Gothic 720
Printed and bound in Great Britain by
CPI Bath
Colour separations by
Radstock Reproductions Ltd,
Midsomer Norton

Photographs page 1: *Asparagus on
buttery toast with melting Parmesan
cheese* (page 30);
page 2 left: *Mustard-brushed flounder
with steamed leek greens* (page 42);
right: *Cointreau champagne raspberries*
(page 172);
page 3: *Grilled chicken with a
warm bacon and broad bean salad*
(page 136)

Acknowledgements

Assembling these recipes has been
nothing but a pleasure, discovering
the best of British produce, and more,
that joins us through the seasons.
Finding and enjoying all these
flavours would not have been possible
without the help of the following, to
whom I pass on my warmest thanks:
Wayne Tapsfield, Lissanne Kenyon,
all Rhodes' restaurant teams, Rick
Stein, Sîan Irvine, Jo Pratt, Sharon
Hearne, Nicky Copeland, Charlotte
Lochhead, Andrew Barron, Nick
Vaughan-Barratt, Siobhan Mulholland,
Claire Popplewell, Borra Garson
and Lynda Seaton (*Fresh Produce Journal*).

spring into summer

contents

summer meat **136**

summer fruit and puddings **154**

Basics 175

Putting this book together has been a new experience for me. But it's not because it contains a host of new recipes, it's that my mind was opened to a sense of seasonality I hadn't consciously thought about for a long time. When cooking in a professional kitchen (still one of my greatest pleasures), I am provided every day with an almost unlimited supply of foods from around the world. With virtually anything you need or want to hand, you can lose sight of the joys closer to home.

At one time we had to rely on the seasons, making do with whatever produce was available at that particular time of the year, but growth of international trade and transport has changed all that and many ingredients are now available out of season. Although strawberries grown in more southerly climates can be sweet and juicy, and enliven a winter dinner table, I'd still rather wait to celebrate the uniquely delicious British strawberries in summer. Another change is that over the years we've become familiar with a huge variety of ingredients that we've absorbed into our food culture; summer was once the berry and cherry season, but today we anticipate and expect the glories of imported apricots, nectarines and peaches, too. These imports, many of them too good to ignore, in no sense supplant or replace our home-grown foods, but rather enrich what is available to us to buy, cook and eat.

I am all for finding new flavours – I shall never tire of the search and I say a big thank you to all our overseas suppliers – but let's not forget that here in our own country we can, and will continue to, produce some of the finest foods in the world. So, with this in mind, writing a seasonal book seemed to be the way ahead.

My cookery year starts with the most colourful of the seasons, with spring and summer. Autumn and winter will follow soon, in the next book. *Spring into Summer* has a section devoted to each season and, as you'll see, some ingredients cross over both seasons. Just because a recipe appears in one section doesn't mean you can't cook it at any other time of the year if you can get the ingredients, it's simply that for maximum flavour it is best to follow the seasons. Within each section I've divided the recipes into vegetables, fish, meat and fruit. Sometimes the lead ingredient is the seasonal one, sometimes it's the accompaniment but, either way, whatever's seasonal has been colour coded to highlight it.

I hope the following pages will inspire you with new ideas for making the best of what's in season. There are lots of good, fresh flavours to play with in spring, and don't forget that the last of the winter favourites are still with us at this time, too. Summer offers us a positive wealth of ingredients as the land and sea abound with produce, as do the shelves of supermarkets and food shops. There is an abundant supply of the 'Best of British' produce, and it should all be taken full advantage of.

I also hope you'll appreciate the softer and lighter approach in the recipes, with one or two touches of extra depth and zest. I've kept as close to our own British produce as possible, but have chosen not to deprive us of a selection of 'in season' imports. The real purpose of these pages is not to dictate a strict seasonal list of ingredients, it's really to provide you with a new culinary road to travel down as you consider the flavours and bounty of the British seasons and all they have to offer.

Before you set to work on the recipes in this book, here are a few tips and guidelines that will help you achieve the best possible results.

Ingredients

Butter Unsalted butter is mostly used because it gives greater control over the seasoning of a dish.

Egg sizes All eggs used are large, unless otherwise stated.

Groundnut oil This particular oil is a product sourced from peanuts. As an alternative, vegetable oil can be used.

Herbs All herbs are fresh. All soft herbs, such as tarragon, flatleaf parsley and basil, are best torn by hand to prevent them bruising and breaking the texture. If you replace fresh herbs with dried, remember to use only half the amount specified.

Instant sauces and stocks There are a number of sauce and stock recipes included in the book (with a quick *Instant stock* recipe on page 175), but there are also many good bought alternatives (carton, fresh, dried or cubed) available in supermarkets.

Seasoning Or 'season' simply means seasoning with salt and pepper – preferably freshly ground white pepper, unless otherwise stated.

Vinegars I use a selection of vinegars in this book. Red wine vinegar is a favourite. Because many of those available are thin and not very red-wine-flavoured, I urge you to spend a little more and buy a vinegar that bears the hallmark of a good wine – a Bordeaux, say, or my current favourite, Cabernet Sauvignon. If balsamic vinegar is a personal favourite, the older it is, the thicker and better the flavour.

Techniques and guidelines

Cooking green vegetables All green vegetables can be cooked at the last minute. However, with many other things happening on the stove, it can become overcrowded. Pre-cooking vegetables gives you time to ensure that they are perfectly tender and full of flavour.

To reheat them, most green vegetables can simply be dropped into simmering water for 30 seconds to a minute, then drained and seasoned. Cabbages, greens, spinach and other leafy vegetables are best rewarmed with a knob of butter and just a few tablespoons of water – the water creates steam. Dropping leafed vegetables in a large saucepan of water to reheat them will only spoil their texture. A modern choice is to microwave. This is a very successful route to take, particularly for all leafed vegetables and broccoli. If microwaving them, once they have been cooked and refreshed in iced water, the vegetables can be drained, seasoned and buttered, before microwaving and serving.

There are a few golden rules that should never be broken when cooking green vegetables. Always use a large saucepan up to three-quarters full of boiling salted water and never use a lid at any time during the cooking; even when the water has boiled and the vegetables are cooking. This guarantees that the rich colour is kept. One more small point – try not to cook too many green vegetables at once. If you do, the water temperature decreases and then takes too long to return to boiling point, which often results in the loss of colour.

Once cooked, drain immediately, seasoning and buttering before serving. If cooking in advance, drain the vegetables and plunge into iced water. This stops the cooking process and preserves the flavour and colour of the vegetables. It is also important not to leave the vegetables sitting too long in the iced water, after a period of time they will absorb it, becoming watery. So once cold, drain immediately and refrigerate until needed.

Measurements Follow one of the measurements only; do not mix metric and imperial. All spoon measurements are level unless otherwise stated.

- a tablespoon is 15g (½oz) for solids and 15ml (½fl oz) for liquids
- a dessertspoon is 10g for solids and 10ml for liquids
- a teaspoon is 5g for solids and 5ml for liquids

Oven temperatures Be aware that if you are using a fan-assisted oven the temperatures may need to be adjusted and lowered to your oven manufacturer's recommendations.

Removing pin bones from fish Fine pin bones are found in round fish fillets, that is red mullet, trout, salmon, cod and so on. The bones run down the centre of most of these fillets and are easily removed with fine pliers or tweezers. It's worth spending the time needed to remove them, as the fish then becomes more comfortable to eat.

Sterilizing jars It is important to ensure that any jars to be used for jams etc., are sterilized. First wash the jars in soapy water and rinse well. Place in a large saucepan, cover with water and bring to the boil. Cover with a lid and continue to boil for 15 minutes. Remove from the heat, leaving the lid on, and allow to cool slightly. Remove jars and stand upside down on a clean tea towel to drain.

Jars must still be hot while filling with the just-cooked jam. (Alternatively, heat the sterilized jars in a moderate oven for 5–10 minutes before use.)

Once the jars are filled, cover the preserve or chutney with waxed paper before closing and placing in a cool dark place, making sure the jars are not touching. Most jams and marmalades will have a 12-month shelf life, providing the right quantity of sugar has been used. Once opened, any jar should be kept refrigerated.

Using a gas gun Powerful butane gas canisters can be used as a blow torch in the kitchen to give a crispy glaze to many dishes. They are available from almost any hardware store and can also be found in the kitchen sections of department stores. Follow the instructions and use carefully and, of course, keep away from children.

spring

Spanning the months of March, April and May, spring carries the image of a glistening sun, waiting to rise and sparkling over the morning dew, but still bringing with it a chill in the air. In recent years, spring does seem to have adopted a more sodden outlook, with the dew becoming puddles, maturing into pools and sometimes even streams. Unpredictable is probably the word to use when describing this season, but with it comes the excitement of the first of the year's new-season produce.

We shouldn't deprive ourselves of the vast variety of imported goodies in our shops, but so often they have been packed while still unripe and we buy them because, on dark cold days, we are lured by their bright colours and perfect shapes. When the grocer or supermarket buyer knows what they are buying, you can be lucky and find really good imported products to enliven your spring meals, but often British-grown seasonal produce is overlooked. Spring offers us many exceptional ingredients and all that these feature ingredients really need, and justly deserve, is a little extra thought and menu-planning to create outstanding seasonal dishes.

March, especially, probably needs a little extra thought as many winter root vegetables, such as parsnips, swedes and turnips may have started to take on a spongy texture, and if the weather has been particularly bad even potatoes will be suffering. But there's a host of newcomers joining us at this time, which we can take advantage of to enliven our menus.

Spring cabbages and greens start appearing in March: the more open-leafed varieties are the ones to look out for. Spring onions also appear on the scene, and along with purple sprouting broccoli are the two main stars of this month. The sprouting broccoli may have a slightly untidy appearance, compared to the bigger, neater calabrese which arrives later, but it carries a distinctive flavour that the more tailored variety just cannot match.

Rhubarb is with us through late winter into early mid-spring in its pale-coloured, forced, 'champagne', variety, grown under cover. The outdoor, garden rhubarb season runs through into summer giving us the deeper red, more piquant variety. The 'champagne' label is a British speciality, dating back to the nineteenth century. It apparently takes several years of production before perfecting and reaching its vintage title. The champagnes have a more delicate colour, with a softer, less sharp flavour that gently fizzes, rather than shocks, your taste buds.

Morel mushrooms, every chef's favourite, are making an entrance in March, too. Having a short life span, they really should be tried when in season. They are not cheap, but if you know somebody who knows their mushrooms, you can often find them to pick. They have a flavour like no other, with possibly only ceps matching them. Morel mushrooms have a great ability to infuse their flavour into other ingredients, as well as absorb others too. Dried morels are available throughout the year, and can also be used, but they do need pre-soaking in water before use.

Sea kale is the other feature ingredient available in March and on into April. A celery-like vegetable, and rare to find today, it used to be one of Britain's most popular. It can be eaten almost as you would asparagus spears, and can take on many other flavours, as it does in the *Blood orange and chive sea kale* (page 25).

Other March flavours include very young spinach leaves, fresh sorrel and very young wild salmon. Scallops are a good price to buy and try. Imported kumquats, the small, oval orange-flavoured fruits, are worth sampling at this time, too.

Flounder is a fish, so often ignored. Its season generally runs from March to November and, if super fresh, will eat as well as its counterparts – dab, Dover and lemon soles, halibut and plaice among them. If you find any of these during March, use them, as they are at their plumpest, with a sweeter taste than the often muddy and earthy autumn catch.

The wild ransom or wild garlic leaves also hit the scene during this month, and last through the whole of spring. These onion-like leaves thrive on damp soil and are consequently usually found in open woodland areas, often close to streams. A few leaves, broken or shredded and simply tossed into a salad, provide a garlic flavour that spreads throughout the other leaves. They are well worth finding and using, and add a milder garlic flavour than their cultivated friends.

Spring brings us Easter, and with it the rich flavour of chocolate. With few home-grown fruits around at this time, chocolate becomes a very popular substitute, so rich chocolate cakes, flans and mousses are a must.

Spring lamb is another Easter speciality. The succulent young meat is at its best towards the end of April and usually originates from the West Country, which is the warmer part of Britain at this time. As spring turns to summer lamb from more northerly Scottish lands comes into season.

In April, lemon soles are still in very good order and red mullets are appearing. I adore cooking monkfish, which once upon a time was cheap to buy because it was looked upon with total disregard. This meaty fish is available all year round but does seem to be a prize-winner during this month. Mostly found off the coasts of Scotland and Cornwall, its dense white meat carries a sweet flavour almost like that of lobster.

After heavy winter months, shellfish returns to form, with crab in particular featuring. The common crab is around, but what about the even sweeter and more delicious spider crab? It's not the easiest to find but a pre-order with your fishmonger will help. There's a recipe for *Warm spider crab linguine with orange and tarragon sauce* on page 52 that takes advantage of all the flavours the meat and shells have to offer (common crab can also be used), so give it a try.

Purple sprouting broccoli, cabbages, spring greens, and spring onions are still available in April, with cauliflowers and a selection of herbs – mint, chives, rosemary, thyme and sage – making an entrance. Arriving towards the end of the month are Jersey Royal potatoes and, with good weather, asparagus.

May brings really appetizing ingredients at long last. Asparagus steals the limelight with the British variety becoming the star of the show and running through this last month of spring, and into the last week of June.

It is so important during this spell to take advantage of these home-grown green sticks. They often need nothing apart from a splash of melted butter and maybe a bowl of steaming baby Jersey Royal potatoes. This combination is a meal in itself. To enjoy asparagus at its best and experience its maximum flavour, it really needs to be picked and cooked within a couple of hours. White asparagus, mostly imported, also hits the scene about now, offering a different texture and flavour.

One or two ingredients, sometimes found towards the end of May, are not always available on a regular annual basis. One is imported apricots, and if you shop wisely and avoid underdeveloped, over-firm fruits you may find the first of the season's perfectly ripened, sweet treasures. Another is broad beans. Although you sometimes have to wait until summer, you can be lucky with a spot of good weather, and find this tasty vegetable showing its tiny young face early.

The more unusual, salty vegetable samphire can sometimes be found in late spring, too. It has an aromatic, seasoned flavour with a definite salt bite, and I have utilized this quite unique saltiness in several recipes to enhance other flavours in the dish.

By the end of spring, Jersey Royal potatoes are becoming cheaper and more plentiful, and the first radishes, strawberries and imported cherries are arriving, brightening up the end of this season and heralding the advent of summer.

Serves 4
- 8–10 young leeks
- salt and twist of pepper
- 8 tablespoons *Vegetable vinaigrette* (page 180)

For the variation with morels and Parmesan
- 175–225g (6–8oz) fresh morel mushrooms
- 8–10 tablespoons *Vegetable vinaigrette* (page 180), featuring extra diced fennel only, or *Sweet port red wine dressing* (page 182)
- 1 heaped tablespoon chopped mixed herbs (such as chervil, parsley, tarragon, etc.)

- knob or 2 of butter
- salt and pepper
- leeks, prepared and cooked as below
- Parmesan cheese shavings, made using a vegetable peeler

Warm leeks with vegetable vinaigrette

Leeks are often called 'poor man's asparagus' just as marsh samphire (page 116) often is. For me, though, the leek stands alone, quite proud, with its texture and flavour (and price) lending itself to many dishes.

Here leeks are served as a simple starter or side dish. They are generally with us from the autumn to mid-to-late spring. Although they are coming to the end of their season, don't ignore them at this time, as spring leeks tend not to carry the sometimes woody centres found in summer ones. For this recipe it's best to choose thinnish leeks as these offer a softer and more gentle finish to the dish. It's best to cook the leeks until almost overdone. If too *al dente*, the leek will have a leathery texture and over-peppery flavour.

A little more extravagant, but adding such flavour, the variation recipe offered here with morel mushrooms and Parmesan shavings, is a quite outstanding combination to accompany leeks. The morels join us between the months of March and April – perfect timing for this recipe.

Method Trim away the tough dark green tops of the leeks. Split the leeks lengthwise and wash and rinse thoroughly, removing the outside layer if it feels too tough. Cook in boiling salted water, uncovered, for 6–7 minutes, then check for tenderness. If too firm, continue to boil for a further 3–4 minutes. Remove the leeks from the pan directly onto a kitchen cloth to collect excess water. Season with salt and pepper and arrange on plates, then spoon over the vinaigrette.

● Fresh herbs can be added to the dressing, along with quartered black olives.

● Mascarpone cheese can be added to this recipe: its soft creamy texture melts across the warmed leeks.

Method for the variation Prepare the morels as described on page 26. Mix the vinaigrette or dressing with the chopped herbs and set aside.

Melt a knob of the butter in a frying pan. Once bubbling well, add the mushrooms and fry for a minute or two until tender. Season with salt and pepper. Remove from the heat and add a touch more butter to emulsify all the flavours in the pan.

Spoon and scatter the morels over and around the cooked plated leeks. Parmesan shavings can now be strewn across the dish, before finishing with the butter and dressing.

Serves 4 as a main course or supper dish

For the garnishes

- 12 asparagus spears, trimmed of spiky ears and base stalk
- 450g (1lb) baby carrots, peeled or scraped, leaving 1–2cm (½–¾in) of stalk intact
- 450g (1lb) new potatoes
- olive oil (optional)
- salt and pepper

- bunch of radishes, trimmed
- bunch of spring onions, trimmed
- lots of crusty bread

For the fondue

- 1 garlic clove, split in two (optional)
- 300ml (½ pint) white wine
- 450g (1lb) cheese (see below), grated or crumbled
- 1 level teaspoon cornflour or arrowroot
- twist of pepper
- freshly grated nutmeg
- juice of ½ lemon

Blue cheese fondue with spring dips

From the French, 'melted', fondue is a term used in many recipe titles. This recipe is based on the Swiss classic cheese fondue – Swiss cheese melted in wine – but uses blue cheese instead. One particular blue cheese I enjoy is Beenleigh Blue, which is not the easiest to find particularly at this time of the year, but if you do it will prove to be worthwhile. It's basically a ewe's milk cheese, quite full-flavoured without too dense a texture.

Another blue ewe's milk cheese is Lanark Blue, which resembles Roquefort in strength, needing to be calmed with another milder cheese for this recipe. There's also the more well-known Wensleydale, which is made from a combination of ewe's and cow's milk. Another favourite is the heavenly cow's milk Cashel Blue from Ireland.

To balance the richness of these strong-flavoured cheeses the quantity can be halved and the difference made up with Swiss Gruyère, the soft texture of which gives a smoother finish.

The spring garnishes are baby carrots, new potatoes and asparagus, along with radishes, spring onions and lots of crusty bread. The carrots, potatoes and asparagus can be served warm or cold; warm they do create a nice contrast with the other garnishes.

If you're not a fan of blue cheese at all, simply use all Gruyère. The spring vegetables then become the main feature.

Method The vegetable garnishes can all be cooked ahead, ready to reheat when needed. Cook the asparagus in boiling salted water for 2–4 minutes until tender but crisp. Refresh immediately in iced water. Cook the carrots in boiling salted water for 3–10 minutes, depending on their thickness. Refresh as above. Cook the new potatoes in boiling salted water for approximately 20 minutes. Drain and allow to cool naturally. If refreshed in cold water they do tend to become very soggy.

These can all be reheated in boiling water or in a steamer when needed, then drizzled with olive oil, if using, and season with salt and pepper.

To make the fondue, rub the inside of a flameproof casserole with the garlic halves, if using. Add the white wine and bring to a gentle simmer over a medium-to-low heat. Gradually add the cheese, stirring as you do until melted. Loosen the cornflour or arrowroot with a little water and mix into the melted cheese, adding just enough to reach a fondue consistency. Season with pepper, nutmeg and enough lemon juice to cut into the cheesy flavour.

Once the fondue is at a very gentle bubble transfer it to a spirit lamp on the table. The vegetables and the salad radishes and spring onions can be presented with the fondue, also offering crusty bread.

● *A tossed side salad eats very well with a fondue, its freshness cleansing the palate between dips.*

● *If you decide on a pure Swiss fondue, using just Gruyère, the lemon juice should be replaced with 2–3 tablespoons of kirsch for the classic flavour.*

Serves 4

- 675g (1½lb) large potatoes
- 25g (1oz) butter, plus 2 knobs
- bunch of spring onions, finely chopped
- 125–150g (4½–5oz) plain flour, plus more for dusting
- 1 egg, plus 1 extra yolk
- salt and pepper
- freshly grated nutmeg
- iced water
- 225g (8oz) podded broad beans
- 1–2 tablespoons olive oil, plus more for drizzling
- 100–150ml (3½fl oz–¼pint) single cream (optional)
- 100–175g (4–6oz) crumbled blue cheese (see below) or Parmesan cheese shavings or Gruyère slices
- squeeze of lime juice (optional)

Champ potato gnocchi with broad beans and blue cheese

Gnocchi are Italian dumplings, made either from semolina, choux pastry or, as with this recipe, potatoes. Champ is an Irish potato dish, consisting of mashed potatoes, spring onions and lots of butter. The oniony flavour, as we know, works well with almost any cheese, biting into its rich flavour.

Blue cheese is suggested here – Stilton, Roquefort or Irish Cashel Blue all work well. Other cheeses to use, although not blue, are Parmesan (melting shavings over the gnocchi to a golden brown), or slices of Gruyère (just melting them).

The new season's young broad beans are merely boiled and buttered with the gnocchi just before serving. This dish is a good vegetarian option, as a starter or main course (with a salad), supper dish or savoury dessert.

Method Cook the potatoes whole in boiling salted water. While they are boiling, melt half of the 25g (1oz) butter in a frying pan. Once bubbling, add the spring onions and cook for just a minute barely to soften.

Once the potatoes are tender, peel while still warm and mash to a smooth consistency. Mix in 125g (4oz) of the flour, along with the spring onions, remaining measured butter, whole egg and egg yolk. Season with salt, pepper and nutmeg.

The gnocchi mix should now feel moist, but if too sticky add a little more flour. The dumplings can now be moulded and this is best achieved while the mix is still warm, shaping them by hand into 2cm (¾in) balls. The gnocchi are now ready to pre-cook in batches in salted simmering water. As they are placed in the water, they will sink and then rise to the surface when cooked. They cook in 3–4 minutes, maximum 5 minutes. Once cooked, it's important the balls are firm to the touch. Refresh in iced water. When cold, dry on a kitchen cloth or paper. The gnocchi can now be refrigerated until needed.

The broad beans can also be pre-cooked, blanching them in boiling salted water until tender. If making this dish during the month of May, the broad beans will be quite small, taking just a minute or two to cook. Later in their season, the beans may well need up to 5 minutes. Refresh in iced water, then peel the rich green beans from their shells. To reheat, the beans can be warmed in a minute or two in a few tablespoons of water with a small knob of butter. Season with salt and pepper.

To fry the gnocchi, melt a knob of butter with a little olive oil in a frying pan. Once bubbling, add the dumplings. (These can be cooked in batches so as not to overcrowd the pan. If so, place them in a moderate oven to keep warm while the rest are cooked.) Fry on a moderate heat until golden brown and completely warmed through.

Mix the warmed broad beans with the gnocchi, then spoon into one large or four individual ovenproof dishes. If using the single cream, warm 100ml (3½fl oz) of it with half of the cheese, adding the remaining cream if too thick. Spoon the cream over the gnocchi and broad beans and top with the remaining cheese before grilling. If not using the cream, just sprinkle with the crumbled blue cheese, Parmesan shavings or Gruyere slices and place under a hot grill, until the cheese melts.

A drizzle of olive oil, mixed with a squeeze or two of lime juice to finish, if using, offers a shiny glaze.

Serves 4

- 12–16 or 24–28 (depending on size) white asparagus spears, prepared as below
- salt and pepper
- iced water
- knob of butter
- 12 chestnut mushrooms (button mushrooms can also be used)

- 5 tablespoons hazelnut, walnut or olive oil (nut oils will enhance the naturally nutty chestnut mushrooms)
- 2 tablespoons sherry vinegar
- 100ml (3½fl oz) *Vegetable stock* (page 177) or *Instant stock* (page 175)
- squeeze of lemon juice

- 2–3 spring onions, outside layer of skin removed
- 1 tablespoon flatleaf and curly parsley, loosely chopped

White asparagus with a warm casserole salad of mushrooms and spring onions

English spears of white asparagus can be found between mid-to-late spring and, although rare, are worth looking out for, but the Dutch variety is the more common during this season. The spears themselves can often be particularly thick, and will need to be peeled, trimming away the stalk ends. If you are lucky enough to find the thinner stalks, then perhaps they will still require a very light peeling and trimming for guaranteed tenderness.

Three to four thick spears per person will be plenty as a starter, or six to seven if smaller. The 'casserole salad' is purely a description of the loose stock-style of dressing that binds the thick chestnut mushrooms with the asparagus.

Method Blanch the asparagus spears in boiling salted water, allowing 4–5 minutes for the thin and 5–6 for the thicker. (It's best to cook them in batches – too many spears will reduce the temperature of the water, leading to stewing rather than boiling.) Remove from the water and plunge into iced water, which will instantly stop the cooking process. Once cold (the time in iced water need only be equal to the cooking time), remove and dry lightly on kitchen paper. The asparagus can now be refrigerated until needed. However, for this particular dish I'd suggest serving the spears at room temperature or lightly warmed with a brushing of butter under the grill or gently in a frying pan. Another warming method is to heat the spears in a tablespoon or two of water with a knob of butter.

Quarter each of the mushrooms. Heat 2 tablespoons of the oil in a large frying pan and season the mushrooms with salt and pepper. These can now be fried for a few minutes until golden brown and tender. Remove the mushrooms from the pan and keep warm.

On a medium heat, add the sherry vinegar to the pan. This will almost instantly reduce and, at the same time, release all the flavours from the pan. Add the stock and bring to the boil. Add the remaining oil and a squeeze of lemon juice to taste. Season with salt and pepper. The 'casserole' liquor will now be in a loose vinaigrette form, with enough piquancy to enhance the dish. Split the spring onions lengthwise and, at quite an acute angle, cut the halves into long, very thin slices.

Divide the spears between plates or bowls and sit the mixed mushrooms and spring onions on top of each portion. Add the chopped parsley to the dressing and spoon over each serving.

- *The nut oils are more expensive and not essential to the dish, but can add a touch of luxury to the finished flavour.*

- *If sherry vinegar is unavailable, sherry itself can be used, or red wine vinegar. Pure lemon juice can also stand as the only acidity in the liquor.*

Serves 2
- 2–3 eggs
- 1 generous teaspoon sesame seeds
- 12–16 medium asparagus spears
- groundnut, vegetable or olive oil, for brushing
- squeeze of lemon juice
- 50g (2oz) butter
- coarse sea salt or salt
- twist of pepper
- 1 teaspoon chopped chives (optional)
- drizzle of sesame oil or olive oil

Grilled asparagus with soft hard-boiled eggs and toasted sesame dressing

This delicious starter is a slight variation on the classic asparagus dish of hard-boiled eggs and nutty brown butter strewn across the rich green spears. Here the tips are grilled not boiled, with the nutty flavour provided by the toasted sesame seeds.

Cooked for only 7–8 minutes, the eggs maintain a moistness which provides nothing but sheer pleasure – compared to the traditional pale, hard-boiled, yellow crumble.

Method Place the eggs in boiling water and bring back to a rapid simmer. Cook for 7–8 minutes. Remove and place under cold running water for just 2–3 minutes to stop the cooking. Now remove from the water and leave to cool a little further before shelling.

Sprinkle the sesame seeds in a pan and toast under the grill or place over a medium heat and colour to a golden brown. This takes very little time and, once coloured, the seeds must be removed immediately from the pan to prevent any burnt bitter edge.

Preheat a grill plate. Trim the spiky ears from the asparagus spears, and snap or cut away between 2–4cm (¾–1½in) of the grey/white base. Brush each spear with the oil, place on the preheated grill plate and cook until tender, allowing them to take on bold dark grill lines. Turn the spears when necessary.

While the asparagus is cooking, in a small saucepan bring 3 tablespoons of water and a good squeeze of lemon juice to the boil. Quickly whisk in the butter to create an emulsion of the two, providing an instant butter sauce. Remove from the heat (never reboil a sauce once butter has been added as this will separate the oils from solids), season with salt and pepper and add a squeeze more lemon juice if needed. Add the sesame seeds and chopped chives, if using.

Cut the eggs in halves or quarters lengthwise and present with the asparagus spears divided between two plates. Season with a twist of pepper and coarse sea salt before spooning the sesame seed butter over and drizzling with the sesame or olive oil.

● *If a grill plate is unavailable, the asparagus can be blanched and quickly pan-fried to a light golden edge, or simply boiled for a few minutes.*

- 8 medium or 12 small new potatoes, cooked
- salt and pepper
- 1 shallot, finely chopped
- 12–16 asparagus spears
- iced water
- 225–350g (8–12oz) mixed salad leaves (such as dandelion, baby chard, lamb's lettuce, curly endive, spinach, lollo rosso, oak leaf, watercress, etc.)

- 8–10 radishes, washed and cut into thin wedges

For the lemon oil dressing
- 3 tablespoons olive oil
- 3 teaspoons lemon juice

For the sour cream dressing
- 2 tablespoons soured cream or crème fraîche
- 1 level teaspoon Dijon mustard
- ½ level teaspoon caster sugar
- 1–2 teaspoons lime juice or white wine vinegar

Flat asparagus salad with new potatoes and radishes

All the main components here are fortunate enough to share the same seasons, spring and summer. The 'flat' in the recipe title is purely a description of a very simple scattering of these ingredients flavoured with the dressings. Any of the new potatoes that are finding their way to us by the end of spring will work here, such as Jersey Royals, pink fir apple, etc., along with the choice of salad leaves on offer. Once the salad leaves have been picked and washed it's important they are left to drain well.

Method Quarter the hot cooked new potatoes, or halve if small, place in a bowl and season with salt and pepper. Make the lemon oil dressing by mixing the olive oil, lemon juice, salt and pepper and spoon half over the still warm potatoes with the chopped shallot. If the potatoes have been well cooked to a soft tender stage and are still warm, the dressing flavours will be absorbed.

For the sour cream dressing, whisk all of the ingredients together and season with salt and pepper. If too thick, loosen to a coating consistency with a drop or two of water.

Trim the pointy ears from the asparagus spears and snap or cut away the tough base of the stalks. Cut each spear in half and cook in boiling salted water for 2–3 minutes. When tender, refresh in iced water and pat dry.

All of the previous preparation can be done several hours in advance, keeping the potatoes at room temperature. To serve, mix the asparagus, salad leaves and radishes together adding the remaining lemon oil dressing, gently spreading the flavour evenly. Spoon a little sour cream dressing onto the plates and scatter the asparagus salad and potatoes over it. Finish with trickles of the remaining sour cream dressing.

- 2 bunches of sea kale
- salt and pepper
- 50g–75g (2–3oz) butter
- juice of 1 lime or ½ lemon

Simple sea kale

Sea kale is a vegetable that has become quite a rarity on our plates. Often found in abundance during its short season between late February and late April, it grows wild on the coasts of the United Kingdom. However, it is also commercially grown inland on a small scale, from where it will be sold bunched in local greengrocers and now and again in large supermarkets. Sea kale resembles individual young celery sticks, usually 23–25cm (9–10in) in length, with a small white, yellow to green leaf sitting around the top. The flavour resembles that of white asparagus, with a mild, crisp finish and an almost soft sweetness. Sea kale makes a nice alternative starter served, as you would asparagus, with hollandaise sauce or just melted butter. This simple recipe is along the lines of the latter, with just a squeeze of citrus juice to sharpen the finish.

Sea kale suits just one basic cooking method, which is simply to boil it for a few minutes in salted water. After this, other cooking methods, such as frying or grilling can be effective. Steaming is an alternative to boiling, but this does need a longer cooking time.

Method Trim away the base to each stalk of sea kale and wash well to remove any soil or sandy grit. To cook, drop the stalks in boiling salted water and cook for a few minutes. This cooking time will leave them tender although still very crisp. If you prefer a softer finish, simply continue to cook for a few minutes more, ten being the maximum. Lift from the pan with a slotted spoon and transfer to a large clean pan. Add the butter, which will emulsify with the residual moisture as it is shaken into the pan. Season with salt and pepper, and add the lime or lemon juice. Divide the sea kale between plates and spoon the butter over each.

● *Once seasoned with pepper each portion can be lightly sprinkled with coarse sea salt for a crunchier finish.*

● *Lots of freshly chopped parsley or a selection of herbs can also be added to the sauce.*

Serves 4 as a starter or accompaniment

- 2–3 blood oranges (1–2 of these segmented, saving all juices)
- 1 sugar cube or a pinch of caster sugar (optional)
- 6 tablespoons *Vegetable stock*, (page 177) or water
- 2 bunches of sea kale
- salt and pepper
- 75g (3oz) butter
- squeeze of lemon juice
- 1 heaped tablespoon finely chopped chives

Blood orange and chive sea kale

Blood oranges are imported and with us through the late winter and early spring months. This quite stunning fruit can be used in so many sweet or savoury dishes. It is probably most famous used in *Sauce maltaise* (page 178), a buttery hollandaise sauce finished with a strong reduction of blood orange juice and finely grated zest.

Here the juice is used to flavour a simple butter sauce, garnished with diced segments of the fruit and lots of chopped chives to add their oniony bite.

Method To make the sauce, finely grate the zest from a quarter of the unsegmented orange, then halve and juice. Pour the juice into a small saucepan along with the grated zest and juices saved from segmenting. Bring to the boil and reduce by two-thirds. It is not essential to segment two oranges, one will probably be enough, however, I do love the fruit and two will provide extra flavour. Cut each segment into two or three pieces and keep to one side. Taste the reduced orange liquor; if too sharp and bitter, add the sugar cube or sugar to taste, and stir until dissolved. Add the vegetable stock or water to loosen the syrupy orange, and strain off the orange zest. (This reduction stage can be done well in advance, just to be reheated and finished with the butter when needed.)

To prepare the sea kale, remove the base from each kale stem, washing and rinsing away all soil and sandy grit. Plunge into the boiling salted water and cook until tender. Drain well once cooked and divide between four plates.

While the kale is cooking, bring the blood orange reduction to a simmer and whisk or stir in the butter, a knob at a time, until completely emulsified. Season with salt, pepper and a squeeze of lemon juice. Add the orange segment pieces and warm through, then add the chopped chives. Spoon the sauce over the sea kale and serve.

● *A drizzle of olive oil or a nutty hazelnut or walnut oil can be trickled around the plate to finish.*

● *About 8–12 green peppercorns can be halved and added to the finished sauce for a warm piquant bite.*

Serves 4

- 350g (12oz) young spinach, washed and stalks removed
- salt, plus coarse sea salt
- iced water
- 100g (4oz) fresh morel mushrooms, well washed with large ones split in two
- 25–50g (1–2oz) butter
- 50–75ml (3–5 tablespoons) whipping cream or crème fraîche
- twist of black pepper
- freshly grated nutmeg
- 4 eggs
- dash of balsamic vinegar or sherry vinegar

Fried egg and spinach with morel mushrooms

This serves either as a starter or a lunch/supper dish, perhaps accompanied by a few new potatoes. For an even more seasonal feel, the spinach can be replaced with spring greens.

The addition of the morel mushrooms makes it a spring recipe, but these can be replaced with almost any other mushroom, wild or cultivated, for an all-year-round recipe. Morel mushrooms need to be carefully well washed and rinsed, not steeping them in the water. If left submerged they will overabsorb and become spongy. Cleaning them becomes a lot simpler, quicker and thorough if the mushrooms are halved, but leaving them whole obviously maintains their unique shape, although they will take a little longer to cook.

Method The spinach can be cooked in advance by blanching in rapidly boiling salted water for just a minute, until tender, before refreshing in iced water then draining. Gently squeeze to remove excess water. The cooked leaves can now be refrigerated until needed, ready to reheat in butter or quickly microwave.

Trim away the base of the morel stalks (keeping them for later use when making stock). Split the large mushrooms in half lengthwise. Gently brush and then lightly wash and rinse them to make sure they are completely clean and free of grit.

To assemble the dish, the spinach can be reheated if pre-blanched or, if cooking to order, melt a knob of butter in a large saucepan and, once this is bubbling, add the spinach leaves. Cook on a fairly high heat and stir. Any moisture within the leaves will help steam the the leaves, speeding up the cooking time. After a minute or two the spinach will be ready. If sitting in too much natural water, quickly drain away the excess. Add 3 tablespoons of the cream or crème fraîche and stir in. Season with salt, pepper and nutmeg; keep warm to one side.

Fry the eggs for a few minutes in a good knob of sizzling butter, seasoning with coarse sea salt and black pepper when cooked.

Serve the spinach on plates or bowls. If it's slightly too thick, loosen with the remaining cream or crème fraîche. Place a fried egg on top of each portion. Quickly return the pan to a high heat and add a knob of butter. Add the morels and quickly fry to warm through and tenderize. Sprinkle with a dash of vinegar – this will quickly evaporate just gently adding a piquancy to the mushrooms. Season with salt and pepper and add the remaining butter. When bubbling, spoon it over the eggs and spinach before serving.

● *If using spring greens these should always be pre-cooked in boiling water. The torn leaves take about 3 minutes to become completely tender. Refresh in cold water and drain well. Season and reheat when needed before stirring in the warmed cream.*

● *If you have truffle oil just a few drops will take this dish even further. Dried morel mushrooms can also be used. Soak 50g (2oz) in cold water for 30 minutes then rinse, squeeze dry and use as above.*

Serves 4 as a light starter or accompaniment

- 450–675g (1–1½lb) purple sprouting broccoli spears
- 1 tablespoon very finely chopped shallot or onion
- juice of 2 large oranges
- 1 teaspoon finely grated orange zest
- 2–4 wild garlic leaves
- 100g (4oz) butter
- salt and pepper

Steamed purple sprouting broccoli with melting wild garlic and orange butter

The rich green broccoli – calabrese – is a fairly recent addition to our culinary repertoires, having become readily available here only in the late 60s and early 70s. Before being blessed with such an outstanding vegetable from Calabria, the Italian region in which it was developed, purple sprouting was the variety more likely to be available.

This springtime variety, best eaten in March and April (although it can be found as early as January), can be treated like asparagus with which it is often compared. Although mainly coloured purple, pale green and white varieties can also be found, all with much the same flavour.

This dish, using the large or smaller sprouts, makes a good starter or vegetable accompaniment, which works well with most types of fish and seared scallops, all white meats, chicken, pork, veal, etc., as well as roast lamb.

Most Italian recipes suggest garlic, herbs, anchovies and olives as garnishes for broccoli, or a simple lemon butter is another classic. Taking a little from both of those ideas, I'm using wild garlic as a strong herb flavouring, accompanied by the citrus touch of orange.

The early spring months, March in particular, are perfect for wild garlic. If it still cannot be found, substitute 1–2 crushed garlic cloves cooked with the shallots.

Method If small trimmed broccoli sprouts can be found, 450g (1lb) will be plenty. If larger, then simply break the spears from the thicker central stalk. If very fresh and young, the actual stalks need not be peeled. This is best tested by taking a raw bite: if good and tender to eat, then leave them unpeeled; if slightly chewy, the skin is best peeled by hand or carefully with a small knife or peeler. Steam the broccoli when needed, above boiling water for just a few minutes until just tender but still with a bite.

To make the butter (which when made in this quantity can be frozen, keeping for several months), rinse the shallot or onion in a sieve under cold running water as this helps wash away the very raw oniony bite. Drain and place in a saucepan with the orange juice. Bring to a rapid simmer and allow to boil to reduce until almost dry. Remove from the heat, add the orange zest, then leave to cool.

The quantity of wild garlic is really down to personal taste. Both quantities work for me, the four leaves offering the right flavour when I'm in a real garlicky mood. Wild garlic leaves are powerful to eat and don't quite betray their strength by nose alone. Chop the leaves carefully and mix two into the butter along with the orange shallots or onions. Season with salt and pepper. Taste for wild garlic flavour and add more chopped leaves if needed. Roll and wrap the flavoured butter in cling film, then refrigerate or freeze until needed.

To serve, stack or lay the warm steamed broccoli spears on plates and top with a generous knob of the garlicky orange butter to melt and flavour the vegetables.

- *Olive oil or Lemon oil (page 183) can be drizzled around the plate to finish.*

- *For a wild garlic and orange butter sauce, heat 3 tablespoons of water and, once bubbling, remove from the stove and whisk small knobs of the flavoured butter in until a buttery sauce consistency is achieved.*

Serves 4 as a starter or accompaniment

- 675g (1½lb) St George's mushrooms, preferably small
- 2 tablespoons olive oil
- 2 garlic cloves, thinly sliced or finely crushed (more can be added for a stronger garlic finish)
- juice of ½ small lemon
- large knob of butter
- salt and pepper (coarse sea salt can also be used)
- 1 tablespoon chopped curly or torn flatleaf parsley

St George's mushrooms with garlic, lemon and parsley

Garlic mushrooms, finished with chopped parsley and a squeeze of lemon juice, are better known in France as *champignons à la Bordelaise*. I absolutely love to eat them – and lots too – just sitting in a bowl with good crusty bread to mop up the juices. This particular recipe you'll only be able to make from the 23rd April (St George's Day, hence the mushrooms' name) through to June. However, don't forget there are so many other tasty mushrooms, cultivated and wild, available throughout the year – chestnut mushrooms, for instance, are not so distinctive, but can be used as an alternative.

Method Trim the stalks from the mushrooms and rinse them quickly under running water. They are best washed well in advance and then placed on several layers of kitchen paper to drain. The dryer the mushrooms, the better the finished flavour will be, as they will fry and not stew in the pan.

Heat the olive oil in a large frying pan or wok. Add the mushrooms. (They may have to be cooked in two pans or two batches, as too large a quantity will cool the pan, causing stewing rather than frying.)

Fry the mushrooms, not turning them too often as this tends to cool the pan, for a few minutes until well coloured and tender. Add the garlic and continue to fry for a further minute. Add the lemon juice, stirring it quickly in amongst the mushrooms. Add the butter, season with salt and pepper, and finish with the chopped parsley before serving.

● *The garlic mushrooms will also eat well on thick slices of buttered toast. An attractive finish is to flavour the mushrooms with a splash of sherry and finish with cream. To do so, once the garlic has been added also add 2–3 tablespoons of medium sherry. Simmer for a few minutes, then add 100–150ml (3½fl oz–¼pint) of double cream. This will begin to thicken very quickly. Stir and season, before finishing with the lemon juice and chopped parsley.*

Serves 2 as a starter
- 12–16 asparagus spears
- 2 thick oval slices of French stick
- knob of butter, plus more for spreading and finishing
- salt and black pepper
- 25–50g (1–2oz) fresh Parmesan cheese shavings or grated Parmesan

Asparagus on buttery toast with melting Parmesan cheese

There are very few ingredients in this dish – thick toast, fresh English spears and lots of Parmesan – but an awful lot of flavour. Asparagus crosses over the seasons, so you'll find it in both spring and summer.

Method Trim the pointy ears away from the asparagus spears and snap or cut away 2–4cm (¾–1½in) of the tough stalk base. Cook the spears in boiling salted water for just 2–3 minutes (4 minutes maximum), until tender but still with a bite.

While the asparagus is cooking, brush both sides of the bread slices with butter and toast beneath a hot grill. Once golden, turn the slices and toast the other sides. Place the buttery toasts on plates.

Remove the asparagus from the water immediately when cooked and place in a separate pan with a knob of butter. Season with salt and pepper and lay on top of the toasts. Scatter the Parmesan shavings or grated Parmesan over the spears just before serving. For a softer finish place under the grill and warm to a melting stage.

● *The French bread can be rubbed with garlic before buttering and toasting.*

- 2 small or 1 large head of celeriac
- juice of ½ lemon
- 50g (2oz) butter
- 5–8 leaves of wild garlic
- 750ml (1¼pint) milk
- 150ml (¼pint) whipping or single cream
- salt and pepper
- freshly grated nutmeg

Celeriac soup with wild garlic

Celeriac is predominantly an autumn–winter vegetable, and despite being at the end of its season now, I wanted to remind you that it is during the first months of spring that you will still find the last of the British-grown on the shelves. Celeriac marries well with the wild garlic leaves which are just arriving.

Method Cut away the root and skin of the celeriac and chop into rough 2cm (¾in) dice. Toss the celeriac in a bowl with the lemon juice to help retain its white colour.

Melt the butter in a saucepan and, once bubbling, add the celeriac and cook on a low heat, covered with a lid and stirring from time to time. After 8–10 minutes, add five of the wild garlic leaves. Add the milk and bring to a soft simmer. Cook at this temperature for 20–25 minutes until the celeriac is completely tender.

At this point the wild garlic leaves can either be left in to be puréed with the celeriac, or removed for a slightly milder finish.

Purée to a smooth consistency in a blender or liquidizer, add the cream and season with salt, pepper and a touch of nutmeg. The soup should now have a creamy but not over-thick consistency. If necessary add a little more milk to loosen. For the silkiest smooth of finishes, strain through a sieve. The remaining wild garlic leaves, if using, can now be finely shredded and sprinkled across each portion.

- *A trickle of walnut oil to finish adds a rich nutty flavour, that brings out all the others.*

- 6 rashers of streaky bacon
- 12–16 medium flat mushrooms, wiped and stalks trimmed
- salt and pepper
- 1 red onion, finely chopped
- 1 garlic clove, finely chopped
- 1 tablespoon olive oil
- 200ml (7fl oz) red wine
- 1 sugar cube
- 25g (1oz) butter, diced
- 1–2 handfuls of young spinach leaves (or torn large ones), washed
- 4 *Poached eggs* (page 186)
- 1 dessertspoon chopped curly parsley
- squeeze of lemon juice (optional)

Mushroom and spring spinach Bourguignonne with poached eggs

Flat mushrooms have such a meaty texture they can replace actual meats quite easily. Basically comprised of red wine, baby onions, fried bacon pieces and mushrooms, the Bourguignonne label is normally associated with braised beef, steaks or chicken dishes.

The mushrooms in this version have become the main feature with bacon and red onions, which are also in season during these spring months, helped along by the addition of wilted young spinach and red wine. For a vegetarian option, the bacon can be omitted.

This dish eats very well as a starter, lunch or supper dish, but can also make a substantial main course by using the quantities above to serve two. Flat mushrooms come in many sizes; if large are the only ones available, two per portion will be plenty. For medium mushrooms (6–7.5cm/2½–3in in diameter) three or four each are ideal.

Method Cut the bacon rashers into thin strips. Heat a large frying pan and add the bacon. The strips will now release their own fat content and fry to a crispy finish. Spoon the bacon from the pan, leaving the fat in which to fry the mushrooms. Place the mushrooms in the pan and cook over a high heat for 3–4 minutes on each side until well coloured, seasoning with salt and pepper. Remove from the pan and keep warm.

Mix together the chopped red onion and garlic. Add the olive oil to the pan and fry the onion mixture for a few minutes until softened. Pour over the red wine, which will begin to sizzle, lifting all residue in the pan.

Add the mushrooms, along with any juices. Increase the heat and allow the red wine to boil until reduced by half. Add the sugar cube and the butter, gently shaking the pan until both have dissolved and mixed in. Add the spinach and bacon pieces and warm for just a minute until the spinach has wilted. Check for seasoning.

Reheat the pre-made poached eggs by plunging them into rapidly simmering water for 1 minute. Divide the mushrooms and spinach between plates and top each with a warm poached egg. Add the chopped parsley to the Bourguignonne sauce, along with a squeeze of lemon juice, if using, and spoon a little over each dish.

fish

Serves 4 as a main course

- 1kg (2¼lb) monkfish (weight on the bone)
- 1 spring cabbage
- 50g (2oz) butter, plus 3 knobs
- salt and pepper
- iced water (optional)
- freshly grated nutmeg
- 40 clams, well washed
- 2 shallots or ½ onion, finely chopped
- 1 garlic clove, finely crushed (optional)
- pinch of caster sugar
- 150ml (¼pint) white wine
- flour, for dusting
- 2 tablespoons olive oil
- 1 tablespoon chopped flatleaf parsley
- 1 teaspoon chopped tarragon

Roast monkfish with spring cabbage and clam casserole

Monkfish and clams are available all year round, but it is during mid-spring that monkfish is at its best. At the same time we also have young spring cabbages, which need no more than softening and buttering. It is important that clams are well washed before use, discarding any that will not close when lightly tapped.

Method The monkfish must first have its dark skin removed. This will come away quite simply, if you pull it sharply from the thick end to the thin end of the tail. Two fillets can now be cut away from the central bone. The fillets will still have a thin membrane coating so trim it away with a sharp knife. Try to get your local fishmonger to do all this for you.

Each fillet can now be cut into two portions providing four pieces in total, each approximately 175g (6oz). These can now be refrigerated until needed.

Quarter the cabbage and remove the stalks from the leaves. Tear the leaves into bite-sized pieces. While the fish is frying, the cabbage can be cooked in a knob of butter and 5 tablespoons of water, until tender. The alternative is to pre-cook it (to reheat later), by plunging it into boiling salted water and cooking for a few minutes until tender, then refreshing it in iced water and draining well in a colander. If reheating later in the microwave, at this point the leaves can be buttered adding the salt, pepper and nutmeg.

Pour 300ml (½pint) of water into a large saucepan and heat until bubbling. Add the clams, cover with a lid and cook on a high heat, shaking the pan. After 2–3 minutes, the clams should all be open (discard any that

aren't). Drain, saving the cooking liquor. All of the clams can be removed from their shells or leave 4–5 per portion still in shell for a more rustic finish. Keep to one side.

While the clams are cooking, melt a knob of butter in another pan and add the shallots or onion and garlic, if using. Cook for a few minutes until beginning to soften. Add the caster sugar and white wine, bring to the boil and reduce by two-thirds. The drained clam liquor can now be poured in through a fine sieve or muslin cloth, before bringing back to the boil. Reduce by a third to half for a good intense flavour, then keep to one side.

Lightly flour the monkfish fillet portions and season with salt and pepper. Heat the oil in a large frying pan or roasting tray. Fry the fish fillets in the hot pan for 6–7 minutes, colouring on all sides, and then remove the pan from the heat. The fish will now continue to cook while the remaining flavours are put together.

Reheat the cabbage in pan with a knob of butter and season with salt, pepper and nutmeg (or microwave).

Return the sauce to the stove and bring to a simmer. Add the 50g (2oz) butter and whisk in well. The clams, in and out of shell, can now be added to warm through, but not allowed to boil. Add the fresh herbs.

This dish is best served in a bowl, placing the cabbage in the centre, spooning the clams and sauce around, and presenting the monkfish fillets on top of the cabbage. It is also quite nice simply to plate the cabbage and fish, offering a bowl of clam casserole on the table.

- *A squeeze of lemon or lime juice can be added to the finished sauce, or a drizzle of* Lemon oil *(page 183).*

Serves 4 as a main course

- 1 × 750g (1¾lb) monkfish, filleted and portioned as below
- 550g(1¼lb) St George's mushrooms
- 2 tablespoons olive oil
- salt and pepper

- flour, for dusting
- 50g (2oz) butter plus a knob for the mushrooms
- 1 tablespoon torn flatleaf parsley
- 1 heaped teaspoon chopped chives

For the court-bouillon

- 3 small carrots
- 4 button onions, sliced
- 100ml (3½fl oz) white wine
- juice of 1 orange
- juice of ½ lemon
- ½ teaspoon light brown or demerara sugar

Monkfish steaks with court-bouillon and mushrooms

Court-bouillon is the acidic stock usually made for cooking fish and seafoods, but which also works very well with vegetables and some meats. The one used here is much milder, omitting the vinegar and replacing it with the sweet acidic bite of fresh orange and lemon juices, and the white wine, so now all of the flavours work with the mushrooms. Having joined us during that last week of April, St George's mushrooms reach their healthy plump prime during the month of May, and the monkfish is also at its prime through both of these spring months.

A 750g (1¾lb) fish, will be needed for this recipe. Once filleted from its central bone and trimmed (see method, page 35), the fillets are best cut at an angle, starting from the point of the tail, to provide good portions throughout, cutting each fillet into 4–6 slices, to create 2–3 steaks per portion.

Method To clean the mushrooms, trim away the base stalk and rinse the mushrooms in cold water. Leave them to dry on kitchen paper, while the court-bouillon and fish are being prepared and cooked.

To prepare the court-bouillon, cut the carrots into very thin round slices. (Before slicing, the carrots can be shaped with a cannelle cutter knife which, when pulled along the carrots, will create a groove. About 3–5 grooves offer a floral shape and look to the finished slices.) Place the carrot and onion slices, white wine, 50ml (2fl oz) of water, the juice of the orange and lemon, and sugar in a saucepan. Bring to a simmer and cook for 1–2 minutes, then remove from the heat and leave to cool.

Heat the olive oil in a large frying pan (or two). Season the monkfish steaks with salt and pepper and lightly dust with the flour. Once the pan is hot the fish can be carefully placed in it, taking care not to overfill the pan as this will reduce the temperature, boiling the fish rather than frying it.

Fry the fish for 2–3 minutes until golden brown, then turn and fry the other sides for a further 2–3 minutes. Once cooked, remove the fish from the pan and place in a suitable ovenproof dish. The steaks can now be kept warm in the preheated oven while the mushrooms are frying.

Rinse the frying pan and place it back on the heat. Once hot, add the knob of butter and the mushrooms. Fry on a high temperature for a few minutes until beginning to soften.

Return the court-bouillon to a simmer while the mushrooms are cooking. Add the 50g (2oz) of butter, shaking it into the court-bouillon until blended to a silky finish. Add the chopped herbs and season with salt and pepper.

Divide the mushrooms between four large bowls. Remove the monkfish steaks from the oven and arrange on top of the mushrooms. Any juices released from the fish can be added to the court-bouillon, before spooning it around the fish and mushrooms.

● *Cultivated or other wild mushrooms (ceps, chanterelles, etc.) can be used in place of the St George's variety featured here.*

Serves 4 as a starter
- 450g (1lb) wild salmon fillet, pin-boned (page 11)
- knob of butter
- 1 dessertspoon groundnut oil
- coarse sea salt
- twist of black pepper

For the sauce
- 100ml (3½fl oz) dry vermouth
- 150ml (¼pint) *Salmon stock* (page 177) or *Fish stock* (page 176)
- 2 tablespoons double cream
- 100ml (3½fl oz) crème fraîche
- 25g (1oz) sorrel leaves
- salt and pepper
- 25–50g (1–2oz) butter (optional)
- squeeze of lemon juice

Wild salmon slices with sorrel crème fraîche

This combination of flavours, salmon and sorrel, was brought to us in the late 70s by the Troisgros brothers, based at 'Les Frères Troisgros' restaurant in Roanne, France. The three Michelin-starred chefs produced a simple dish of gently pan-fried, thinly sliced, salmon sitting on a herbed sorrel cream sauce and a new classic was born. The beauty of this dish is that it will see you through the spring and summer months as both ingredients are readily available.

Wild salmon is with us from early spring to late summer and early autumn. It is during the summer months of June and July that you'll find it in more abundance, at a better price, but to get the first in spring is a real treat. If you find the wild salmon hard to come by, then simply replace it with farmed salmon, a product improving with every 'season'.

Young sorrel leaves are at their best from early March, the herb itself carrying a natural lemon flavour which can be helped along with a squeeze of the fruit itself. Instead of frying this fish, the thin slices will be plated cold, ready to be lightly oiled or buttered and then quickly warmed under a hot grill. As the top warms, it cooks but leaves a moist medium-rare finish underneath. The plates can be dressed with the fish well in advance, ready to finish when needed.

It is often best to purchase the whole salmon and enjoy its flavour in many different recipes over a two- or three-day period. This will also provide you with the salmon carcass from which to make your stock. The tail pieces can then be sliced for this particular dish, leaving the prime fillet for main-course portions.

Method Slice the salmon thinly, approximately 3–4mm (⅛–⅙in) thick. Place an open 15–17.5-cm (6–7-in) flan ring on the centre of each heatproof serving plate and carefully arrange the fillet slices to cover the space, creating a circle inside the rings. Remove the rings and cover the fish lightly with cling film and refrigerate until needed.

To make the sauce, boil together the vermouth and stock until reduced by half to two-thirds. Add the cream and return to a simmer. Add the crème fraîche and whisk to emulsify with the stock. The sauce can be left at this stage until needed. It will be reasonably loose, not over-creamy and coating, resulting in a lighter finish.

Preheat the oven and grill. Gently wash and pick the stalks from the sorrel leaves. Shred these, just before serving. Melt the knob of butter in a frying pan with the groundnut oil. Remove the cling film from the fish plates and brush each portion with the buttery oil. The plates can now be placed in turn under the preheated grill for just a minute or two to warm the tops of the slices. To continue this process, place the warmed plates on a lower shelf of the oven to retain the heat. While warming the wild salmon, reheat the sauce, season with salt and pepper and whisk in the butter, if using. Just 30 seconds before serving, add the shredded sorrel leaves and squeeze of lemon juice to enhance the rich lemon herb flavour.

To serve, brush the salmon again lightly with the buttery oil if needed, to leave a shiny finish. Sprinkle with coarse sea salt and a twist of black pepper, and then spoon the sauce around the salmon.

- *This dish also works very well with sea trout.*

Serves 4 as a starter
- 75g (3oz) podded peas
- iced water
- 450g (1lb) fillet of sea trout, pin-boned (page 11)
- flour, for dusting
- 1–2 tablespoons olive oil
- knob of butter
- ½ lime

For the cauliflower cream
- 25g (1oz) butter
- ½ cauliflower (or 1 small), cut into small florets
- 200ml (7fl oz) milk
- salt and ground white pepper
- squeeze of lemon juice (optional)

For the herb oil (makes 150ml /¼ pint: recipe can be halved)
- 1 tablespoon chopped curly or torn flatleaf parsley
- 1 tablespoon torn chervil leaves
- 1 tablespoon chopped dill
- 1 tablespoon chopped chives
- 1 tablespoon chopped tarragon
- 100ml (3½fl oz) olive oil
- 3 tablespoons groundnut oil

Fillet of sea trout on cauliflower cream with a fresh herb-pea dressing

This recipe will serve four as a starter, but it does also eat very well as a main course, simply multiplying the ingredients 1½–2 times. The herb oil certainly will not need to be increased, as quantities given make 150ml (¼pint). The oil keeps very well refrigerated for up to a week or more, retaining its rich herb flavour and green colour. The fresh peas will be beginning to show their faces during the last spring month of May; if unavailable, frozen peas can also be used or simply carry the recipe through to their prime time of summer. The main feature of this recipe, the sea trout, is as good as salmon, and also with us through the months of spring into summer – well worth catching.

Method To make the cauliflower cream, melt the butter in a heavy-based saucepan. Add the florets, cover with a lid and cook on a very low heat, without colouring, for 10–15 minutes, until beginning to soften. Add the milk and, once gently simmering, return the lid and cook for a further 15 minutes until the cauliflower is cooked and collapsing. Season with salt and white pepper. If the cauliflower has taken on a greyish muddy pink colour, don't worry, once liquidized the purée will whiten.

Blitz the cauliflower in a liquidizer, adding a spoonful at a time and loosening with the milk in which it was cooked. With continual liquidizing, a very soft smooth finish will be achieved. If using a food processor, the purée may well need to be pushed through a sieve for a completely smooth finish. Seasoning can now be added, and a squeeze of lemon juice as an optional extra, for a gentle citrus bite. This purée will eat at its best if served warm.

To make the herb dressing, reserve a level teaspoon of each herb to garnish the peas. Place all of the remaining chopped herbs in a liquidizer. Heat the olive and groundnut oils together in a small saucepan until just warm. Pour on top of the herbs and liquidize to a smooth purée. Strain the oil through a sieve. Kept refrigerated, the oil will last for up to two weeks.

To cook the fresh peas in advance, plunge them into boiling salted water and cook until tender. Drain and refresh in iced water before redraining. To reheat, the peas can either be microwaved or plunged back into boiling water for a minute.

Cut the sea trout fillet into four equal portions, checking the flesh has been pin-boned. Now score the skin side with a sharp knife, cutting just 2–3 lengths. Season the flesh side of the fillets with salt and pepper, and the skin side with salt only. Lightly dust the skin side with flour. Heat a frying pan and add the olive oil. Once bubbling, place the fillets in, skin-side down, making sure the fish is left alone and not moved. Cook for 4–5 minutes (6 minutes maximum), then add the knob of butter. Turn the fish and remove the pan from the heat. The residual heat of the pan will finish the cooking process without overcooking the fish.

Warm the peas, then add them to just 4–6 tablespoons of the fresh herb oil. Add the reserved chopped herbs and juice from the half lime. Adjust the seasoning with salt and pepper. Spoon the warm cauliflower purée into the centre of plates or bowls. Spoon the peas and dressing around, creating a border. Sit the sea trout on top of the cauliflower cream and serve.

Serves 4

- 2 × 350–400g (12–14oz) red mullet, pin-boned (page 11), scaled and filleted, all the trimmings saved
- 3 knobs of butter
- 2 shallots or ½ small onion, finely chopped
- good sprig of rosemary, plus more sprigs for garnish
- 150ml (¼pint) white wine
- 100ml (3½fl oz) whipping cream
- salt and pepper
- lemon juice, to taste
- flour, for dusting
- 2 tablespoons olive oil

For the potatoes

- 275–350g (10–12oz) new potatoes, well scrubbed
- 2 garlic cloves
- 2–3 tablespoons olive oil
- squeeze of lemon juice

Red mullet with a rosemary cream sauce on broken new potatoes

The combination of the red mullet and rosemary was made famous by a Swiss chef – Frédy Girardet. During the 80s this man was reputed to be the number one chef in the world, and a true master he was too. The beauty of this concept lies within its simplicity, utilising the maximum flavour from the fish itself, which is at its best in early spring and peaks again in August. The potatoes are a nice added extra, just cooked, then lightly forked with the mildest of garlic hints coming through. Here the quantities are for a starter. For a main course, simply double everything.

Method If your fishmonger is filleting the red mullets for you, ask for the central pin bones of each fillet also to be removed. Melt a knob of butter in a saucepan, and add the shallots or onion. Cook for a few minutes, until softened. Chop the red mullet head, bones and trimmings and add along with the rosemary. Continue to cook, without allowing to colour, for a further few minutes. Add the white wine and once boiling, reduce by three-quarters. Add 150ml (¼pint) of water and bring back to a simmer. Cook for 10–15 minutes, then increase the heat and reduce by half. Strain the fish stock through a sieve, squeezing all flavour and juices from the bones. Add the cream and return to a simmer, then cook for a few minutes until slightly thickened. Remove from the heat and season with salt, pepper and a squeeze of lemon juice to taste – just to lift other flavours, not to overpower them and make it a lemon sauce. The sauce can now be rewarmed when needed, not allowing it to overthicken, and finished with a knob of butter.

To prepare the potatoes, cook them in boiling salted water with the addition of one garlic clove, split in two. This will only give a slight garlic perfume to the potatoes. Once cooked, drain and, if not well scrubbed, it's best to peel them. Cut each potato into quarters. Split the remaining garlic clove and rub it around the inside of a bowl, leaving the halves in it. Add the potatoes, olive oil and a good squeeze of lemon juice, then season with salt and pepper. The potatoes can be left at this stage; simply toss all the flavours together and keep warm until needed.

To cook the fish, lightly season the mullet fillets with salt and lightly flour the skin sides. Warm the olive oil in a frying pan over a medium heat. Once hot, place the fish in the pan, skin-side down, and fry for 4 minutes, seasoning with salt and pepper. Turn the fillets in the pan, add a knob of butter to melt it and then remove from the heat. The residual pan-heat will finish the cooking without toughening the flesh, relaxing and softening it instead.

While the mullets are cooking and resting, the sauce can be warmed and the potatoes finished. Remove the two garlic halves from the bowl of potatoes and break down the potatoes with a fork. These can be as crumbly or smooth as you wish. However, with many new potato varieties, trying to oversmooth will create too much stickiness. The potatoes can now be either laid under the fish fillets or shaped/spooned at the top of the plates. Arrange the mullet fillets on the plates and pour the sauce around. Garnish each with a sprig of rosemary.

- *If serving as a main course, the best accompaniment is fresh peas or a green salad.*

Serves 4 as a main course
- 12 × 50–75g (2–3oz) flounder fillets, skinned
- salt and pepper
- flour, for dusting
- 2–3 tablespoons olive oil
- large knob of butter

- ½ quantity *Mayonnaise* (page 180, made with half vegetable oil and half olive oil)
- 1 heaped tablespoon chopped sorrel leaves
- squeeze of lemon juice (optional)

For the chips
- 4–6 large floury potatoes, preferably Maris Piper, King Edward or Desirée, peeled
- cooking oil, for deep-frying (vegetable, groundnut or olive for luxury chips)
- salt

Flounder fillets with boiled chips and sorrel mayonnaise

Flounder is a small flat fish similar in shape and look to plaice, dab and even lemon sole. Most fish is best when absolutely fresh but sadly this particular fish really suffers if it is not. Flounder is around to use during this time and marries well with the sorrel, which is plentiful in late spring through to summer. If unavailable, any of the similar fish mentioned can be used to replace the flounder in this recipe.

The boiled chips in the title is purely a description of the blanching method used before frying, to crisp and finish them. Classically, chips have always been pre-blanched in a lower-temperature fat, gently frying until tender before cooking, and then finished in hotter fat when required. The method does work well, but quite often the potato is greasy. Introducing the boiled method counters this problem, and instead the chips become tender and are ready to fry, with a clean, crisper finish.

Mayonnaise and chips are everyone's favourites. The addition of fresh lemony sorrel offers an extra complement to the fish itself. Making the *Mayonnaise* with equal parts of vegetable and olive oil reduces the sometimes over-powerful olive flavour, which with this particular recipe would tend to mask the fresh sorrel. Individual fillets of flounder will generally weigh 50–75g (2–3oz), so it is best to serve three fillets per portion, meaning you need three flounders for four portions.

Method To prepare the chips, trim the potatoes to a rectangular shape. Cut these into 1cm (½in) thick long slices, then cut each slice into sticks the same width. Blanch in boiling salted water for 4–6 minutes or until just tender. Carefully drain and leave to cool naturally, laid on a kitchen cloth. This will absorb any excess water, with the steam also removing any unwanted moisture as it rises.

Heat the oil to 180°C/350°F. While cooking the fish (see below), finish the boiled chips in the hot fat for just a few minutes, until golden brown and crispy. Shake off any excess fat and sprinkle with salt before serving.

Season the flounder fillets with salt and pepper and dust with flour. Heat a tablespoon or two of olive oil in a frying pan, and once hot, fry the fillets for 1–1½ minutes on each side until golden brown. Just before removing from the pan, add a little of the butter to finish. Remove the fish and keep warm while repeating the same process with the remaining fillets.

To finish the mayonnaise, simply add the chopped sorrel, along with a squeeze of lemon juice to further enhance it if needed.

Present the flounder fillets on plates, drizzling with a little of their cooking oil and butter, together with the chips and sorrel mayonnaise.

● *Lemon or lime wedges can also be offered or presented on the plate.*

● *It is not essential to add sorrel to the mayonnaise; it will also work very well plain.*

Serves 4 as a main course

- 1½lb (675g) leeks
- knob of butter, plus more for greasing
- salt and pepper
- 4 × 350–450g (12oz–1lb) flounders, filleted and skinned
- 2 teaspoons English or Dijon mustard (wholegrain mustard can also be used)

- 2 tablespoons *Mayonnaise* (page 180), or bought variety
- squeeze of lemon juice
- 4–6 tablespoons *Chive and tarragon oil* (page 182, optional)

Mustard-brushed flounder with steamed leek greens

Known among most fishermen as 'poor man's plaice', flounder is available from March to early winter. This flat fish, much the same shape as plaice, dab or lemon sole, is best eaten within the first two months of its season. Being a fairly well-travelled fish, quality can deteriorate after too many exhausting journeys. If you do manage to find this fish during March and April, do take advantage of its availability. When very fresh, it will eat as well as any plaice during this short spell. Used mainly as bait by fishermen, this will give you an indication of its more than competitive price.

To enhance and set off what this fish has to offer, this recipe, which I first came across in the USA, works very well. It simply involves a combination of mayonnaise and mustard brushed over the fillets before grilling. The leeks lift the fish with their oniony bite, and in the month of March are just ending a more than successful season.

An optional extra is the *Chive and tarragon oil*. Both flavours also match well with mustard and leeks. If you're not too sure about the blanching and blitzing, both herbs chopped and added to olive oil will work almost as well.

Method Remove the bases of the leeks and split each leek in two lengthwise. Remove the tough outside layer, then shred the leeks finely, including the maximum quantity possible of the green tops. Wash well and leave to drain in a colander.

To cook the leeks, melt the knob of butter in a large saucepan. Add the leeks and cook on a fairly high heat. The moistness of the leeks will create steam, cooking them in just 2–3 minutes until tender. Once cooked, season with salt and pepper.

While the leeks are cooking, season the flounder fillets with salt and pepper. Butter a large baking tray (you may need two) and place the fillets on it. Mix the mustard into the mayonnaise and finish with a squeeze or two of lemon juice. Brush this liberally over each of the fillets. Place the fillets under a preheated grill and cook for just 2–3 minutes, until golden brown and cooked through. The fillets can now be arranged on plates, followed by the leeks. To finish, drizzle with the chive and tarragon oil, if using.

- *A teaspoon of extra chives and tarragon can be added to the flavoured oil just before serving.*

Serves 4 as a main course
- 4 × 175g (6oz) portions of cod fillet, pin-boned (page 11), with skin left on
- 150–175g (5–6oz) coarse sea salt
- 3 small young spring greens
- salt and pepper
- iced water (optional)
- knob of butter
- flour, for dusting
- 2 tablespoons vegetable oil

For the orange sauce
- 2 shallots, finely chopped (or 1 heaped tablespoon finely chopped onion)
- 100ml (3½fl oz) white wine
- juice of 1 orange
- 2 tablespoons single cream
- 50g (2oz) butter, diced

For the red wine dressing
- 150ml (¼pint) red wine
- 1–2 sugar cubes
- 1 tablespoon olive oil

For the candied orange
- 3 oranges
- 50g (2oz) caster sugar

Crispy cod with candied orange spring green hearts

Cod is one of Britain's most popular fish, its flaky texture taking many a 'battering' during its time, however, its flavour comes more alive when it is fried or grilled. Straightforward poaching or steaming, unless the fish comes almost direct from the boat, can often leave you searching for something to happen. Having said that, the steaming process the fish experiences when battered and fried is quite a different kettle of fish altogether.

For the spring greens, I'm choosing the central heart cores, cutting each into halves or quarters. The fresh flavour of the spring greens is lifted, picking up a bitter-sweet bite from the oranges.

Method To make the candied orange peel, remove the rind from all three oranges with a vegetable peeler. Slice the pieces of rind lengthwise into very thin strips. Cover with cold water and bring to a simmer. Drain and refresh in cold water. Repeat the same process twice more.

Squeeze and strain the juice from all three oranges. Pour into a saucepan with the sugar and blanched orange strips. Slowly bring to a simmer and cook on a low heat for 30 minutes, reducing it to a syrup. As the syrup cooks, the orange rind becomes tender. Remove from the heat and leave to cool. This quantity gives more than is needed here, but if refrigerated will last almost indefinitely.

Score the cod skins with a sharp knife in strips 5mm (¼in) apart. Sprinkle the coarse sea salt on a suitable platter and place the fish, skin-side down, on top. Leave for 30 minutes to draw excess moisture from the skin. When cooking the fish, the skin then very quickly becomes crispy.

Remove the outside leaves from the spring greens, splitting the central hearts and cutting them into quarters. These can now be cooked to order, or pre-blanched. Whichever option you wish to take, simply plunge them into rapidly boiling salted water and cook for just 2–4 minutes until tender. If pre-cooking, refresh in iced water. The spring greens can now be microwaved or heated in a knob of butter and a little water, then seasoned with salt and pepper.

To make the orange sauce, place the shallots or onion in a saucepan with the white wine. Bring to the boil and reduce until almost dry. Add the orange juice, return to the boil and reduce by half. Add the cream and, once warm, stir in the diced butter. Season to taste.

To cook the cod, remove the fillets from the salt, rinse and wipe dry, then dust with flour and season with a twist of pepper. Heat the oil in a frying pan and, once hot, carefully place the fillets in, skin-side down. Cook for 6–7 minutes, until golden brown and crispy. Turn the fish in the pan and cook for just another minute. Remove the fish and keep warm.

Drain any excess oil from the pan, then pour in the red wine. Boil and reduce by two-thirds, then stir one sugar cube in, tasting for sweetness. If still too harsh, add the other sugar cube, then add the olive oil. Strain through a tea strainer.

Arrange the cod fillets and 3–4 pieces of spring greens per portion, side by side on plates. Sprinkle 6–7 strands of candied orange over each portion of spring greens and spoon the orange sauce over. The red wine dressing can now be spooned around the fish.

Serves 4 as a main course
- 1 quantity *Nutty Béarnaise sauce* (page 179)
- 450–675g (1lb–1½lb) purple sprouting broccoli spears
- iced water (optional)
- 4 × 175–225 (6–8oz) portions of turbot fillet, skinned
- flour, for dusting
- 1 tablespoon olive oil
- salt and pepper, plus coarse sea salt
- knob of butter
- 1 teaspoon chopped flatleaf parsley
- 1 lemon, quartered

Pan-fried turbot with nutty Béarnaise sprouting broccoli

Turbot begins its British season in April, going through to February. This flat fish carries the reputation of being the king of all fish. Its own distinctive flavour needs little help, just drizzling it with butter and a sprinkling of salt can be more than enough. In France the fish was traditionally cooked in a *turbotière*, a large diamond-shaped piece of equipment, used to steam or poach the fish. The simple accompaniment would be a sauce hollandaise. I'm not moving too far from this elegant simplicity; a green vegetable with the buttered fish creates an instant friendship. With purple sprouting broccoli also at its best at this time of the year, the combination of the two seemed more than logical.

The *Nutty Béarnaise sauce* (page 179) holds flavours with which both are familiar. The turbot has always enjoyed a sauce in the style of a hollandaise, and the nutbrown butter flavour of this particular variety is one that this fish (and many others) is often paired with when shallow-fried.

The concept of this dish will work with almost all flat white fish (lemon sole, plaice, halibut, flounder, etc.), as well as with cod, salmon and skate. It's also not essential to serve the nutbrown variety of the sauce; a plain *Béarnaise* (page 178) or *Simple hollandaise* (page 178) works well, or even just melted butter.

Method Make the nutty Béarnaise sauce in advance, as instructed in the recipe, adding the chopped tarragon and the parsley just before serving.

To prepare the broccoli, cut the large spears from the tops and continue to cut away the smaller surrounding spears, leaving any small tender leaves attached. If the spears are young and tender, their stalks need not be peeled (this is best tested by taking a raw bite; if crisp and tender, then simply leave). If slightly chewy, it is best to peel away the outer skin by hand or with a peeler. The broccoli will now just take a few minutes to cook in rapidly boiling salted water, and will change in colour from purple to two-tone (purple top and green spear), finishing with rich green spears. If cooking the broccoli in advance, once tender quickly plunge into iced water, then drain and refrigerate until needed. To reheat, either microwave or plunge into boiling water for just a minute or two.

Lightly dust the skinned sides of the fish with flour. Heat the olive oil in a frying pan. Once hot, place the fillets in, floured-sides down, and season the exposed sides with salt and pepper. Fry the fish over a moderate heat for 5–6 minutes until a light golden brown. Add the knob of butter, then turn the fish over in the pan and remove from the heat. The fish will now finish cooking, needing just another minute or two in the pan, without becoming overcooked or leathery. Sprinkle each fillet with a little coarse sea salt.

Meanwhile, the warmed broccoli spears can be presented on plates and topped with the finished nutbrown Béarnaise sauce.

Arrange the turbot next to the broccoli, spooning a little of the cooking butter over each and garnishing with the lemon quarters.

Serves 4 as a main course

- 4 × 550g (1¼lb) lemon soles, each divided into 4 skinned fillets
- 15–25g (½–1oz) butter, to finish sauce, plus a knob for the spinach and more for greasing
- salt and pepper
- 450g (1lb) baby carrots, peeled or scraped, leaving 1–1½cm (½–¾in) of stalk on top
- 1 vanilla pod, split and seeds scraped out
- sprig of rosemary, plus ½ teaspoon picked leaves, cut into shorter sticks
- 1 level teaspoon caster sugar
- 2–3 tablespoons double cream
- squeeze of lemon juice
- 675g (1½lb) baby spinach, washed and stalks removed if necessary

Lemon sole and spinach with vanilla-rosemary carrots

Vanilla is a spice that will work with many vegetables, and the baby carrots and young spinach available to us in late spring both accept its quite aromatic touch. Rosemary is a herb that can be so overpowering, but here lends just enough to complement all the other flavours. With this recipe the baby carrots are going to be well cooked, taking on a gentle softness so as not to fight the tenderness of the delicate sole fillets.

Method Preheat the oven to 190°C/375°F/Gas 5. Fold each sole fillet into a looped cravat shape. Place on a large roasting tray lined with buttered and seasoned parchment paper and refrigerate.

Place the carrots in a large saucepan and barely cover with water. Add the vanilla pod and seeds, along with the sprig of rosemary, caster sugar and a pinch of salt. Bring to a simmer and cook for 8–10 minutes, or longer if the carrots are not so thin, until cooked through. Remove the carrots from the pan and keep to one side.

Boil the cooking liquor to reduce by three-quarters. Remove the vanilla pod and rosemary. Add the double cream and bring to a simmer. When needed, the sauce can now be finished, adding just 15g (½oz) of the measured butter. For a thicker and richer finish add the remaining measured butter. Finally, add a squeeze of lemon juice, along with the cut rosemary leaves.

Season the fish with salt and pour a little water into the tray to barely cover the base of the roasting tray. Bring to a simmer on the hob, cover with foil and finish in the preheated oven for just a few minutes, five maximum. Once cooked, remove the fillets from the oven.

While the fish is cooking, melt the knob of butter in a large saucepan and, once bubbling, add the spinach leaves. These will cook in literally just a minute or two, becoming tender almost immediately. Season with salt and pepper, then drain off any excess water.

The carrots can now be reheated in a tablespoon or two of water or in a microwave for a few seconds. Arrange the sole fillets on plates, with the carrots and spinach sitting either side. Spoon the sauce over the carrots or simply around the plates to complete the dish.

- *If baby spinach is unavailable, a few extra minutes will need to be added to the larger spinach leaves' cooking time.*

Serves 4 as a main course
- 2 × 675g–750g (1½–1¾lb) plaice or lemon soles, filleted and skinned
- flour, for dusting
- knob of butter, plus more for greasing and buttering
- salt and pepper
- 900g (2lb) fresh young spinach, washed and stalks removed

For the champagne cream sauce
- knob of butter
- 3 shallots, finely chopped
- 175g (6oz) button or chestnut mushrooms, sliced
- 200ml (7fl oz) champagne or sparkling white wine
- 100ml (3½fl oz) Noilly Prat dry vermouth

- 200ml (7fl oz) double cream
- 100ml (3½fl oz) crème fraîche
- 1–2 teaspoons lemon juice
- salt
- cayenne pepper
- 2 egg yolks

Grilled plaice or lemon sole fillets with champagne-glazed spinach

Either of these two flat fish can be used in this recipe, both available to us during the spring month of May.

It's not over-essential to use extravagant champagne, white wine will also blend with the other flavours. However, champagne or sparkling white wine does seem to add a little extra fizz to the end result, working alongside a Noilly Prat vermouth.

Method To create an extra grilling effect with the plaice or lemon soles, they can first be marked with a hot skewer. Although not essential, it helps the finished presentation and imparts a slight bitter grilled flavour. To achieve this, simply heat thin metal skewers on a naked flame or under a hot grill.

Lightly flour the filleted presentation side of each fish fillet (you'll have two smaller fillets from each of the large ones, giving two pieces per serving) and mark at an angle by laying the hot skewer across it to form the deep lines, reheating the skewer as needed. Once all are marked, lay on a buttered and seasoned tray, then lightly butter and salt the fillets.

For the sauce, melt the knob of butter in a frying pan and add the chopped shallots. Cook for a few minutes until softened but not coloured, then add the mushrooms. Continue to cook until these are also softened. Add the champagne or sparkling wine and vermouth and bring to a simmer. Cook on a high heat to reduce by three-quarters. Add half of the double cream along with the crème fraîche, and bring back to a simmer. Cook for 2–3 minutes, then add the lemon juice with salt and cayenne pepper to taste. Strain the sauce into a clean pan, keeping the mushrooms and shallots to one side.

While making the sauce, melt a knob of butter in a small saucepan. Add the spinach leaves and cook for a few minutes until wilted and tender. Season with salt and a twist of pepper, squeezing away any excess water.

Add the reserved mushrooms and shallots from the sauce to the spinach and divide either between individual ovenproof dishes big enough to carry two pieces of fish each, or two large dishes that will hold four fish pieces each when served.

Preheat the grill. Lightly whip the remaining double cream to soft peaks, then mix with the egg yolks. Fold this into the champagne cream sauce and pour over the spinach. Glaze to a golden brown under a preheated very hot grill.

The fish will now take just 3–4 minutes to cook under the preheated grill. The grilled fillets can now be presented on plates or sitting on top of the glazed spinach and mushrooms.

● *The fish can also be plainly steamed, presenting the natural white fillets on top of the glazed spinach and mushrooms.*

Serves 4

- 4 mackerel fillets, taken from 2 × 350–400g (12–14oz) fish, pin-boned (page 11) and skinned
- flour, for dusting
- 1–2 tablespoons cooking oil
- knob of butter

For the gooseberry and mustard seed sauce

- 2 level teaspoons white/yellow or black mustard seeds
- juice and finely grated zest of ½ lime
- 225g (8oz) gooseberries, topped and tailed
- 1 tablespoon caster sugar
- 25g (1oz) butter
- salt and pepper

Seared mackerel with gooseberry and mustard seed sauce

The combination of mackerel and gooseberries goes back a long way, surviving many changes of fashion and culinary style with the tartness of the fruit cutting into the oily flesh of the fish. The gooseberry fruit does tend to appear during the last week or two of spring. It's extra firm and tart at this time (until it gains its summer sweetness), and this is what's needed for this particular dish. If gooseberries are not available in your local area around this time, then simply hold on to this recipe until the following season.

Many recipes opt for the puréed finish to the sauce. With this recipe, however, the fruits are only taken to the 'popping' stage, when they are just beginning to break down, with the juices sweetened with a touch of sugar. The bite of mustard seed provides warmth, giving the finished sauce a loose chutney-like appeal.

This dish can be served as a starter or main course, either working very well with the *Creamy new potatoes with goat's cheese* (page 92).

Method To make the sauce, first soak the mustard seeds in the lime juice, adding a drop or two of water if needed. This will cause the seeds to swell, releasing their warmth and flavour. Place the gooseberries, sugar, lime zest and 5 tablespoons of water in a saucepan and bring to a simmer. As the gooseberries are cooking, they will begin to soften and pop, approximately 7–8 minutes depending on the size of the fruits. At this point remove the pan from the heat. Allow the sauce to relax for 10–15 minutes, then stir and check the consistency and sweetness. If too thin, return to the stove and continue to simmer to a softer and slightly thicker consistency. It is best not to make the sauce too sweet, but if over-tart, add sugar to taste. Once finished, add the mustard seeds with the lime juice and butter, stirring both in thoroughly, and season with a pinch of salt and a twist of pepper.

Season the mackerel fillets with salt and pepper, then dust the skinned sides with a little flour. Heat the oil in a large frying pan, and place the fillets in, floured-side down. Fry for up to 4 minutes, then add the knob of butter. Turn the fillets in the pan and remove the pan from the heat. Leave to bubble in the warm pan for a minute or two, during which time the fish will finish cooking and its texture will relax. The fillets can now be offered with the gooseberry sauce.

● *A light, green salad will eat very well with this dish, along with hot new potatoes.*

Serves 4 as a generous starter
- 2 heaped tablespoons salt (or 3.5 litres /6pints *Court-bouillon* (page 176)
- 4 × 675g–1kg (1½–2¼lb) spider crabs
- knob of butter
- 225g (8oz) cooked linguine pasta or noodles
- 1 large orange, segmented and each segment cut into 3–4 pieces
- 1 heaped teaspoon chopped tarragon

For the sauce
- 1 tablespoon olive oil
- 1 small fennel, cut into roughly 5mm (¼in) dice
- 1 small carrot, cut into roughly 5mm (¼in) dice
- 1 small onion, cut into roughly 5mm (¼in) dice
- 1 garlic clove, crushed
- 350g (12oz) crab claw and leg shells from the spider crabs, finely chopped

- juice of 2 oranges and 3 strips of peel
- 4 tomatoes, roughly chopped
- 2 sprigs of tarragon
- glass of white wine
- pinch of saffron (optional)
- 300ml (½pint) water or fish-flavoured *Instant stock* (page 175)
- 2–3 tablespoons whipping cream
- salt and pepper
- squeeze of lemon juice
- 25g (1oz) butter

Warm spider crab linguine with orange and tarragon sauce

Mid-to-late spring, and the spider crab becomes available. Sadly this wonderfully sweet and tender shellfish is not so commonly found and available as the brown crab. It would seem most of this almost spider-shaped culinary treat is exported to Europe, to be enjoyed in France and Spain.

Cooking and picking the meat from crabs does seem to become laborious, the spider crab probably the most fiddly, and perhaps this is why we send them on to our European friends. Whatever the case, should you manage to stumble upon these richly flavoured creatures, treat yourself and cook and clean them, even if just to add them to a salad. You won't be disappointed.

This recipe makes starter portions, the crab and pasta served back in the shell topped with a home-made bisque-like cream sauce. For a light finish, the sauce is blitzed with an electric hand blender, leaving you with a frothy foam to spoon over the crabs, hiding a very tasty surprise underneath. The crabs for this recipe are best between 675–1kg (1½–2¼lb) each. The larger ones probably provide enough for main courses, the smaller ones suiting generous starter/supper portions. The crabs can be cooked in salted water or court-bouillon (the latter will obviously lend more flavour to the crabs, enhancing their natural sweetness).

Method Bring 3.5 litres (6pints) of salted water or court-bouillon to the boil. Place the crabs in the pot, making sure they are well covered. Bring back to the boil, lower the temperature slightly and simmer for approximately 8, maximum 10, minutes. Remove the pot from the stove and allow the crabs to cool in the stock for a further 8, maximum 10, minutes. There is a particular flavoursome bonus if court-bouillon is used, as when the shellfish relaxes, the meat absorbs the rich fragrant spicy flavours. Once cooled the crabs can be cracked from their shells.

First remove the claws and legs and break them open with a nutcracker or with a sharp tap from the back of a knife. Many small spider crabs will not have much, if any, meat in their thin legs. However, it's best to crack them open anyway, as you don't want to waste or lose any of the meat. Once all the claw and leg meat has been removed, the flesh can be torn into strands, checking carefully for any shell splinters. The next stage is to detach the body of the crab from the back shell. Once turned onto its back, the bony pointed flap can be pulled away. Insert a strong knife between the shell and body and twist firmly to release the meat. Any grey-looking gills, or dead man's fingers as they are also known, should be detached and discarded. Before spooning the brown meat from the shell remove the stomach sac (intestines) and discard. This can easily be achieved by applying pressure to the small piece of shell situated just behind the eyes. Press, discarding both the bone and intestines. Pour away any excess water from the shell. The brown meat can now be spooned from the central body, rinsing under cold water quickly on removal. This brown meat can now be pushed through a sieve to help remove any crushed shell and provide a smoother finish. Keep it separate from the white meat.

The central body can now be quartered, carefully

removing all of the white meat with a pick, skewer or cocktail stick. (This stage does take some patience, but it's worth every minute.) Each quarter can be halved to check for any extra strands of meat. Check the meat for any broken shell, before adding it to the white claw meat. The claws, legs and central body shell can be chopped and used to make the sauce. The round crab shells can now be well rinsed, ready to present the finished dish. The shell edge can be trimmed, if needed, with scissors to remove any thin 'beard'.

To make the sauce, warm the olive oil in a saucepan and add the chopped fennel, carrot and onion along with the crushed garlic. Cover with a lid and cook on a gentle heat for 8–10 minutes, stirring from time to time, until soft. Add the finely chopped crab claws and legs along with the orange peel and cook for a further 5 minutes. Add the chopped tomatoes and tarragon and, after a few more minutes, the white wine. Bring to the boil and reduce by two-thirds. Add the orange juice and bring back to the boil again and reduce by two-thirds. Add the saffron, if using, and then the water or fish-flavoured instant stock. Bring to a simmer and cook for 10 minutes. At this point, the sauce can be passed through a sieve or liquidized for a smoother result. For the smoothest of finishes, push through a fine sieve.

Add the whipping cream and return the sauce to a simmer. Season with salt and pepper and a squeeze of lemon juice, then stir in the 25g (2oz) of butter to finish. The sauce needs to be of a glossy loose consistency. If too thick, the sauce will not blitz to a light frothy finish.

To finish the dish, warm the brown crab meat in 1–2 tablespoons of the cream sauce. Melt the knob of butter in a large pan. Add the cooked pasta or noodles and season with salt and pepper. Warm gently, adding the orange pieces, the chopped tarragon and the white crab meat, along with a few tablespoons of cream sauce. This will now loosen the pasta, warming the complete dish. Check the seasoning again.

Spoon the brown meat into the base of each washed shell. Divide the crab, orange and tarragon noodles between each shell, then blitz the finished sauce and liberally spoon over each. The finished shells are best presented on a folded napkin on a plate or in a soup plate, the cloth preventing the shell from sliding. The shells have a 'pillow' presentation of creamy sauce sitting on top of the creamy crab noodles.

● *A splash of brandy or Grand Marnier can be added to the finished sauce for an even livelier flavour.*

● *It is not essential to blitz the sauce to a frothy consistency. Simply loosen the noodles with a few extra spoonfuls and this will provide equally good finished flavours.*

Serves 4 as a starter
- 225g (8oz) whole North Atlantic prawns, preferably raw
- 175g (6oz) (approx 8–10) cleaned scallops
- knob of butter
- salt and pepper
- 1 quantity *Simple hollandaise sauce* (page 178)
- 10 green peppercorns in brine, cut in halves (optional)
- 1 quantity *Prawn dressing* (page 118)
- handful of rocket leaves or watercress (optional)
- drizzle of olive oil (optional)

Warm scallops and prawns hollandaise

Potted prawns and shrimps are the ones set in butter and served accompanied by brown bread or warm toast. It is from this concept that this dish was born.

Scallops are reaching the end of their British season at the beginning of the spring. This is often a good time to buy, with the prices lower than during the winter months. Their texture softens the finished dish, with the firmness of the prawns preventing an over-milky finish.

The butter connection with the two seafoods is to be found with a sauce hollandaise, offering its creamy consistency as their binder. An extra flavouring touch is the *Prawn dressing*, its lemon/bisque bite cutting into the overall taste. It's not essential to add the dressing, a sauce hollandaise with scallops and prawns is a pretty sound dish alone, but an alternative finish that maximizes the prawn flavour really shouldn't be ignored.

The quantities given here are measured so as to not offer too much of an over-rich start to your meal. These portions can of course be increased, with plenty of hollandaise and dressing to share.

Method If raw, the prawns first need to be plunged into boiling salted water for 30 seconds, then removed and left to cool. Shell the prawns, saving 50g (2oz) of the shells for the dressing. Refrigerate the prawns until needed, using the shells to follow the dressing method on page 118.

If the scallops are bought in the shell, prise them open with a knife and detach the scallop from the lower shell. The surrounding membrane can now be pulled away and discarded (unless using to flavour a stock or sauce). Rinse the scallops and dry on kitchen paper or a cloth. The coral can now be separated from the 'meat', utilizing it as noted below. The scallops can now be cut into quarters if small and eighths if larger. Also refrigerate until needed.

Melt the knob of butter in a small saucepan with 2 tablespoons of water over a low heat. Once melted, add the scallops and prawns. Heat gently until just warmed.

It is important not to boil the seafood, as this will toughen and dry their texture. Once warmed, season with salt and pepper and transfer the shellfish to a bowl. Any juices left in the pan should be quickly boiled and reduced to just a tablespoon, then poured over the shellfish. Add 4–6 tablespoons of the hollandaise sauce, just enough to bind without over-masking (any excess can be offered separately).

Spoon the seafood between plates or bowls. If using, place five green peppercorn halves around each portion (these provide a perfumed bite to the complete dish) and drizzle the prawn dressing around the portions. Season the rocket or watercress with salt, pepper and a drop of olive oil, if using, and then arrange 4–5 leaves on top of each.

● *The scallop corals can be kept frozen, to be used in future scallop salads or other dishes. If blitzed and blended with an equal quantity of butter before freezing, the butter can then be used as a fish sauce thickener and enhancer. Only very little of this particular butter needs to be added to a fish sauce and once it is whisked into a hot sauce it must not be reboiled, or this will result in a grainy consistency.*

Serves 4–6 as a main course
- 1 lemon
- 1 × 1.5–1.75kg (3½–4lb) new season's leg of lamb, trimmed of excess fat
- salt
- 1 tablespoon finely cracked black pepper (mignonette)
- 1 tablespoon picked thyme leaves
- cooking oil, plus more for greasing

- 1 tablespoon runny honey
- glass of white wine (approximately 150ml/ ¼pint)
- 300ml (½pint) *Instant stock* (page 175) or water
- ⅛ stock cube (optional)
- 150ml (¼pint) double cream (optional)

For the potatoes
- 900g–1.25kg (2–2½lb) large potatoes, preferably Maris Piper, King Edwards or Desirée, peeled
- 50g–100g (2–4oz) melted butter, plus extra for brushing (optional)
- salt and pepper

For the sprouting broccoli
- 1kg (2¼lb) purple sprouting broccoli spears
- knob of butter

Roast lemon peppered lamb with baked potato cake

The new season's lamb is with us, offering a sweet tender finish that really needs no help at all. However, the lemon and pepper do offer a slightly fiery, piquant bite, only complementing and not fighting with, the sweet succulent slices.

The baked potato cake is a French classic, usually known as *pommes Anna*, and consists of lots of potato slices layered in a tin and baked with the roasting lamb.

I'm also including young purple sprouting broccoli in this recipe. It is at its best between the months of March and April, so I thought we'd take advantage and include it. Should the broccoli be unavailable, freshly buttered spring greens (page 63) are the perfect substitute.

Method To cook the potatoes, preheat the oven to 220°C/425°F/Gas 7. For a neater finish, it's best to peel three or four of the larger potatoes leaving them a smooth, almost cylindrical, shape. Slicing these length-wise, before drying on kitchen paper, provides the right length of slice to line the cake tin. It is also best to cut two of these potatoes 2mm (⅟₁₆in) thick. A mandolin slicer will obviously make this a lot easier. All remaining potatoes are best sliced lengthwise very thinly. This will make them more pliable and easier to use.

Use a 17.5 × 8–10-cm (7 × 3–4-in) cake tin and brush well with some of the melted butter, saving the remain-der to work through the potatoes. (100g/4oz is listed as an optional total quantity to use, which does look and sound extravagant – and that it is too. It is not essential but will leave you with a very rich and memorable

flavour.) For the most attractive of finishes a disc of 5cm (2in) can be cut from one of the slices and placed in the centre of the base of the tin. Arrange the thicker potato slices overlapping neatly around this to cover the base of the tin. Place the thinner slices, also overlapping and standing upright, around the edge of the tin, making sure 1cm (½in) is folded and pressed onto the base. This helps the whole cake turn out with a gâteau-like presentation.

To finish, place all the remaining potato slices in a bowl, season with salt and pepper and mix with the remaining melted butter. Pack and press these into the tin until all are used. Any overhanging side slices can now be folded back in and pressed onto the 'cake'. Cover with foil, pressing it down firmly against the potatoes and place in the oven. The potatoes will take approximately 1 hour 20 minutes to 1½ hours. This will be perfect timing, considering the lamb's roasting and relaxing time (see overleaf). After 30 minutes, remove the foil from the cake tin and continue to cook until tender and golden brown. To check the potatoes are completely tender, pierce with a knife.

It's always best to allow a resting time of 5–10 minutes before turning out the cake. To do so, gently loosen the edge from the tin with a small knife, then place a large flat baking tray over the cake tin and turn over. The cake will now fall from the tin onto the tray. The top of the cake may well still be a little opaque and not completely coloured. If so, lightly brush with butter, place under a preheated grill and finish to a rich crispy golden brown.

To prepare the lamb, finely grate the zest from the lemon before cutting the fruit in two. Rub one of the lemon halves over the leg of lamb, squeezing the juice. Now sprinkle the leg with the lemon zest, salt, cracked black pepper and thyme leaves. Put on a lightly oiled roasting tray and then place in the oven. Roasting from cold, without preliminary frying, will always take longer. (For medium-rare meat, cook for up to 1 hour and 15 minutes, for medium up to 1 hour 30 minutes, for medium-to-well-done 1 hour 40 minutes, and for completely well done 1 hour 50 minutes to 2 hours.) After the first 30 minutes of cooking, the lamb should be basted every 20 minutes. For extra flavour and finish to the lamb, 20 minutes before its cooking time is complete remove the leg from the oven and tray and pour away any excess lamb fat. Return the leg to the tray and spoon over the honey. Return to the oven and baste frequently. As the honey cooks it will reduce, leaving a slightly caramelized finish.

Remove the leg from the oven and roasting tray and allow to rest for a minimum of 15–20 minutes. Pour away any extra excess fat from the tray leaving all residue behind. A very sticky finish can be achieved by heating the tray on the stove. Doing this will boil, reduce and thicken the residue for an even stronger caramelized flavour. Pour in the white wine which will instantly boil and sizzle, lifting the flavours from the pan. Once the wine is reduced by half, add the water or stock. After just a few minutes of sizzling, the lamb-stock cooking liquor is formed. This should now be tasted and, if shallow in flavour, add the piece of stock cube. The liquor can be strained and served as a loose gravy.

For a lemon cream sauce finish, allow the stock to reduce by a third, then add the double cream and cook for a few minutes to thicken. Add just enough of the juice from the remaining lemon half to enhance the flavour, and strain as for the loose gravy above.

The broccoli needs little preparation and cooking time. The finer spears can be picked from the large central stalk, leaving any small leaves attached to them. The large flower on top can now be cut off, leaving a good 5cm (2in) of stalk attached.

Place the large pieces in rapidly boiling salted water and cook for just 2–3 minutes before adding the smaller pieces. Cook for a further 1 minute, drain, season and finish with the knob of butter.

The complete presentation of a whole potato cake and bowl of sprouting broccoli with the roast leg of lamb and gravy is quite spectacular. To carve the lamb, it is best to cut it at a 45° angle, starting at the thin shank end. As you carve, the slices grow and the meat becomes pinker. The potato cake will slice into 6–8 wedges.

● *The purple sprouting broccoli can be cooked in advance, refreshing it in iced water once tender. To reheat, simply plunge back into boiling water for a minute or microwave. The Steamed purple sprouting broccoli with melting wild garlic and orange butter (page 28) or the Nutty Béarnaise sprouting broccoli (page 46) or simply buttered greens, all eat well with this dish.*

● *It is not essential to surround the edge of the cake tin with the upright potato slices. Although these will obviously enhance the presentation, once the base is laid the rest can simply be packed on top for speed.*

Serves 4 as a main course

- 1 shoulder of lamb, boned and rolled (about 675g/1½lb)
- salt and pepper
- 2 tablespoons cooking oil
- 1 lemon
- 300ml (½pint) white wine
- 900ml (1½pint) *Chicken stock* (page 175) or *Instant stock* (page 175)
- 20 sorrel leaves
- 1 dessertspoon clear honey
- 1 level tablespoon ready-made English mustard
- 1 heaped teaspoon butter, plus a knob for the samphire
- 1 heaped teaspoon plain flour
- 90ml (3floz) whipping or single cream
- 675g (1½lb) samphire

Pot-roasted lamb with sorrel and samphire

This dish has quite a combination of flavours, but all work with, and for, one another. There is also a honey-and-mustard glaze as an extra with which to finish the lamb, providing a sticky, hot, sweetness to the meat. The fresh sorrel lends a lemony touch, that works well with honey and mustard, and finishes the light cream sauce.

Marsh samphire, a salty vegetable, grows by seashore rocks and is often found in the East Anglian marshes. It is most usually served with seafood, however young marsh-land lamb is often served with samphire as a salty garnish, too. This shoulder may not be of the marshland variety but it does eat well with this well-seasoned vegetable and the creamy sorrel sauce. If you can't find samphire, extra-fine French beans or flat runner beans sliced thinly could act as a substitute, but they are best seasoned with rock salt to get the abundance of flavour required.

Method Preheat the oven to 160°C/325°F/Gas 3. Season the rolled shoulder with salt and pepper. Heat the cooking oil in a roasting tray, placing in the lamb. Cook over a moderate heat until the joint is well coloured all over.

Place the lamb in an ovenproof braising pot and rub with the juice from half the lemon. Add half of the white wine with the chicken or instant stock, bring to a gentle simmer and cover with a lid. The lamb can now be pot-roasted in the preheated oven for 2½ hours. After the first 2 hours, add fourteen of the sorrel leaves to the pot. As the lamb continues to cook, the sorrel flavour will influence the stock. The joint will now be very tender. Remove the meat from the pot and place on a roasting tray.

Strain the cooking liquor through a sieve, and skim away excess fat. In a saucepan, boil the remaining white wine and the juice from half of the lemon, and reduce by three-quarters, then add 200ml (7fl oz) of the cooking liquor. Whisk in the honey and mustard, then spoon this over the lamb and place the tray on top of the stove. On a medium heat, boil and reduce the liquor, turning the lamb as it glazes. This can be a little untidy, due to spitting, but does help the lamb accept the glaze very quickly. Once the liquor is completely reduced and sticky, remove the lamb from the heat and leave to rest for 15–20 minutes.

In a clean saucepan, the remaining cooking liquor can now be boiled and reduced, if necessary, leaving you with approximately 300ml (½pint). Mix together the teaspoon of butter with the flour, then whisk this in bit by bit. The butter and flour combination is a thickening agent known as *beurre manié* (kneaded butter). This small quantity will just start to thicken the sauce. Simmer gently for a few minutes then add the cream. Any remaining last few drops of lemon juice from the two halves can also be added. Season with salt and pepper. Finely shred the remaining six sorrel leaves and add them to the sauce.

The samphire can be prepared in advance, washing it well and snipping away any woody stems. Plunge the samphire pieces into boiling unsalted water (the samphire is very salty). Once reboiling, drain and season with a twist of pepper and add the knob of butter.

To serve, carve the shoulder into thick slices and offer them with the samphire and sorrel cream sauce.

- Mashed potatoes *(page 186) or new potatoes will eat well with this dish.*

Serve 4–6 as a main course

- 1 × 1.5kg (3–3¼lb) lean brisket of beef, salted and soaked (see below)
- Chicken stock (page 175) or beef- or chicken-flavoured Instant stock (page 175) or water, to cover the beef
- 2 small onions
- 1 bay leaf
- sprig of thyme
- 1kg (2¼lb) carrots, peeled and cut into 2cm (¾in) thick pieces
- salt and pepper
- 2 teaspoons snipped tarragon leaves
- 25g (1oz) butter (optional), plus a knob for the carrots

Cauliflower champ

- 25g (1oz) butter, plus a knob for the spring onions
- 1 large or 2 small cauliflowers, cut into florets
- 300ml (½pint) milk
- salt and ground white pepper
- squeeze of lemon juice
- 6 spring onions, thinly sliced

Braised beef brisket with tarragon carrots and cauliflower champ

This sounds like a very wintry dish, but we all know mid-spring has never offered summery conditions. So this dish will suit our April days perfectly.

Lincolnshire spring cauliflower seems to offer the best of flavours around this time. However, the champ recipe will work well with almost all cauliflowers, from all countries, all year round. It's basically taken from the Irish potato champ – creamy, buttery and finished with spring onion. The carrots are cooked in the pot with the beef, becoming overcooked and very tender, and offering their sweetness to the cooking liquor.

Beef brisket, a cut taken from the breast, is perfect for slow braising or stewing, but does have quite a fat content. Usually this cut is sold pre-rolled, which is fine, but do ask for a lean piece and, if necessary, for it to be unrolled and the fat removed. The meat will cook equally well in its natural shape. It can be sold salted or plain, and either will work here. To help reduce the salt content, a salted joint can be blanched in water as described below. The dish is best planned a day in advance, allowing for the pre-soaking of the meat for 24 hours in cold water before rinsing and blanching the following day.

Method To blanch the brisket of beef, rinse it under cold water, place in a large saucepan and cover with fresh water. Bring to the boil and simmer for 2 minutes, then remove from the stove and rinse under cold water. This will help remove any excess salt content.

Place in a suitable large pot and cover with stock or water. Add the onions, bay leaf and thyme and bring to the simmer. Skim away any impurities floating on the

surface before covering with a lid and cooking gently for 3 hours. The beef can also be cooked in an oven preheated to 160°C/325°F/Gas 3. After 3 hours, skim away any excess fat or impurities, adding the carrots and continuing to cook for a further hour. During this cooking time, the carrots will overcook. It is like this that they will eat at their best for this dish.

During this last cooking hour, make the cauliflower champ. Melt the 25g (1oz) of butter in a saucepan until bubbling. Add the cauliflower florets and cook, covered, on a low heat until they begin to soften without colouring. Add the milk and bring to a simmer. Re-cover and cook until the cauliflower is at a purée stage. Transfer the florets, without the milk, to a liquidizer and blitz to a smooth purée, adding any of the remaining milk to loosen, if needed. Season with salt, ground white pepper and a squeeze of lemon juice.

The spring onions can be quickly softened in the knob of butter and added to the purée just before serving, to ensure they don't discolour.

Once the meat is cooked, remove from the heat and allow to rest for 20–30 minutes. During this time, the meat will relax and become tender. While it's resting, the carrots can be removed with some of the stock, ready to reheat and season before serving the beef, finishing them with the tarragon and the knob of butter.

Strain 600ml (1pint) of beef cooking liquor into a clean saucepan. If you like, add the optional butter for a softer buttery finish. Slice the brisket (it could almost be carved with a spoon it is so tender), presenting it with the beef cooking liquor, tarragon carrots and cauliflower champ.

Serves 4

- 10–12 baby turnips
- 10–12 button mushrooms, preferably same size as the turnips
- juice of ½ lemon
- 3 tablespoons olive oil, plus more for brushing
- salt and pepper
- 4 × 75–100g (3–4oz) beef fillet slices
- 1 heaped tablespoon chopped herbs (such as chives, chervil, dill, tarragon and parsley)

For the dressing

- 1 cooked medium beetroot, peeled and finely chopped
- 1 tablespoon balsamic vinegar or red wine vinegar
- 2–3 tablespoons olive oil

Grilled beef fillet with baby turnips, marinated mushrooms and a beetroot dressing

A great late spring dish as beetroots and turnips are just coming into season, this offers an alternative starter with the hot and cold combination of grilled (or seared) beef fillet, garnished with raw sliced mushrooms and turnips bound with a herby lemon and olive oil. The dressing is quite sweet with the double act of beetroot and balsamic vinegar working together.

Method Trim the turnip tops to just a short stem. The mushrooms are best wiped clean with a damp cloth rather than washed. Trim the stalks flush with the bases of the mushrooms. Now cut the turnips and mushrooms into thin slices. Mix the lemon juice with the olive oil, and season with salt and pepper. Spoon this marinade over the sliced turnips and mushrooms and gently mix. It's best to prepare to this stage 15–20 minutes before eating, turning every few minutes or so to help impregnate the marinade's flavour.

To make the dressing, place the chopped beetroot, vinegar, 2 tablespoons of the olive oil and 2 tablespoons of water in a liquidizer. Blitz to a smooth purée, then add the remaining tablespoon of olive oil if necessary, to loosen the consistency. Season with salt and pepper, then push through a sieve if necessary for a smoother finish.

Brush the beef fillets with olive oil and season with salt and pepper, then place on a preheated very hot griddle plate or frying pan. Cook for just 45 seconds to 1 minute, then, if using a griddle, turn the fillets 90° to create a grilled crisscross pattern. After a further 45 seconds, turn the fillets over and cook for just a further minute for a rare pink finish.

While cooking the beef, add the chopped herbs to the marinated vegetables and divide between four plates, placing them towards the top of the plate. Present the beef fillets in front of the mushrooms and turnips, then spoon the beetroot dressing around. Excess marinade can also be drizzled around the beef, mingling it with the beetroot dressing if wished.

Serves 4 as a main course
- 450g (1lb) spring greens
- salt and pepper
- iced water
- 4 tablespoons black peppercorns
- 75g (3oz) butter
- 4 shallots, sliced
- 2 tablespoons olive oil
- 4 × 225g (8oz) skirt steaks, preferably batted (see below)
- 5 tablespoons cognac
- freshly grated nutmeg

Steak au poivre *with buttered spring greens and shallots*

The skirt steak, although one of the cheaper cuts of meat, is one you'll probably have to order in advance. It is one of the most popular steaks served in brasseries all over France, where the cut is known as *bavette*.

This steak requires only a very quick few minutes of cooking in a hot pan. Once rested, it will be tender, and packed with flavour. To help make it even more tender, the skirt steak can be gently batted, using a meat-tenderizing hammer which will break up its fibres and give a softer cooked finish.

The seasonal feature of this dish is, of course, our home-grown spring greens. Sautéed with sliced shallots in nutty butter, they are guaranteed a good relationship with the steak.

Method   Tear the spring-green leaves into 5–7.5cm (2–3in) pieces and blanch in rapidly boiling salted water for 2–3 minutes until tender, then refresh quickly in iced water. Drain in a colander and gently squeeze out excess water.

Crush the black peppercorns before sieving to shake off any excess powder. The peppercorns will now offer a perfumed aroma and warmth; pepper powder only provides excessive heat. Press the peppercorns on both sides of the steaks and sprinkle with salt.

In a large saucepan, melt 15g (½oz) of the butter. Once hot and bubbling, add the shallots. Cook on a high heat for a few minutes until golden brown and tender. Remove from the pan and keep to one side.

Wipe the pan with kitchen paper, return to the stove and add the olive oil. Once this is very hot and at the point of almost smoking, place the steaks in the pan (this may have to be done in two batches). Cook the steaks for 2–3 minutes then turn over. Continue to cook for a further 2–3 minutes for a medium-rare to medium finish. Remove the steaks from the pan and keep to one side.

Now add the cognac to the frying pan, lifting all the sediment and juices. Allow to reduce by half, then pour in any juices collected from the resting steaks. Add 50g (2oz) of the butter. This cooking liquor is not a sauce, but a moistener to pour over the steaks when serving.

While the steaks are frying, reheat the shallots in a large saucepan or wok. Add the remaining butter and, once bubbling, and at its nutty-brown stage, add the spring greens. Cook for a few minutes to heat through and season with salt, pepper and nutmeg.

The steaks can be left whole or sliced before presenting on plates with the greens, and pouring the cognac butter liquor over.

- *An alternative to* au poivre *is a crème fraîche mustard sauce. Cook the steaks as above, omitting the peppercorns and remove to rest. Fry 2 chopped shallots until golden brown, add 100ml (3½fl oz) of white wine. Reduce by half and add 150ml (¼pint) of crème fraîche or whipping cream, scraping up the residue from the pan. Add a further 100ml (3½fl oz) of crème fraîche and a teaspoon of Dijon or English mustard. Stir to a sauce consistency, adding a knob of butter. Pour the sauce over the steaks and serve.*

Serves 4 as a main course

- 1kg (2¼lb) piece of pork belly, boned with rind left on
- 2 large onions
- 1 tablespoon cooking oil
- coarse sea salt and pepper, plus salt for the kale
- 300ml (½pint) *Chicken stock* (page 175) or *Instant stock* (page 175) or water
- 675g–900g (1½–2lb) curly kale
- iced water (optional)
- knob of butter
- 1–2 tablespoons wholegrain mustard (optional)
- 1 quantity *Basic butter sauce* (page 179, optional)
- squeeze of lemon juice (optional)

Softly roasted pork belly with warmed curly kale

Pork belly is a very versatile cut of meat. With this recipe, several hours of slow cooking gives the fat content time to melt through the meat, producing a very tender and moist finish. If the rind is left on the pork it will provide a crisp crackling topping to finish.

Curly kale is one of our greens that reaches its peak during the spring month of March. It is one of the most attractive members of the cabbage family in its raw state, having an almost curly parsley-leaf look. Although similar to spring greens, curly kale has its own texture and taste, loving lots of butter and seasoning.

For this recipe, I'm suggesting a butter sauce finished with wholegrain mustard for a silky warmth to the dish.

Method Preheat the oven to 160°C/325°F/Gas 3. Score the pork belly rind with a sharp knife at intervals of 1cm (½in). Peel the onions, cut them in halves and place in a roasting tray. These will act as a trivet, preventing the pork meat from touching the hot tray. As the belly roasts, its fat content and juices will be absorbed by the onions, almost caramelizing them towards the end of the cooking time. These can then be served with the meat.

Lightly oil the pork rind and sprinkle with coarse sea salt. The meat side can also be seasoned with the salt and a good twist of pepper. Place the meat on top of the onions, and into the preheated oven and roast for 3 hours. During this cooking time the fat content of the meat will provide a self-basting service. After 1½–2 hours it's best to check the onions are not becoming too dry and beginning to stick and burn on the tray. If they are, add a few tablespoons of water to moisten.

Once cooked, remove the pork and onions from the oven and tray and keep warm to one side, while the meat rests. Heat the tray on the stove and add the stock or water. This will instantly bubble up with the heat in the pan, lifting all residue and juices from the onions. Bring to a simmer and cook for a few minutes. If too shallow in flavour, continue to cook the stock and reduce by a third. The stock gravy can now be strained through a fine sieve before serving.

While the pork is roasting, prepare and cook the curly kale. Remove the stalks and wash the leaves well. If cooking the kale in advance, it can be blanched in boiling salted water for 3–4 minutes until tender. Plunge into iced water to stop the cooking process and maintain its colour, and strain. It can be either microwaved or heated in a knob of butter and a few tablespoons of water. This creates an instant liquor, heating the kale through in just a minute or two. Season with salt and pepper. If simply cooking before serving, cook as above and finish with a knob of butter and seasoning.

Add a tablespoon of the mustard to the butter sauce. This will provide an extra warmth to the sauce; for a hotter finish add the remaining mustard. Finish the sauce with a squeeze of lemon juice.

The pork crackling can now be broken and snapped into pieces, then cut chunky portions of the belly and divide both between plates.

Moisten the curly kale with half of the mustard sauce and serve with the pork, trickling the rest of the sauce over and around the leaves. The softly roasted pork is now ready to serve, offering the stock gravy separately.

Serves 4–6 as a main course

- 3 ham hocks (or pork knuckles)
- 2 onions
- 2 carrots
- 1 bay leaf
- few peppercorns
- few parsley stalks
- 175g (6oz) puy lentils
- 1 large carrot, cut into 5mm (¼in) dice

- 1 large onion, cut into 5mm (¼in) dice
- 2 celery sticks, cut into 5mm (¼in) dice
- salt and pepper
- 2 tablespoons chopped flatleaf parsley
- 2 knobs of butter
- 225–350g (8–12oz) girolles, cleaned as below

- 150ml (¼pint) crème fraîche (optional)
- squeeze of lemon juice (optional)
- 1 heaped teaspoon chopped chives (optional)

Boiled ham hock with braised lentils and wild girolles

The ham hock is the same cut of the meat as the knuckle of pork. However, the ham hock has been salted and matured, while the knuckle will be taken from the untreated leg of pork. Either can be used for this recipe, but the ham finish does lend a different taste and texture.

Girolles are also known as chanterelles, and are quite often mistaken as exactly the same. Yes, they are related, but are actually different strains of the same species of mushroom. The girolle is found between the months of May and June, sometimes lasting into July. The chanterelle is available between mid-summer and autumn. Another distinctive difference is in size: girolles do tend to be on the smaller side, lovely to use for both their flavour and garnishing qualities. Apart from these few pointers, the two mushrooms both hold a yellowy orange, sort of apricot, colour and scent and are a delight to eat. To clean a girolle, it's best to scrape the stalk and trim its base and then rinse the mushroom under cold water to remove any grit. Leave to drain and dry. Another method is to quickly blanch the cleaned mushrooms in boiling water, plunging them in and out in seconds. The heat of the water seals the mushrooms, preventing them from becoming waterlogged or bleeding their juices.

Method Cover the hocks with cold water and bring to a simmer. Cook for a few minutes, then drain and rinse under cold water. Return the hocks to the stove, adding the onions, carrots, bay leaf, peppercorns and parsley stalks. Cover with water (no salt, the ham already has enough) and bring to a simmer. Cook over a gentle heat for approximately 2½–3 hours, until very tender

and the small bone within the ham hock becomes loose. Remove the pan from the heat.

To cook the lentils (this is best started 15 minutes before the hocks have finished their cooking time, with the lentils' total stewing time giving the hocks a reasonable resting period), quickly blanch them in boiling water and then drain and refresh under cold water. Place the lentils in a pan with 600ml (1pint) of the ham cooking liquor, straining it over them. Bring to a simmer and cook for 25–30 minutes, topping up the pan with extra liquor if needed. It is best to keep the lentils soft and loose within the finished liquor.

While the lentils are cooking, place the diced carrot, onion and celery in a separate small pan, cover with strained hock-cooking liquor, bring to a simmer and cook for 10–12 minutes. Once tender keep to one side, adding them to the lentils once they are softened. Remove the skin from the hocks, breaking chunks of tender meat from the bone. Add the ham pieces to the lentils, checking for seasoning, before adding the chopped parsley and a knob of butter.

Now fry the girolles very quickly in the remaining butter in a hot pan, for just a minute or two until tender.

To present the dish, spoon the ham lentils onto a large serving plate or bowl then sprinkle with the sautéed girolles and serve.

If using the crème fraîche, once the girolles have been removed from the frying pan, add the squeeze of lemon juice to the pan, along with the crème fraîche, and bring to a simmer before seasoning with salt and pepper. Add the chopped chives and drizzle over and around dish.

Serves 4 as a main course

- 50g (2oz) butter, at room temperature
- 2 teaspoons picked marjoram, stalks removed and saved
- salt and pepper
- 2 guinea fowl
- cooking oil
- 450–675g (1–1½lb) spring greens, stalks removed
- iced water
- freshly grated nutmeg
- 25g (1oz) butter
- 450g (1lb) baby carrots
- generous pinch of sugar
- 300ml (½pint) *Instant stock* (page 175) or *Chicken stock* (page 175)
- 150ml (¼pint) double cream
- 1–2 teaspoons Dijon or English mustard

Guinea fowl with spring greens and carrots and a mustard and marjoram sauce

Guinea fowl, available all year but especially plump at this time, are the slightly gamey alternative to chicken. Smaller in size and a little drier in texture, the bird needs to be 'buttered up' to guarantee moist results.

Compared to a basic domestic chicken, the guinea fowl wins hands down on flavour. For four portions one bird is not quite enough, unless you've found a particularly large bird. It's best to pick two smaller ones, offering half per portion. More fresh herbs are beginning to join us, with marjoram not being too difficult to find.

Method Preheat the oven to 200°C/400°F/Gas 6. Mix two-thirds of the 50g (2oz) of butter with 1 teaspoon of the marjoram and season with salt and pepper. Push the butter under the skin of the breasts, folding the skin beneath the neck ends of the birds. Brush each bird with the remaining butter and season with salt and pepper. Heat a roasting tray with a tablespoon or two of cooking oil. Once hot, lay the birds on one side in the pan. Fry on a medium heat for a few minutes until approaching golden brown. Turn the birds onto the other breast and repeat the process. Sit the birds breast-side up in the pan and roast in the preheated oven for 40–45 minutes, basting every 10 minutes to guarantee a richer finish. Remove the birds from the oven and lightly cover with foil to keep warm. Rest for 15 minutes.

While the birds are roasting, prepare the spring greens. Gently tear the leaves into bite-size pieces and blanch in boiling salted water for approximately 3 minutes until tender. Refresh in iced water before draining and squeezing gently to remove excess water. Season with

salt, pepper and nutmeg, then fold half the 25g (1oz) of butter through the leaves. These can now be micro-waved when needed or heated in a saucepan.

The baby carrots can also be cooked earlier for microwaving or just at the end of the roasting time, while the birds are resting. Peel or scrape the carrots, leaving 1–2cm (½–¾in) of stalk attached. Place in a saucepan and barely cover with boiling water. Add a pinch each of salt and sugar, along with the remaining half of the butter. Return to the boil and simmer rapidly for 3–10 minutes until just tender. (The liquor the carrots have cooked in can be used as the base for the instant stock. If so, drain off 300ml (½pint) and keep to one side, leaving the carrots in the pan with the remaining liquor.)

Remove the birds from the roasting tray, pouring away any excess fat. Place the tray on a medium heat and, when beginning to sizzle, add 300ml (½pint) of chicken stock or stock made with the reserved carrot liquor. Add the saved marjoram stalks. As the water boils it will lift all of the flavours from the pan. Allow the stock to reduce by a third, then pour in the double cream. Bring to a simmer and cook to a loose sauce consistency. Season with salt and pepper, adding any juices collected from the resting guinea fowl. Strain through a sieve. Now add the mustard along with the remaining marjoram leaves. Return the carrots and heat through quickly, along with the spring greens (microwaving or in a saucepan).

Cut the legs and breasts from the birds and present on plates, offering half a guinea fowl on each with the vegetables to the side. Spoon the sauce around or offer separately.

Serves 4 as a main course
- 1 × 1.5–1.75kg (3½–4lb) free-range chicken, cut into 8 pieces (2 drumsticks, 2 thighs, 4 breast halves)
- salt and pepper
- flour, for dusting
- 2 tablespoons olive oil
- 1 tablespoon chopped chives

For the vinaigrette
- 3 tablespoons white or red wine vinegar (tarragon vinegar also works well)
- 2 teaspoons Dijon mustard
- 100ml (3½fl oz) olive oil
- coarse sea salt
- squeeze of lemon juice

For the mushrooms
- 450g (1lb) St George's or chestnut mushrooms
- 25g (1oz) butter

Sautéed chicken steeped in vinaigrette with St George's mushrooms

The chicken pieces are pure simplicity, literally just sautéed until tender before steeping in vinaigrette. St George's mushrooms begin to appear on St George's Day, April 23rd; one of the few mushrooms of spring. They tend to stay with us through to the end of May, offering their services to many a dish, and eating particularly well sautéed in butter with a touch of garlic and parsley.

Method Preheat the oven to 220°C/425°F/Gas 7. Season the chicken pieces with salt and pepper and lightly dust with flour. Heat the olive oil in a frying pan or flameproof braising pan. Once hot, sauté the chicken pieces for approximately 8–10 minutes until well coloured. The pan can now be placed in the preheated oven for a further 10–15 minutes to complete the cooking.

Make the vinaigrette by whisking together the vinegar, mustard and olive oil, and seasoning with coarse sea salt and pepper and a squeeze of lemon juice. Spoon the dressing over the cooked chicken, cover with a lid and keep warm.

While the chicken is steeping, prepare the mushrooms. Trim off the stalks and, if necessary, rinse the mushrooms very briefly, making sure not to leave them soaking as they absorb water very easily. Melt the butter in a large hot frying pan and add the cleaned mushrooms. Sauté on a high heat for a good few minutes until tender. Season with salt and pepper. The sautéed mushrooms can now be added to the chicken pieces, finishing with the chopped chives.

The richness of the dressing, the vinegar and mustard in particular, lifts the flavour of the mushroom garnish. A good tossed salad, with lots of watercress and rocket leaves, provides a simple finish; or perhaps just a spoonful or two of very soft and creamy *Mashed potatoes* (page 186).

Serves 4 as a main course
- 1–2 knobs of butter, plus more for greasing
- 2 large onions (or 3 small), sliced
- salt and pepper
- 6 large potatoes (approximately 675g/1½lb)
- 1 large Bramley cooking apple, peeled and cored

- 2 tablespoons cooking oil
- 4 large duck legs
- coarse sea salt
- 150–200ml (¼pint–7fl oz) chicken-flavoured *Instant stock* (page 175) or *Chicken stock* (page 175)

For the spinach
- 900g (2lb) young English spinach, washed and stalks removed
- 25g (1oz) butter
- 1 teaspoon chopped fresh rosemary
- freshly grated nutmeg
- 50g (2oz) hazelnuts, skinned (see below) and roughly chopped

Duck boulangère *with hazelnut-rosemary spinach*

Boulangère means 'the the style of the baker' and is used for dishes braised or baked with potatoes and onions. The potatoes absorb the stock, leaving a crisply topped but very moist, almost creamy centre. In this recipe, the duck legs will simply be roasted on top of the potatoes, all juices and duck fats becoming absorbed by the layers beneath them. One other added flavour is a thinly sliced large Bramley cooking apple. Its sharpness helps the potatoes along and combines well with the rich duck juices.

During our spring months young spinach appears, very young and tender during the first eight weeks, with coarser leaves arriving in May. Any of these can be used for this recipe.

The hazelnuts for this recipe will need to be skinned (they can be bought pre-skinned). To do so, toast the nuts under the grill or in a moderate oven until the skins darken and become loose. At this point, place the nuts in a cloth and rub together well. This will release the skins. The rosemary flavour is lent to the dish via the butter working into the spinach.

Method Preheat the oven to 190°C/375°F/Gas 5. Melt a knob of butter in a frying pan and, once bubbling, add the sliced onions. These need only to be cooked for a few minutes until just beginning to soften. Season with salt and pepper and leave to cool.

Slice the potatoes very thinly. For a neater presentation, although certainly not essential, shape one or two into cylinders. When sliced, these can be used for the top layer. Cut the apple in half, then cut each into thin slices.

Heat the cooking oil in a frying pan. Season the duck legs with coarse sea salt and pepper, and place them in the pan, skin-side down. Fry on a moderate heat until golden brown and just becoming crispy. This will take approximately 15 minutes.

Butter a suitably large ovenproof baking dish or braising pot, then sprinkle in a spoonful or two of the cooked onions. Now add a layer of potato slices and season with salt and pepper. Repeat with another layer of onion then add some of the apple slices. Top with more potatoes, season and repeat the onion, apple and potato layers until all are used. If using cylindrical potatoes for the top layer, it's best to overlap each slice: start from the outside and work in to the centre. Heat the stock and pour over the potatoes, filling to about 1cm (½in) from the top layer. Break a knob of butter into pieces and dot over the top.

Place the golden brown duck legs, skin-side up, on top of the potatoes. Place in the preheated oven, and cook for 1½–2 hours. After 1½ hours, check the legs: they should be cooked through, with the potatoes very moist and tender. For extra well-done legs, continue to cook for the further 30 minutes. More stock may well have to be added at this point (if all has previously been used, no more should be needed).

Cook the spinach once the duck *boulangère* is completely cooked and resting. Melt the butter in a large saucepan with the rosemary. Once bubbling, add the well-drained spinach leaves. Cook on a medium-to-high heat, stirring, for a minute or two. Season with salt, pepper and nutmeg, before adding the chopped hazelnuts. The nutty spinach is now ready to offer along with the duck legs *boulangère*.

fruit and
puddings

Serves 4–6 as a pudding

For the marmalade (makes about 550–600ml/1 pint)
- 450g (1lb) kumquats, quartered with seeds removed
- 600ml (1pint) orange juice (preferably carton for increased flavour)
- 275g (10oz) granulated, preserving or jam sugar
- generous squeeze of lemon juice (optional)

For the ice-cream
- 225g (8oz) kumquats, halved with seeds removed
- 600ml (1pint) single cream
- 4 egg yolks (6 for a richer custard finish)
- 100g (4oz) caster sugar
- 3 tablespoons Grand Marnier

For the roly-poly
- 225g (8oz) self-raising flour
- 1 teaspoon baking powder
- pinch of salt
- finely grated zest of 1 lemon or orange
- 150g (5oz) vegetarian or beef suet
- 100–150ml (3½–5fl oz) milk
- 150–175g (5–6oz) kumquat marmalade (see below)

Steamed kumquat marmalade roly-poly

Classically, roly-poly is made with jam, but marmalades are close relatives, so find their way into this recipe very easily. Almost any sweet preserve can be rolled in the suet paste and steamed, orange in particular offering a contrasting, but at the same time complementing, combination of sharp tang and bitterness with the sweet syrupy finish.

Imported kumquats, around at this time, are a perfect substitute for the traditional Seville orange, combining all of the assets just mentioned. This is a very simple marmalade recipe, making more than enough for this dessert – the rest will store in sterilized jars (page 11) – and the ice-cream is purely an optional extra.

Method To make the marmalade, place the kumquat quarters in a saucepan, along with the orange juice, sugar and lemon juice, if using. Bring to a very gentle simmer and cook for 1 hour. The fruits should now be tender but still with a slight bite in the zest. To check the setting point, spoon a little marmalade onto a saucer and chill. It should lightly jellify and wrinkle when moved. If still slightly chewy and loose in consistency, continue to cook for a further 10–15 minutes and recheck. Remove from the heat, skim away any impurities and allow to cool for 15 minutes, then spoon into sterilized jars.

To make the ice-cream, place the kumquats in a food processor or liquidizer and purée. For a smooth finish, push the purée through a sieve. Bring the cream to the boil. While heating the cream, whisk together the egg yolks and sugar to a light fluffy ribbon stage. Pour the boiling cream over the eggs, stirring well. Return the custard to the saucepan and cook over a gentle heat

until thick enough to coat the back of a spoon. Remove from the heat and add to the kumquat purée. Leave to cool. Once cold, add the Grand Marnier and pour into an ice-cream machine. It will take approximately 20–25 minutes to thicken. At this point, remove the ice-cream mix from the machine and freeze to set.

To make the roly-poly, sift together the self-raising flour, baking powder and pinch of salt. Add the grated lemon or orange zest, along with the suet and work to a breadcrumb consistency. Add the milk a little at a time, until a soft texture is formed. Wrap in cling film and allow to rest for 20–30 minutes.

Roll the suet dough into a rectangle approximately 35 × 25cm (14 × 10in). Spread the marmalade on the dough, leaving a border 1cm (½in) clear. Brush the border with extra milk or water, then roll the dough from the wider edge and pinch at either end to retain all of the marmalade. Wrap the roly-poly loosely in grease-proof paper, followed by loose aluminium foil and tie with string at either end.

Steam the pudding in a steamer for 2 hours, topping up with hot water, if necessary, during cooking time. Once cooked, unwrap, slice and serve, offering the kumquat ice-cream separately.

● *A large steamer is needed for this recipe. If unavailable, two smaller roly-polys can be made.*

● *Late in the spring and early summer season many kumquats can be tougher in texture, often needing between 1½ and 2 hours cooking time.*

Serves 5–6

- 125g (4½oz) butter, plus more for greasing
- 2 teaspoons flour, plus more for the ramekins
- 125g (4½oz) dark chocolate, chopped
- 2 eggs, plus 2 extra yolks
- 4 tablespoons caster sugar

For the chocolate sauce (optional)

- 100g (4oz) bitter dark chocolate (milk or white chocolate can also be used), chopped
- 150ml (¼pint) single cream
- 25g (1oz) butter

Soft chocolate pudding

Although chocolate is not a seasonal ingredient, Easter Sunday wouldn't be the same without some form of chocolate dessert. This dessert has become a modern classic, which is very popular today and will remain so for many years to come. The mix can be made several hours in advance, poured into the prepared moulds and refrigerated until needed. One important detail is to make sure it is back to room temperature before baking. Once cooked and cut into, it won't be quite cooked through, revealing a thick, soft chocolate centre. I've included a recipe for chocolate sauce to go with the dessert, for real chocoholics. Extra-thick or pouring cream or vanilla ice-cream also work very well. For an orangey accompaniment, the perfect partner is the *Warm syruped kumquats* (page 74).

Method For the pudding, preheat the oven to 220°C/425°F/Gas 7 and liberally butter and flour five or six 150ml (¼pint) ramekins. In a bowl set over a pan of simmering water, melt the chocolate and butter together. It is important that the bowl is not in contact with the simmering water as this will separate the solids and fats from the chocolate. Once warm and melted, remove the bowl from the pan.

While the chocolate is melting, with an electric whisk mix together the eggs, extra yolks and caster sugar to a thick but light consistency. This mix will have taken on a cold sabayon stage, almost a combination of soft peak meringue and cream. Pour into the warm chocolate, and dust the flour in through a sieve. Fold the three components together gently, then spoon into the prepared moulds. (If not cooking immediately, these can now be refrigerated for several hours, if wished, until needed, returning them to room temperature before baking.) Place in the preheated oven for 9 minutes.

Meanwhile, make the sauce, if using. Place all the ingredients together in a bowl set over simmering water until the chocolate has melted.

Remove the puddings from the oven and leave to rest for 1 minute before serving in the ramekins or turning out onto plates. The sides will be set but the filling soft. Serve with the warm chocolate sauce or your chosen accompaniment.

- *The* Cocoa sorbet *(page 78) also eats very well with the warm pudding.*

Serves 4–6

- 225g (8oz) white chocolate, chopped
- 150ml (¼pint) *Pastry cream* (page 188)
- seeds from 1 vanilla pod (optional)
- 200ml (7fl oz) double cream

For the kumquats

- 350g (12oz) kumquats
- 300ml (½pint) orange juice
- 225g (8oz) caster sugar

Vanilla white chocolate mousse with warm syruped kumquats

Although not grown in the UK, the kumquat, the small oval orange citrus fruit, finds itself in season during winter and spring months. This small fruit, like the orange, is not native to the Mediterranean. China is its original home, with the name derived from the Cantonese *kam kwat*, meaning 'gold orange'. The difference between the orange and kumquat is that the tiny kumquat can be eaten rind and all. The zest and pith are quite sweet, with a bitter, sour centre to counter this flavour. These fruits will eat very well with meats, fish and desserts, whether pickled, preserved or poached.

Here, we will poach them in an orange juice and water syrup, serving them warm to go with the rich cold chocolate mousse. They can be poached as whole fruits, or halved and the pips removed before cooking. With young small kumquats it is fine to leave the pips in, but once approaching May, when the fruits become much larger, I would suggest removing them.

As for the white chocolate mousse, it's a very simple recipe that can be set in individual 150ml (¼pint) moulds or simply set in one dish and spooned into portions. One of the ingredients of the mousse is *Pastry cream*. This obviously means tackling that recipe before even thinking about this one. *Pastry cream*, however, is simple to make and forms a base to many other dessert recipes, too.

Method Melt the chocolate in a bowl over gently simmering water, making sure the base of the bowl is not in contact with the water. Once melted, whisk it into the pastry cream with the vanilla seeds, if using. Whip the double cream to soft peak stage, then fold it

into the chocolate custard mix. The mousse can now be spooned into individual ramekins or one large serving dish, Refrigerate until chilled.

Prepare the kumquats. If young and small fruits are available, simply pierce each skin with a cocktail stick; for larger ones, it is best to split the fruits in half and remove the seeds before cooking. Place the orange juice and sugar in a saucepan with 150ml (¼pint) of water and bring to the boil. Reduce the temperature to a simmer and cook for 5–6 minutes. Add the kumquats and bring the syrup back to a gentle simmer.

If halved and young, the fruits may only take 30 minutes of stewing before becoming tender. For whole, or larger 'tougher', fruits, the cooking can take between 50 minutes and an hour, with a maximum cooking time that may be needed of 1½ hours. The kumquats can now be left to cool slightly to a warm serving temperature. As with a lot of fruits cooked in syrup, in particular citrus fruits, storing them in an airtight jar and refrigerating them will give them a fairly long shelf life.

To serve, present spoonfuls of mousse, or each small ramekin, on plates with a spoonful or two of the syruped kumquats. The two flavours and colours of white and orange can stand alone without garnish, just offering their distinctive tastes to one another.

If you prefer to garnish your desserts, here are a few suggestions. Dark *Chocolate shavings or pencils* (page 190) can be presented on top or beside the mousse. Finely shredded mint can be sprinkled over the kumquats, or the Melba toasts, used for the *Grilled raspberry Melba stack* (page 159) will give a crisp biscuit bite.

Serves 4

- 4 ripe, medium-sized peaches
- iced water
- 12, 16 or 20 fresh strawberries (depending on size)
- 1 quantity *Vanilla whipped pastry cream* (page 189) at room temperature, not refrigerated
- icing sugar, for dusting

For the poaching syrup

- 200ml (7fl oz) white wine
- 150g (5oz) caster sugar

Poached peach and strawberry custard creams

Late spring, and the shops are becoming more colourful with imports galore brightening our shelves. Apricots, nectarines and peaches in particular catch the culinary eye. So early, not all are at their best, so do check with a quick squeeze: if too firm, they just don't seem to want to ripen.

Early English strawberries are now looking bigger and redder than ever. Already delicious to eat, they go well with nicely poached peaches, particularly if set amid glazed custard.

Method To make the syrup, pour the white wine and an equal volume of water into a saucepan, along with the caster sugar. Bring to a simmer and cook for just a few minutes.

To skin the peaches, first plunge them into boiling water for just 20–30 seconds, then refresh in iced water. The skins will now have become loose and easy to peel. Halve the peaches and remove the stones.

Place the peaches in the syrup and cover with greaseproof paper. Bring to a simmer and cook for a few minutes, then leave to cool. The peach halves can now be cut again into quarters. The sweet stock syrup is best kept refrigerated, to be used for poaching other fruits or sweetening fruit salads.

If necessary, rinse the strawberries, cutting the larger of the fruits in half, leaving smaller berries whole.

Divide the vanilla whipped pastry cream between four soup plates or flat bowls. Press the peach quarters and strawberries into the custard in no particular fashion, then dust with icing sugar through a very fine sieve or tea strainer. Place each under a preheated grill until the custard has a golden brown glaze.

- *The finely grated zest of 1 lemon or orange, poached to soften in a few tablespoons of the syrup, can be added to the custard for a gentle citrus bite.*

Serves 4

- 3 egg whites
- 175g (6oz) caster sugar
- 300ml (½pint) milk
- icing sugar, for dusting
- 6–8 rhubarb stalks (forced rhubarb will not need peeling)
- 1–2 tablespoons caster sugar
- 4 slices of brioche, approximately 1.5cm (⅝in) thick, crusts removed
- butter, for spreading
- 300ml (½pint) *Crème Anglaise* (page 188, optional)

Oeufs à la neige *on baked rhubarb with brioche and custard*

Also known as 'floating islands', *oeufs à la neige* are basically egg whites that have been mixed with sugar then whisked and poached in milk and water. The young rhubarb is cooked in the oven until tender, and any liquor released poured over the finished dish. The brioche slices are toasted and buttered and as the rhubarb begins to bleed its juices are absorbed into the brioche, giving a moist finish. The *crème Anglaise* custard is an optional extra, but for me is just essential for poached meringues; it also adds a creaminess to the finished dish.

Method To make the meringue, whisk the egg whites to soft peaks in a spotlessly clean bowl. Continue to whisk, adding two-thirds of the sugar. When that has been whisked in, add the remaining sugar and whisk in to give a smooth firm finished texture.

Heat the milk and an equal amount of water in a large wide saucepan, not allowing it quite to reach a simmer. Shape the meringue mixture between two tablespoons, making 12–16 meringues. It is best to cook just six at a time, shaping and spooning them carefully into the milk. Turn the meringues over after 5–6 minutes and poach them for a further 5–6 minutes. Carefully remove them from the milk and place them on greaseproof paper lightly dusted with icing sugar. It is not essential to serve the meringues hot or even warm, room temperature will be enough, helped along by the warm rhubarb.

To prepare the rhubarb, preheat the oven to 190°C/375°F/Gas 5. Cut the rhubarb into 6–7.5cm (2½–3in) pieces, making approximately 4–5 pieces per stalk. Lay on a baking tray, sprinkle with 2 tablespoons of water and the caster sugar. Place in the preheated oven and cook for approximately 10 minutes until tender (thicker rhubarb may need an extra minute or two). Remove from the oven and keep warm while the brioche is toasted.

Brush the brioche slices with the butter, then dust fairly generously with icing sugar and colour under a preheated grill to give a slightly burnt bitter-sweet edge. For a crisper finish it is best not to toast them too quickly. Turn the slices, and repeat this process.

To serve, place the brioche toasts on plates and top each one with 6–8 pieces of rhubarb, saving any syrup left on the tray. Three to four meringues can now be arranged on and around the rhubarb, drizzling with any saved rhubarb syrup. Warm or cold *crème Anglaise* custard can be offered separately.

Serves 4–6

Makes about 1 litre (1¾pints)

- 250g (9oz) caster sugar
- 150g (5oz) cocoa powder, sifted
- 1 tablespoon vanilla essence (if a particularly strong thick essence, add just 1 teaspoon)

For the orange biscuits (makes 16)

- finely grated juice and zest of 1 orange
- 100g (4oz) caster sugar
- 100g (4oz) plain flour
- 50g (2oz) softened butter, plus more for greasing

Cocoa sorbet with orange biscuits

The spring Easter extravagance of chocolate couldn't be overlooked in this seasonal book. This sorbet's bitter chocolate flavour is provided entirely by cocoa powder. The powder can be very bitter but, when balanced with the sugar and water and then frozen, does give a good rich chocolaty flavour. The sorbet can be infused with other flavours by simply omitting 100ml (3½fl oz) of water and replacing it with the same volume of a liqueur. Grand Marnier works very well, offering its orange flavour to work with the biscuits. Other alternatives include amaretto, kirsch or perhaps the coffee-flavoured Kahlúa.

Method Add the sugar to 900ml (1½pints) of water in a pan and bring to the boil. Add the cocoa powder and mix well. Cook on a low heat for 20 minutes, keeping the mix moving during this cooking time. After 20 minutes, the mix will have become rich and thicker in consistency. Leave to cool.

When cool, add the vanilla essence, along with a flavoured liqueur, if using, as mentioned in the introduction. The sorbet can now be churned in an ice-cream machine, for approximately 20 minutes until smooth and at setting point. Transfer to a suitable container and freeze until needed.

To make the biscuits, boil the orange juice until reduced to 2 tablespoons. Allow to cool. Now mix this well with all of the other ingredients. Cover and refrigerate for 2–3 hours to set.

Preheat the oven to 180°C/350°F/Gas 4. Roll the biscuit mix into 16 balls, then press each onto buttered baking trays and flatten them into 6–7.5cm (2½–3in) rounds. It is important to leave plenty of space between each, to allow room for spreading. Cooking 4–6 on each tray should give enough space for the biscuits.

Bake in the preheated oven for 12–14 minutes until golden brown. Allow the biscuits to rest on the tray for 1 minute, then carefully lift them with a palette knife or fish slice onto a cooling rack. Should the biscuits begin to stick to the tray, return them to the oven to rewarm. Once cooled and crisp, the biscuits are ready to serve with the sorbet.

- *Lemon biscuits can also be made using the grated zest and juice from 2 lemons.*

Serves 6 generous portions
- 350g (12oz) *Puff pastry* (page 185), or bought variety
- flour, for dusting
- knob of butter, plus more for greasing
- 550g (1¼lb) rhubarb, washed
- 2 tablespoons caster sugar
- 1 egg, for egg wash
- icing sugar, for dusting
- 150ml (¼pint) cream, for whipping or pouring

For the almond paste
- 60g (2¼oz) butter
- 60g (2¼oz) caster sugar
- 60g (2¼oz) ground almonds
- 1 teaspoon plain flour
- 1 egg

Rhubarb and almond jalousie with rhubarb pulp and cream

Rhubarb, regarded as a fruit, is in fact a vegetable. The fruity title has become established probably due to the acidic tartness of the vegetable needing the sweetness of sugar to balance it. The late-autumn to mid-spring forced rhubarb, or the outdoor thicker garden variety, can be used for this recipe. The forced kind becomes very pink, holding minimal leaves due to lack of sunlight, and has a very tender finish. Our garden stalks grow more robust, redder in colour, but with that need more attention because of their slightly tougher texture. Moving into the summer, they may even need to be peeled before use.

Jalousie is a classic French pastry, usually made with an almond paste, as here, and jam. Jalousie means 'slatted blind', the connection between the two comes with the slatted finish of the pastry, snipped in lines across the top to expose the fruit filling. This is a very attractive dish, with many textures, from the crispy pastry and succulent rhubarb, to the sponge-like almond paste. It can be prepared hours in advance, cooking just 60 minutes before eating. The extra pulp adds more of a fruity finish, making sure that the rhubarb is not lost amongst its rich friends.

Method Roll out a third of the puff pastry into a 30 × 10–12cm (12 × 4–4½in) strip on a lightly floured surface. This can now be placed on a buttered baking tray. At this stage it's not important to trim the strip to a perfect rectangle. Prick with a fork and refrigerate.

Preheat the oven to 190°C/375°F/Gas 5. Cut the rhubarb into approximately twenty 6½–7cm (2½–3in) sticks, starting from the top of each stick and working down. This will probably use about 375g (14oz) of the total. Roughly chop any remaining rhubarb and trimmings.

Lay the twenty sticks on a baking tray and sprinkle them with 1 tablespoon of the caster sugar. These can now be only just softened in the preheated oven for 6–8 minutes, taking away their absolute rawness. If the sticks are particularly thick, this may well take up to 10 minutes. It is important not to overcook, so test by gently prodding the rhubarb, which should respond with a slight give. Some of the sugar will now have dissolved through the sticks, possibly creating a syrup. Remove the tray from the oven, transferring the sticks to a separate plate and leaving to cool. Any juices can be kept to cook with the pulp trimmings.

To make the almond paste, cream together the butter and sugar, adding the ground almonds and flour (this can be done in a food processor). Now beat the egg into the mix. If the paste is very soft, refrigerate to cool and firm.

Spread the almond paste on the pastry strip, leaving a 1½cm (¾in) border all round. Now place the rhubarb sticks lengthwise on top in rows of five. Roll the remaining two-thirds of the pastry into a 32 × 14–15cm (13 × 5½–6in) rectangle, allowing extra width to cover the filling. Fold the strip in half from the long side. At the fold, using scissors or a sharp knife, cut strips approximately 1cm (½in) apart, leaving a 2cm (¾in) border at either end and on the opposite side of the pastry. Brush the egg wash around the almond paste and rhubarb filling on the pastry base. Carefully place the folded

pastry piece along one side of the base before opening it out across the rhubarb and sealing around the edges. Now trim the rectangle to a neat straight-edge finish, leaving as large a border as possible. The edges can now be decorated by markings with a fork, or left plain. Brush the jalousie with egg wash and refrigerate to rest for 20 minutes.

Increase the oven temperature to 220°C/425°F/Gas 7. Before baking, brush the jalousie again with the egg wash and sprinkle a teaspoon of water onto each side of the baking tray to create a steam that will help the pastry rise. Bake for 40–45 minutes. During this time the puff pastry will become well risen, very crispy and cooked through, leaving a light pastry edge to surround the soft moist centre.

To finish with a glossy glaze, dust the cooked jalousie liberally with icing sugar and place under a preheated grill – keep a watchful eye at this stage, as the sugar caramelizes very quickly. This stage can be repeated once or twice more for an even crisper golden glaze finish. The dessert is now best left to cool until warm as, if piping hot, the fruit and almond paste will have had no time to relax and change texture.

While the jalousie is cooking, melt a small knob of butter in a saucepan. Once bubbling, add the smaller rhubarb pieces along with the remaining caster sugar and any rhubarb juices. It's also best to add 3 tablespoons of cold water to help create a soft finished consistency. Cook on a low heat, allowing the rhubarb to soften and break down to a pulp. This will usually take just 8–10 minutes. Offer the pulp with the jalousie either hot, warm or cold along with whipped or pouring cream.

Serves 4–6
- 350g (12oz) rhubarb, cut into 1½cm (¾in) pieces
- 2 tablespoons caster sugar

For the mascarpone cream
- 3 egg yolks
- 75g (3oz) caster sugar
- 5 tablespoons orange juice
- 1 heaped tablespoon orange marmalade
- 175g (6oz) mascarpone cheese
- 3 tablespoons Grand Marnier (optional)
- 150ml (¼pint) double or whipping cream

Softened rhubarb with orange mascarpone cream

The simmered, sweetened and cooked rhubarb pieces, almost softening to a pulp, are finished with an orange sabayon, enriched with mascarpone cheese and whipped cream. It's a sort of cold variation of rhubarb and custard, with a few touches here and there. Orange and rhubarb are a lovely combination and, if Grand Marnier is available, the two are lifted even higher.

Method Place the rhubarb and sugar in a large saucepan with 3 tablespoons of water. Cook on a low heat, allowing to simmer gently for 6–8 minutes until tender, and approaching a pulp. The maximum cooking time is usually about 10 minutes. If the rhubarb is too syrupy once cooked, drain in a sieve and reboil the juices until reduced and thickened. The syrup juices can now be remixed with the fruits. Leave to cool. Once cooled the softened rhubarb can be spooned into glasses (cocktail glasses are very attractive for this dessert).

To make the mascarpone cream, place the egg yolks, sugar and 3 tablespoons of the orange juice in a bowl. Sit this over a pan of simmering water and whisk vigorously (an electric hand whisk will make life a lot easier) until at least double in volume, the whisk leaving a ribboned trail across the sabayon's surface. Remove from the heat and continuously whisk until cold (an electric mixing bowl and whisk attachment can help here).

Warm the remaining 2 tablespoons of orange juice with the marmalade, then strain through a sieve or tea strainer. A microwave oven will obviously warm the two together very quickly. If a fine-cut or smooth marmalade has been used, it needn't be strained.

Beat the mascarpone until smooth, mixing in the softened marmalade and Grand Marnier, if using. This can now be folded into the cold egg sabayon. Whip the cream until thickened but not firm (more of a soft peak stage). Fold into the mascarpone and sabayon mix, and spoon on top of the softened rhubarb.

The dessert can be served immediately or chilled for several hours.

If chilled the consistency of the cream changes, producing a more dense finish, which is equally good to eat.

● *Small almond or pistachio* Tuile biscuits *(page 189), 2–3 per portion, will eat very well, offering another texture and flavour to the dish.*

Serves 6

- 225g (8oz) *Sweet shortcrust pastry* (page 184) or *Puff pastry* (page 185), or bought variety
- flour, for dusting
- butter, for greasing
- 1 egg yolk
- 1 level tablespoon dried semolina
- 750g–1kg (1¾–2¼lb) fresh apricots (depending on size of fruits)
- 50–100g (2–4oz) caster sugar

For the almond ice-cream

- 300ml (½pint) whipping or single cream
- 300ml (½pint) milk
- 100g (4oz) ground almonds
- 1 vanilla pod, split
- 4 egg yolks
- 100g (4oz) caster sugar
- 3 tablespoons amaretto (almond liqueur) or water
- few drops of almond essence (optional)

Apricot tart with home-made almond ice-cream

Spanish apricots begin their welcome summer visit during the last month of spring. This recipe needs the firmer, earlier apricots to get the best result as the fruits hold their shape during cooking.

Most of the world's round golden fruits are cooked into preserves. Here, the rich fruits are placed raw in a cooked pastry case and baked until tender. The softness of the fruit provides the tender touch to accompany the crispy pastry, with no sponge or cream base necessary.

The almond ice-cream is also not really necessary, but is a pleasure to eat with this particular fruit. Almonds and apricots are a classic combination – perhaps it is the apricot's almondy central kernel that brings the two together, and that's why they've been paired for so long. If you haven't the time to make the ice-cream, then simply offer pouring or whipped cream.

Method To make the ice-cream, heat together the cream, milk, ground almonds and split vanilla pod. While this is heating, whisk the egg yolks, sugar and amaretto or water together until light and fluffy. When just below the boil, pour the hot milky cream and almonds over the eggs, whisking well. Return the almond custard mix to the saucepan and cook over a low heat, stirring continuously, until thick enough to coat the back of a spoon. Remove from the heat, pour the custard into a bowl and leave to cool. Once cold, strain through a sieve, scraping out any vanilla seeds left in the pod halves and adding them to the strained mix along with the almond essence, if using. Now churn the flavoured custard in an ice-cream machine for 20–25 minutes, until thickened

and increased in volume. Transfer the ice-cream to a suitable container and freeze for an hour or two to set.

For the tart, preheat the oven to 200°F/400°C/Gas 6. Roll out the pastry on a lightly floured surface, and use to line a buttered 20-cm (8-in) loose-bottomed tart pan. Any excess pastry can be left hanging over the edge. Prick the base of the case with a fork and refrigerate for 30 minutes, then line with greaseproof paper and fill with baking beans or rice. Bake the tart case blind in the preheated oven for 20 minutes. Remove the beans and paper and return to the oven for a further 5 minutes.

Once cooked, any excess pastry can be trimmed off, leaving a neat finish. Now brush the case with egg yolk to seal, and sprinkle the base with the dried semolina. This will absorb some of the juices as the fruits cook, preventing the pastry from becoming soggy. Leave the oven on, increasing the setting to 230°F/450°C/Gas 8.

Cut the apricots in half and remove the stones. Place the apricot halves in the tart case, standing them upright and squeezing them closely together. Sprinkle with the caster sugar. Late spring (May) fruits will need 100g (4oz) to help soften and sweeten their firmer, slightly under-ripe texture. Once into the summer season, just 50g (2oz) will be enough. Bake the tart for 30–40 minutes, until golden brown and crispy. Cooking at such a high temperature will tinge the fruits, almost burning the tops, adding an extra bitter-sweetness to the finished dish.

Remove the tart from the oven and leave to cool slightly before removing from the tart pan. The apricot tart is now ready to serve and will eat at its best warm, offering the almond ice-cream separately.

summer

As summer arrives, Aladdin's cave is opened wide. Without doubt, the months of June, July and August will bring us the most colourful treasures of all the seasons. The warm sunshine gives us all manner of produce that is so ripe and full of flavour that it only requires the simplest of culinary methods to enhance it.

As the weeks pass, an abundance of fruits will join us, whether they be home-grown red or black berries or the beautiful succulent imported apricots, nectarines and peaches. Imports provide us with a year-round wealth of goodies, offering rich exotic flavours, but summer also introduces home-grown varieties of so many of these once-imported jewels. British aubergines and sweet peppers should be tried, too.

In June, asparagus is still with us, with plenty of these green bundles left for us to enjoy, and broad beans and peas are coming to the fore followed closely by the English courgette. All these vegetables work so well and add a bite to all sorts of vegetarian, meat and fish dishes.

Wild salmon carries a reasonably long season, but it's during the summer months that it really must be sampled. Sea trout is definitely a summer fish, and has taken on similar eating habits to that of the salmon, living mostly off crustaceans, which give it its firm pink-red flesh. It is as good to eat as wild salmon, holding a sweet bite that marries so well with other summer flavours, in particular warm Jersey Royal potatoes.

Cherries will be arriving in June, along with gooseberries in abundance. These will slowly lose the rich, acidic, deep green bite they had in late spring, and take on a sweeter, yellowing touch.

Strawberries are now at their peak and, with not many other red fruits quite yet ready to show their bounty, it's a good time to make the most of them. Take the family to pick your own, to get the freshest, best-quality fruits and have a greedy, fun day out!

Raspberries are definitely my favourite berries and towards the end of June they are beginning to ripen into luscious gems. I prefer to wait until July and August before really tucking in by the ladleful, as they are absolutely superb by then.

Strawberries, raspberries, blackberries, red and blackcurrants and blueberries all find their way into my *Summer fruit family slice* (page 154). Their summery flavours mix and mingle in a dish that is quite stunning to build, and one that won't let your taste buds down with its crispy biscuit pastry, lashings of custard and seasonal red fruits to finish.

As the weather really warms up, cooking and eating simple dishes is a real delight. The simplest of combinations is often the best, so don't be afraid to serve up bowls of salads, softly buttered wild salmon, plates of asparagus with generous dollops of home-made mayonnaise, and towers of fresh fruits with lashings of fresh cream – these simple offerings could well become the ingredients for your finest dinner party.

July is the time for eating and cooking 'al fresco', so don't forget that the barbecue is always an option for cooking fish, meat and vegetables. The dinner table will be at its most colourful in mid-summer, with fresh tomatoes, courgettes and even sweet red peppers towards the end of the month. These combine beautifully to form the classic ratatouille.

Herbs are plentiful now. Wild marjoram (fresh oregano) blooms between July and October, and will add an Italian touch to many dishes. Basil and coriander are two other herbs just waiting to be picked. And there are imported nectarines, peaches, apricots and plums around now, too.

Salads leaves are plentiful, and broad beans, peas, runner beans, beetroots, radishes, cucumbers and even cauliflowers all work so well with them. Baby summer turnips and artichokes also make an appearance and it's during the summer months that our culinary imaginations can run riot.

With the August sun shining brightly, all the July vegetable produce is still with us during this last official month of summer. Sweet red peppers have reached their prime and they are joined by the British aubergines or eggplant, so try my *Ratatouille* feuilleté *with fresh tomato confit and basil sauce* (page 100).

Fresh herrings and sardines are looking plump, juicy and inviting to eat, and sardines especially make a welcome sight on the open grill. The touch of the two seasonings in the *Rock-salt-and-pepper sardines in bitter lemon, tomato courgette linguine* (page 112) helps them along.

The recipes in this summer section will show you how to make the best of this luscious month. August sees lots and lots of tomatoes, fresh herbs, aubergines, courgettes, runner beans and beetroots (and the list goes on!), all of which carry distinctive British flavours to accompany their fish, meat or dairy partners.

August has quite a juicy reputation with plums reaching their best, along with the greengage. This absolutely delicious fruit holds a short, barely two-month season so really must be tried at this time. Peaches and nectarines are absolutely flooded with their own juice (the beautiful white peach is also available) and with all of the British red fruits still in abundance, the shops are full of the very best produce you can eat. So, enjoy the wealth of produce the summer season has to offer.

Sit on a cushion
And sew a fine seam,
And feed upon strawberries
Sugar and cream.
(Anonymous)

vegetables

**Serves 4 as a main course or
6 as a starter**
- 2 large or 3 medium onions
  (red if available), sliced
- 3 tablespoons olive oil
- salt and pepper, plus coarse sea
  salt
- ½ garlic clove (optional)
- butter, for brushing

- 2–3 large courgettes, cut into
  5mm (¼in) slices
- 225g (8oz) goat's cheese,
  skinned (if applicable) and sliced
- 5–6 tomatoes, preferably plum,
  cut into 5mm (¼in) slices
- 3 heaped tablespoons grated
  Parmesan cheese or 75g (3oz)
  diced Italian fontina cheese (rind
  removed)

For the basil oil
- large bunch of loose basil
  (if in plastic packets, 3 bunches
  will be needed)
- salt
- 100ml (4fl oz) olive oil
- 3 tablespoons groundnut oil

Hot tomato, courgette and cheese bake with fresh basil oil

This recipe is wonderful in the warmer summer months, and you could even perhaps replace the goat's cheese with slices of mozzarella. These flavours have been combined so many times before, but we never seem to grow bored of good classics.

Method To make the basil oil, pick all of the leaves and place in a liquidizer with a pinch of salt. Warm the olive and groundnut oils gently together in a small saucepan bringing them to just above room temperature. Remove from the heat, pour over the basil leaves and liquidize until smooth. The flavour and colour of the leaves will now have joined company with the oils. Strain through a sieve and leave to cool. Refrigerated, this oil will keep for up to 2 weeks.

Preheat the oven to 200°C/400°F/Gas 6. To make the bake, fry the onions in a tablespoon of the olive oil for 5–6 minutes until golden brown and softened. Season with salt and pepper. Rub an ovenproof, preferably earthenware, dish with the garlic, if using, then brush with butter. Then place the onions in the dish.

Heat another tablespoon of olive oil in a large frying pan. Sear the courgette slices quickly on one side only, allowing them to colour lightly but not cook. It is important that the pan is very hot and not too many slices are placed in the pan at the same time. Repeat with the remaining slices, heating another tablespoon of oil if necessary. Once all are coloured, leave to cool.

Cover the onions with the slices of goat's cheese and season with salt and pepper. Arrange the tomato slices and courgettes either overlapping or in alternate lines on top of the cheese. Season with coarse sea salt and pepper.

Bake in the preheated oven for 20 minutes. Sprinkle over the Parmesan or fontina cheese and return to the oven for a further 10 minutes until rich golden brown. If the colour is a little light, the bake can be coloured further under a preheated grill. Serve each portion drizzled with the basil oil.

- *A tossed salad eats well with this dish, along with crusty bread or toast, or just buttered new potatoes.*

- 675g (1½lb) new potatoes, scrubbed
- 50–100g (2–4oz) soft goat's cheese, skin removed
- 5–7 tablespoons single cream or milk
- 25–40g (1–1½oz) butter
- salt and pepper

Creamy new potatoes with goat's cheese

The combination of melting goat's cheese rolled around new potatoes is very rich but also very good. It's important that a soft goat's cheese is used as this will then melt easily with the cream or milk and butter. This dish works as a good accompaniment to many meat, fish and vegetarian main courses. It can also have many more added ingredients – sautéed courgettes and tomatoes bound with the cheesy potatoes is a little more work, but results in a complete dish. Spooning the coated potatoes through a selection of green leaves, with a squeeze of lemon juice and drizzle of olive oil, makes a perfect warm salad.

Method Cook the new potatoes in boiling salted water for 20 minutes or until soft and tender. While the potatoes are cooking, chop the goat's cheese and melt it gently with the cream or milk and butter: 50g (2oz) of cheese along with 5 tablespoons of cream or milk and 25g (1oz) of butter will provide just enough to bind the potatoes. The extra quantities will make the mixture sauce-like.

Once the potatoes are cooked, drain and halve while still hot. Season with salt and pepper, then stir in the soft creamy cheese.

● *A selection of chopped herbs, in particular chopped chives can be added, offering an oniony bite and marrying the two old friends of cheese and onion. Raw, chopped shallots can also be added to this recipe.*

Serves 4 as a starter

- 100g (4oz) fresh peas (podded weight)
- 225g (8oz) new potatoes (Jersey Royals, Pink Fir Apple, etc.), overcooked
- 1 banana shallot or 2 small shallots, sliced into very thin rings
- coarse sea salt
- pepper
- 2 tablespoons olive oil
- juice of ½ lime
- 225g (8oz) soft goat's cheese, cut into rough 1cm (½in) dice
- 1–2 handfuls of rocket leaves
- 4 tablespoons soured cream or crème fraîche, for drizzling (optional)

For the dressing

- 1 teaspoon mint jelly
- 2 dessertspoons white wine vinegar
- 3 tablespoons olive oil
- 3 tablespoons groundnut, grapeseed or vegetable oil
- salt and pepper
- 4 mint leaves, chopped

Warm goat's cheese, potato and fresh pea salad with sweet mint dressing

The best type of goat's cheese for this dish is a rindless soft creamy variety which will soften quickly when warmed under the grill. The potatoes can be chosen from any of the new varieties available, cooking them until overdone for a softer texture. The dressing is flavoured with fresh mint but to provide the sweetness in place of sugar, and to augment the mint flavour, clear mint jelly is also added.

This salad works very well as a starter, or as a main course when topped with sea trout or wild salmon gently fried in butter. An extra 'dressing', that is not essential but does help draw everything together, is soured cream or crème fraîche. Just a drizzle or two is enough to finish the dish.

Method To make the dressing, warm the mint jelly through in the microwave for a few seconds to soften and moisten or heat very gently in a pan with the vinegar. Mix the jelly and vinegar with the remaining ingredients and season with salt and pepper (this can be easily achieved in a screw-top jar with lots of shaking). If a sweeter or more piquant finish is preferred, add a touch more softened jelly or vinegar. The fresh mint should be added just before serving.

To cook the fresh peas in advance, plunge them into boiling salted water and cook until tender. Drain and refresh in iced water before redraining. To reheat, the peas can either be microwaved or plunged back into boiling water for a minute.

Peel the cooked potatoes if the skins are tough, or leave the skins on if they were well scrubbed. Roughly halve or quarter the potatoes, depending on their size and place in a bowl along with the shallot rings. Season with coarse sea salt and pepper. Mix the olive oil with the lime juice, pour over the potato pieces and gently spoon around the bowl. Cover and keep warm for 10 minutes. The lime oil flavour will be absorbed by the warm potatoes and shallots, the gentle lime bite working well with the mint dressing.

Scatter the marinated potatoes over the plates along with the goat's cheese. Warm under a preheated grill or in a hot oven, allowing the cheese only to gently soften. While warming the plates, reheat the peas.

To serve, spoon the peas over the potatoes and goat's cheese. Add the chopped mint to the dressing and sprinkle a teaspoon or two over the rocket leaves. Drizzle the remaining mint dressing across all the plates, top with rocket leaves and drizzle with soured cream or crème fraîche, if using.

Makes between 30 and 35 puffs to serve 6–8 as a starter or snack

For the sauce
- 225g (8oz) fresh uncooked beetroots
- 100ml (3½fl oz) *Mayonnaise* (page 180), or bought variety
- 100ml (3½fl oz) soured cream or crème fraîche
- salt and pepper
- squeeze of lemon juice

For the choux pastry
- 5 tablespoons milk
- 100g (4oz) butter
- ½ teaspoon salt
- ½ teaspoon caster sugar
- 150g (5oz) flour

- 3 medium eggs, plus 1 egg, beaten, for brushing
- 100g (4oz) finely grated Cheddar or Gruyère cheese
- pinch of cayenne pepper
- oil, for greasing

Baked cheese puffs with fresh beetroot sauce

These cheese puffs are made from a flavoured choux pastry which soufflées to a crispy coat and soft interior. In France they're classically made with Gruyère cheese and piped into a circle to create a Gougère ring.

Beetroots are so good to eat in mid-to-late summer. Here they are cooked, chopped and puréed in a food processor along with mayonnaise and soured cream or crème fraîche. This strawberry-pink sauce is packed with fresh beetroot flavour and makes the perfect dip for the puffs. An alternative dip is the *Greengage and walnut chutney* (page 187). August is the month for this green plum to join us, having a short life which finishes in mid-to-late September. The beauty of the chutney recipe is that it will last a lot longer, holding on through the autumn months.

Method It is best to make the sauce well in advance so that it is ready and waiting for the warm puffs. Cook the beetroots in rapidly simmering water for 40–60 minutes. For this recipe, it's best to slightly overcook them, without allowing them to become soggy. This will help blend the beets well. To check they are cooked, lift a beetroot from the water and if the skin pulls away easily by the thumb they are ready. If not, continue to cook, checking every 5–10 minutes. Once tender, remove from the water and leave to cool. When still warm, peel and roughly chop them. Place in a food processor and blitz. Add the mayonnaise and soured cream or crème fraîche and continue to purée until smooth. Season with salt, pepper and a squeeze of lemon juice. If still too coarse, the sauce can be strained through a sieve for a smoother finish.

To make the pastry, preheat the oven to 200°C/400°F/Gas 6. Bring the milk, 5 tablespoons of water, butter, salt and sugar to the boil and simmer for 1 minute. Remove from the heat and beat in the flour to make a smooth paste. Return the pan to the heat and stir for 1½–2 minutes. Once the paste has totally left the sides of the pan, remove from the heat. Add three of the eggs, one at a time, beating each until smooth before adding the next. Once the eggs have been mixed in, add three-quarters of the grated cheese and season with a pinch of cayenne pepper. The choux pastry is now ready to pipe, or cover with cling film until needed.

Pipe the pastry into small balls approximately 2.5cm (1in) in diameter on a lightly greased non-stick baking tray, leaving at least 3cm (1¼in) between each. Up to this stage can be done in advance and the pastry balls refrigerated until ready to bake.

Brush the balls lightly with the beaten egg, and sprinkle with the remaining cheese. Bake in the pre-heated oven for 15–18 minutes until golden brown and crispy, keeping them warm if baking in batches. Once all the puffs are cooked, serve warm with the beetroot sauce.

- *For perfect dome-shaped choux buns, the mix can be piped into your hand (which may need to be lightly greased or floured) before rolling into 2.5cm (1in) balls. Place the choux balls on a non-stick baking tray and cook as instructed.*

- *Pre-cooked beetroots can be used. If so, reduce the quantity to 175g (6oz) rather than 225g (8oz).*

Serves 6 as a generous starter or main course

- 3 ripe salad tomatoes, cut into eighths
- juice of 2 lemons
- salt and pepper
- 1 teaspoon coriander seeds (optional)
- 1 bay leaf (optional)
- 6 globe artichokes
- 2 knobs of butter
- 2–3 tablespoons olive oil, plus more for reheating the artichokes (optional)
- 350g (12 oz) mushrooms (a mixture of chestnut, button and wild, such as oyster and chanterelle, can be used in this recipe, or simply any of these)
- 1 medium onion, finely chopped
- 6 *Poached eggs* (page 186)
- 1 quantity *Simple hollandaise sauce* (page 178)
- 1 tablespoon chopped mixed herbs such as tarragon, chives, parsley, chervil (optional)

Artichoke, mushroom and poached egg Benedict

Home-grown artichokes can be found between mid-summer and early autumn, with any after that usually imported.

This may look quite a long recipe with lots of flavours, and not one you're going to make a habit of 'knocking up' for an easy supper, but it does have many advantages. The first is that it is a basic recipe for cooking artichokes, a vegetable that can be used in many dishes and one that works particularly well with summer ratatouille-style vegetables, such as courgettes, aubergines and sweet peppers, or simply cold in a good salad.

The other advantage to this recipe is how far in advance the components can be prepared. The artichokes will keep well for 2–3 days refrigerated, with the mushrooms holding for 24 hours. The *Poached eggs* can be cooked and kept refrigerated for several hours and the *Simple hollandaise sauce* kept warm for between 30–60 minutes. The 'Benedict' title I've taken from the classic eggs and ham Benedict which I just adore to eat.

Method Place the chopped tomatoes, juice of 1 lemon and salt in a saucepan with 450ml (¾ pint) of water, along with the coriander seeds and bay leaf, if using. Bring to a simmer and cook for 5 minutes, then remove from the heat. The cooking liquor is now ready. The tomatoes and lemon juice will have spread their sweet acidic flavours, which will help maintain the natural colour of the artichokes.

Break the stalk from the base of each artichoke and cut 3–4mm (⅛–⅙ in) from the base to reveal the artichoke bottom. Hold the artichoke on its side and, with a sharp knife, cut around to remove the outside leaves. The pointed tops can now also be cut away, leaving you with 2.5–3cm (1–1¼ in) bottoms. Trim off any excess green from the bottoms (this tastes bitter), then scoop out the furry 'chokes' from the centre. To prevent any of the artichokes from discolouring, squeeze half of the juice of the remaining lemon into 150ml (¼ pint) of water and as each artichoke bottom is prepared, rub it liberally with the remaining lemon half and put to steep in the acidulated water while preparing the next.

Return the cooking liquor to the heat and, once simmering, add the artichokes. Cover with greaseproof paper. The artichokes will now take 20–25 minutes to become completely tender. Remove from the heat and leave to cool.

Once cool, lift the artichokes from the liquor and strain the liquor through a sieve. The chokes can now be kept refrigerated until needed, steeped in the strained stock. To reheat, the artichokes can be simply warmed in the liquor for a few minutes, before removing and rolling in a knob of butter; alternatively they can be sautéed from cold in a tablespoon or two of olive oil with a knob of butter, giving them a golden brown edge, and then seasoned with salt and pepper.

Wipe clean or rinse the mushrooms, then roughly chop them into small dice. This is best done by hand to help maintain their texture. They can be 'chopped' in a food processor, but this does tend to tear and bruise rather than chop. Place the mushroooms in a large saucepan and cook on a medium heat, stirring from time to time until all the juices have evaporated.

While cooking the mushrooms, melt a knob of butter in a large hot frying pan. Once bubbling, add the onions and cook on a high heat for 5–6 minutes until tender. Add the onions to the cooked mushrooms, season with salt and pepper, then spoon into a sieve, reserving all of the juices. These can be reduced by two-thirds before adding them back into the mushrooms, which can now be refrigerated until needed.

To reheat, simply place the mushrooms in a saucepan and warm until the mushrooms are heated through.

With all components ready (the poached eggs and hollandaise sauce, made as described on pages 186 and 178, should be warmed through) the dish can be assembled. Spoon ½ teaspoon of hollandaise sauce in the centre of each of six plates or bowls. Fill the artichoke bottoms with the cooked mushrooms and place them on top. The hollandaise will help prevent the chokes from sliding across the plate. Place the warm and seasoned poached eggs on the mushrooms, then spoon a tablespoon or two of hollandaise sauce over each. If using the 2–3 tablespoons of olive oil and herbs, mix them together and drizzle them on top and/or around. The dish is ready to serve and worth every minute.

Serves 4 as a main course or 6 as a generous starter

- 175g (6oz) *Puff pastry* (page 185), or bought variety
- flour, for dusting
- ½ tablespoon olive oil, plus more for brushing
- 1 red onion, thinly sliced
- ½ teaspoon caster sugar
- salt, plus coarse sea salt if available
- twist of black pepper
- 4–5 large courgettes, topped and tailed and cut into 3–4mm (⅛–⅙in) slices
- 1 egg yolk, loosened with a drop of milk (optional)
- 1 teaspoon picked thyme leaves
- squeeze of lemon juice

For the salad
- 7–8 plum or salad tomatoes
- iced water
- 3 tablespoons olive oil
- 1 teaspoon aged balsamic vinegar (for a vinegar of lesser strength add ½–1 teaspoon more)
- 5–6 basil leaves
- 25–50g (1–2oz) Parmesan cheese shavings

Crisp courgette tart with a tomato and basil salad

This recipe makes the most of two main favourites of English summer – courgettes and tomatoes, both in abundance throughout this season. The salad also benefits from the experience of the fresh basil leaves accompanied by a few shavings of Parmesan cheese. In all, a classic combination.

Method Preheat the oven to 230°C/450°F/Gas 8. Roll out the puff pastry on a lightly floured surface to a thickness of about 2mm (⅛in) and cut into a 25cm (10in) disc. Use a large round cake tin or plate as a guide. Place on a lightly greased baking sheet and refrigerate.

Heat the ½ tablespoon of olive oil in a frying pan and, once hot but not smoking, add the red onion. Cook on a medium heat for a few minutes until softening and with a little colour. Add the sugar and stir to dissolve. Season with salt and pepper and remove from the pan. Leave to cool.

Plunge the courgettes into a large pot of rapidly boiling salted water for just 30 seconds. (This begins the cooking process, and enhances the green colour of the skins.) Drain immediately and leave to cool and dry on a clean kitchen cloth or paper.

Prick the base of the rolled chilled pastry with a fork, then spoon the cooked onions over, leaving a 5mm (¼in) border. The onions will spread very loosely not actually covering the complete base (too many onions will create a steaming effect rather than allowing the courgettes to bake). Arrange the courgette slices overlapping around the pastry, from the outside into the centre, finishing with one central slice. Brush lightly with a little olive oil,

season with salt and pepper and brush the pastry border with egg yolk to glaze, if using. Refrigerate until needed or bake the tart in the preheated oven for 20–25 minutes. Remove from the oven after 15–20 minutes and sprinkle with the thyme leaves. Return to the oven and continue baking for the remaining 5–10 minutes.

To serve, brush with just a touch more olive oil for a shiny finish, transfer to a large plate and sprinkle with a little sea salt (if available) and a squeeze of lemon juice.

To make the salad, while the tart is baking, remove the eyes from the tomatoes, cut a cross at each base and then blanch in boiling water for just 10 seconds. Plunge into iced water. Once cold, the skin will peel away easily. Cut the tomatoes into about 5mm (¼in) rings, slicing horizontally across the tomatoes.

Arrange the slices on a large plate in the same fashion as the courgettes. Season with a twist of pepper and sea salt. Whisk together the olive oil and balsamic vinegar and season, then spoon over the tomatoes. Tear the basil leaves and sprinkle over the tomatoes along with the Parmesan shavings. The salad and tart are now ready to serve.

● *The dressing, basil leaves and Parmesan should not be sprinkled over the tomato plate until just before serving.*

● *For a richer golden brown, the courgette slices can be very quickly seared, on one side only, in a hot pan drizzled with olive oil. Leave to cool before placing them on the onions.*

Serves 4 as a main course
- 450g (1lb) *Puff pastry* (page 185) or bought variety
- flour, for dusting
- 1 egg, beaten
- 450g (1lb) tomatoes
- iced water
- 1 tablespoon olive oil, plus more for the vegetables
- salt and pepper
- ¼ teaspoon caster sugar (optional)
- 1 baby aubergine
- 6 baby courgettes
- 3–4 baby red peppers
- 3–4 baby yellow peppers
- 2 small red onions
- 4 *Poached eggs* (page 186)

For the basil sauce
- 2 tablespoons white wine vinegar
- 4 tablespoons white wine
- 4 tablespoons crème fraîche
- 50g (2oz) butter
- salt and pepper
- 8 basil leaves, snipped or shredded

Ratatouille feuilleté *with fresh tomato confit and basil sauce*

Feuilleté translated represents the layers in puff pastry. It's the *pâte feuilleté* (puff pastry) that is to be used in this recipe. Squares of it, cooked like vol-au-vents, are filled with a ratatouille selection of summer vegetables, including baby sweet red and yellow peppers, courgettes, aubergines and red onions, all of which seem to be quite easily obtainable from most large food stores. Should these not be available, the larger standard version of each can be used, cutting them into wedges, slices or dice. Whichever is used, the vegetables can be grilled, cooked on a griddle or pan-fried until tender, before being stacked in the pastry shell on top of spoonfuls of cooked fresh tomatoes. To finish, they are topped with a warm poached egg bleeding its rich yolk, coated with a basil and crème fraîche butter sauce.

Method Preheat the oven to 220°C/425°F/Gas 7. Roll out the puff pastry on a lightly floured surface, to a thick square approximately 18–20cm (6–8in). Quarter this into four 9–10cm (3½–4in) squares. Place these on a baking tray lined with greaseproof paper. Refrigerate for 15 minutes to allow to rest. Now gently cut a border into each pastry square about 5mm (¼in) in from each side. This will make lids that will be removed once the pastry is cooked. Brush carefully with the beaten egg, preferably not allowing it to drip down the sides as this can prevent the pastry from rising when baking.

Bake in the preheated oven for 30–40 minutes until risen, golden brown and crispy. If not quite crisp or coloured, brush once more with the beaten egg and continue to bake for a further 5–6 minutes. Remove

from the oven and leave to cool. The central lids can now be cut out, also cutting and trimming away any excess undercooked central layers. This will leave you with crisp empty pastry cases ready to be filled with the ratatouille.

To make the tomato confit, remove the eyes from the tomatoes with a sharp knife, cut a small cross at the base and then blanch in boiling water for 10 seconds. Plunge into iced water and, once cold, peel the tomatoes. Halve them and scoop the seeds and juices into a sieve over a bowl. Gently press any excess liquid from the seeds and discard the seeds. The tomato liquid will be used in the cooking of the tomatoes as they reduce, making an even more intense flavour. Cut the tomato halves into rough 1 cm (½in) dice. Warm the tablespoon of olive oil in a saucepan, add the tomato dice and cook for a few minutes over a moderate heat, until the tomatoes are beginning to soften. Add the tomato juices and slightly increase the heat. Let the tomatoes cook until the liquid reduces, leaving just a loose pulp. Season with salt and pepper, and the caster sugar if needed to sweeten the finished flavour.

Lower the oven temperature to 180°C/350°F/Gas 4. To prepare the vegetables, cut the baby aubergines and courgettes into quarters lengthwise. Split the red and yellow peppers in half, cutting away the stalk and membrane, and deseed. Now cut each half into three or four strips. Divide the red onions into 8–12 wedges. As mentioned in the introduction, these can now all be grilled, cooked on a griddle or pan-fried. Whichever method is chosen, it's important that the utensil is hot.

If frying, a large roasting tray can be used to provide more space for the vegetables as a lot of cooking space will be needed. However, they can all be cooked in batches and kept warm in the oven. If this is the case, it's best to start with the red onions, searing them in olive oil for a minute or two on each side until tender. Do the same with the aubergines, followed by the sweet peppers and courgettes. All will just take a few minutes to cook. Any remaining cooking will take place in the oven, giving you enough time to assemble the dish.

While the vegetables are cooking, make the basil sauce. Boil the vinegar and white wine together until reduced to 2 tablespoons before adding 3 tablespoons of water. Whisk in the crème fraîche and bring to a simmer. Whisk in the butter and season with salt and pepper. Just before serving at a warm temperature, add the snipped basil leaves.

To serve, warm the pastry cases briefly in the oven, then divide the tomato confit between each. Spoon the vegetables into the cases, showing off their vibrant colours and textures. Rather than overfilling the cases, a selection can also be spooned on the plates as a garnish. Place a warmed and seasoned poached egg on top of each, then drizzle over the basil sauce. The ratatouille *feuilletés* are now ready to serve.

● *For a quicker and easier ratatouille, cut all the vegetables into chunky dice and fry each separately in a wok, keeping each batch warm in the oven while continuing to fry. Once all are cooked, mix with the tomato confit, season and spoon into the pastry cases. Finish as described, with the poached eggs and basil sauce.*

● *Garlic can be added to the tomato confit.*

● *For a perfect square flat top, an extra baking tray can be placed over the pastry vol-au-vents while they are cooking, held up by ovenproof cutters, moulds or egg cups. Once the pastry has risen this far, it will flatten and continue to bake to an equal finish.*

Serves 4
- 675g (1½lb) fresh, ripe tomatoes, quartered
- 3–4 leaves of gelatine, soaked in cold water (these quantities are for 225–300ml/8–10fl oz of tomato water)
- 8 large tomatoes
- iced water
- salt and pepper

For the cream
- 175g (6oz) ricotta cheese
- 1 small garlic clove, crushed
- 1 teaspoon red wine vinegar
- 1 tablespoon olive oil
- 1 teaspoon snipped chives
- 1 teaspoon snipped flatleaf parsley
- 1 teaspoon snipped tarragon

For the garnish (optional)
- 1 tablespoon olive oil
- ½–1 tablespoon balsamic vinegar
- 1–2 handfuls of mixed salad leaves
- 12–16 x 2cm (¾in) pieces of chive
- 12–16 flatleaf parsley leaves
- 12–16 tarragon leaves

Jellied tomato cake with ricotta herb cream

Summer is peaking and tomatoes are in abundance. Plenty of ripe and rich flavours, carrying the added advantage of quite a low price. It is at this time of year that this recipe should be tried. The jelly is made from pure tomato water – just a question of liquidizing the tomatoes and draining them of all their juices. The result is quite an intense flavour for the little jelly.

The ricotta herb cream involves a last-minute blitzing of the cheese, creamed with a bite of garlic, red wine vinegar, olive oil and lots of herbs. To finish this starter, a handful or two of salad leaves and then some herbs can be arranged as a garnish.

Method Liquidize the quartered tomatoes first, enough to break down the texture. Drain through a muslin cloth or fine sieve. To maximize the full flavour and allow the tomatoes to drain completely, it is best to carry out this procedure 24 hours in advance. The minimum time required will be at least 5–6 hours. It is also important not to push the purée through the cloth as this will result in a tomato coulis, too thick and cloudy for this dish. Once drained, a very gentle squeeze will help release the last few drops, resulting in approximately 225–300ml (8–10fl oz) of liquor.

Remove and squeeze excess water from the gelatine leaves, then place them in a small saucepan with a few tablespoons of the tomato water. Warm gently to melt the gelatine, then stir into the remaining tomato water.

To peel the tomatoes, remove the eyes with a sharp knife and then blanch in boiling water for 10 seconds. Plunge into iced water and, once cold, peel them. Cut away the domed tops of four of the peeled tomatoes (opposite the stalk end). Try to make these domes neat and round and approximately 1cm (½in) thick as they will form the tops of the jellied cakes. Quarter and seed the remaining parts of the tomatoes, as well as the other four whole ones. This stage can also be prepared in advance.

To build the cakes, stretch cling film over four 8 × 5-cm (3 × 2-in) metal cooking rings and turn them over. Season the tomato quarters with salt and pepper, only salting the dome tops. Place the pieces in the moulds, layering with the jelly, not overpressing or squashing the tomatoes too tightly. Once all quarters have been used, place the four domes on top. Spoon extra jelly over the tomatoes, leaving a few millimetres of top exposed. Refrigerate until set.

To turn out the cakes, remove the cling film. If left to stand for a few minutes the cakes should, with a gentle push from the domed top, be quite easy to turn out. Another method is holding the metal rings tightly, to lightly warm them with your hands. The quickest method is to quickly warm with a gas gun (page 11).

To make the cream, blend the ricotta cheese to a smooth paste with the crushed garlic, red wine vinegar and olive oil. Season with salt and pepper and fold in the snipped herbs.

To finish the dish, if using the garnish, mix the olive oil and balsamic vinegar together and season. Mix the salad leaves with the chive pieces, parsley and tarragon leaves, and add the vinegar dressing. The three components – tomato cake, ricotta cream, salad leaves – can be placed individually on each plate, forming a trio of flavours and colours.

Serves 4–6 as a starter

- knob of butter
- 1 shallot, finely diced (or ½ small onion)
- 1 garlic clove, chopped
- 1 bay leaf
- 675g (1½lb) red peppers, seeded and chopped into rough 1cm (½in) dice
- ½ teaspoon caster sugar
- 3 tablespoons red wine vinegar
- 3 tablespoons white wine
- 2 leaves of gelatine, soaked in cold water
- 150ml (¼pint) double cream
- squeeze of lemon juice, to taste
- salt and pepper

For the crispy onion strips

- 225g (8oz) puff pastry
- flour, for dusting
- oil, for greasing
- 4 large onions, finely sliced
- knob of butter
- 2 teaspoons demerara sugar
- salt and twist of pepper
- ½ teaspoon picked thyme leaves (optional)
- 1 tin of anchovy fillets (optional)

Red pepper mousse with crispy onion strips

Summer is with us and the English red peppers have joined us too. Obviously this is a recipe that can be made all year round because of imports, but it should certainly be tried and taken advantage of during these warm sunny days.

The onion strips are very quick and easy to make. For a completely vegetarian dish, the anchovy fillets can be omitted. The strips are made from puff pastry and for this particular recipe I recommend the bought variety, fresh or frozen.

The mousse will need up to 2 hours to set, providing plenty of time to make its accompaniment. This recipe eats very well as a starter or can become part of a summer barbecue buffet or picnic. The quantities listed for the onion strips seem quite high, this is basically because once tried they are very moreish. The recipe can be halved, providing just enough for a light starter.

Method Melt the butter in a large saucepan and, once bubbling, add the shallot or onion, garlic and bay leaf. Cover with a lid and cook for a few minutes until the shallots are beginning to soften. Add the red peppers, replace the lid and cook for a further 10–15 minutes, stirring from time to time, until tender. Add the sugar, red wine vinegar and white wine, increase the heat and allow to boil and reduce until almost dry.

Remove the bay leaf and liquidize the mixture to a purée, straining through a sieve for a smooth finish. While still warm, add the soaked gelatine leaves, squeezing them first to release excess water, and stir in well. Leave to cool. Once cold but not approaching a setting point, lightly whip the double cream to soft peaks. Spoon and fold the cream into the pepper purée, adding a squeeze of lemon juice and seasoning with salt and pepper. Now spoon the mousse mix into a suitable bowl, cover with cling film and refrigerate for 1–2 hours until set.

To prepare the crispy onion strips, cut the pastry into four rectangular pieces. On a lightly floured surface roll each piece individually into a long thin strip, approximately 2mm (⅛in) thick and 4cm (1½in) wide.

These can be trimmed to achieve a straighter edge or simply left quite rustic. Place all four on a greased baking sheet and prick along the centres with a fork. Refrigerate.

Fry the onions in the butter (this may need to be done in stages) almost until approaching burnt, then add the demerara sugar. Continue to cook for a few minutes until the sugar is beginning to caramelize. Season with salt and pepper and add the thyme, if using. Remove from the heat and leave to cool.

Once cold, preheat the oven to 200°C/400°F/Gas 6. Spoon the onions along the pastry strips, leaving a 5mm (¼in) border on either side. Cut the anchovy fillets lengthwise into two or three slices, and lay these top to tail along the middle of the onions (cutting the anchovies thinly will balance their strong flavour with that of the onions and pastry).

Bake in the preheated oven for 10–15 minutes until crispy. These will eat at their best warm, but not too hot. The mousse can now be presented on the table along with the strips, cut into 2cm (¾in) slices – just nice bite-size pieces on which to spoon the mousse.

Serves 4 generous portions

- 350g (12oz) podded broad beans
- salt and pepper
- iced water
- 25g (1oz) butter
- 1 tablespoon finely chopped shallot or onion
- 2 sprigs of savory (reserve a few leaves for garnish)
- 600ml (1pint) *Vegetable stock* (page 177) or water
- 100ml (3½fl oz) crème fraîche or single cream (optional)
- pinch of caster sugar

Late broad bean savory soup

Broad beans are with us right up to the last month of summer. Unlike the small moist kidney-shaped young spring bean, which cooks so quickly and eats very tenderly, as the broad bean ages it grows and toughens too. Although you're still able to cook and serve them as a vegetable, I prefer to eat them in a puréed form, hence the soup.

This recipe can be made with just water and the vegetables. Rather than being shallow in flavour, the results are simply fresh and honest. If a greater depth of flavour is preferred, then I suggest using a vegetable stock. The savory within the title actually refers to the summer herb, summer savory (there's also a winter savory, which is more robust in its flavour). The leaves of this purple-to-lilac-flowered plant hold a mixture of herby flavours, ranging from thyme, marjoram and sage to an almost faint nose of mint. Savory is classically associated with dried and fresh bean dishes, with the broad bean holding pole position. It's this herb that can offer our water-based soup a mixed essence of other flavours.

Method Plunge the podded beans into a pan of rapidly boiling salted water. Bring back to the boil and cook for 1 minute. Drain and refresh in iced water. These can now have their tough outer skins removed to reveal the rich green beans beneath.

Melt a knob of the butter in a heavy-based saucepan. Add the shallot or onion and cook until softened, then add the savory and water or stock. Bring to a rapid simmer, then add the broad beans, saving a few per portion for garnish. Cook for 6–7 minutes or until the beans are tender, and remove the savory sprigs. The soup can now be liquidized (in batches if necessary) to a smooth purée, before straining it through a sieve. Add the crème fraîche or cream, if using, and season with salt, pepper and a pinch of sugar. Warm through, stirring in the remaining butter. Sprinkle the remaining beans between bowls, then ladle the soup. Garnish with the reserved savory leaves and serve.

- *A little crème fraîche or single cream can be saved to drizzle on top of the soup before serving.*

- *A flavoured oil – walnut, hazelnut or olive – can be dotted on top of the soup to finish.*

**Serves 4 as a generous starter
or main course**
- 600ml (1pint) water, *Vegetable
  stock* (page 177), *Chicken stock*
  (page 175) or *Instant stock*
  (page 175)
- 450g (1lb) podded peas
  (frozen can also be used)
- salt and pepper
- pinch of sugar
- 100ml (3½fl oz) whipping or
  single cream

For the fish
- 4 × 100g (4oz) portions of
  cod fillet, skinned and pin-boned
  (page 11)
- flour, for dusting
- 1 tablespoon cooking oil
- knob of butter
- 1 heaped teaspoon sesame
  seeds
- 1 tablespoon sesame oil
  (optional)

Pea soup with toasted sesame cod fillet

This must be the quickest and simplest of soups to make. The cod gives this starter just enough depth to make it into a good full lunch or supper dish. The sesame seeds provide a lovely nutty bite to the overall flavour, and you can also trickle the soup with a drop or two of sesame oil if you like. The most natural of pea soups can be made with just water. For a deeper flavour, a stock can be used in its place as listed above.

Method Bring the water or stock to the boil in a saucepan and add the peas. Bring back to the boil and cook for 5 minutes until tender (longer if necessary). Remove from the heat, season with salt, pepper and a pinch of sugar, and liquidize to a smooth creamy soup. For the smoothest of finishes strain through a sieve. The soup at this stage can be cooled over ice (to help maintain its colour), then simply reheated when needed.

If serving immediately, add the cream and return to a gentle simmer, seasoning once again with salt and pepper.

While the soup is simmering, lightly dust the skinned sides of the cod fillets with flour and season with salt. Heat the cooking oil in a frying pan and add the fillets, floured-sides down. Cook for 4 minutes until golden brown, add the knob of butter, then turn and continue to fry for a further 2 minutes. The sesame seeds can be used natural, as they are, or toasted to a golden brown under a hot grill for a richer and nuttier finish.

Place the cod fillets in soup plates and ladle the pea soup around. Sprinkle the fillets with sesame seeds and a drop of sesame oil, if using.

Serves 4 as a starter
- 675g (1½lb) broccoli
- salt and pepper
- iced water
- 25g (1oz) butter, plus a knob for the onion
- 1 onion, finely chopped

- 1 medium potato, cut into rough 1cm (½in) dice
- 600–750ml (1–1¼pint) hot *Vegetable stock* (page 177) or *Instant stock* (page 175)
- 4–5 tablespoons whipping cream (optional)

- 6–8 almond slices per portion (3–4 whole almonds, see below)
- 4 *Poached eggs* (page 186)
- squeeze of lemon juice
- 1 heaped tablespoon chopped parsley
- 1 tablespoon olive oil (optional)

Broccoli soup with poached eggs and toasted parsley almonds

Calabrese is the larger summer variety of the broccoli family. The purple sprouting broccoli of spring was probably the original, as the term broccoli means 'little shoots'. It would seem, however, that this larger member of the family known generally as broccoli has become the most popular.

The soup is very basic and simple, with not too many ingredients in the soup itself. It also eats very well chilled with a touch of soured cream.

As part of the garnish to accompany the softly poached eggs, very small broccoli florets can be cooked separately and added to the finished soup when serving. These provide a fresh taste and texture, enhancing the basic flavour of the dish. The real bonus to the dish is provided by the poached egg: once broken the yolk lifts and enriches everything.

If fresh almonds are available, still within their velvety green coats, then do take advantage of their natural sweet flavour. Once peeled (see introduction, page 156) the small fresh nuts can be sliced in two, providing a thicker and denser texture and flavour. Failing that, dried, skinless, white almonds are the next best choice (also sliced in two), with the dried flakes as a third option. These will work in the soup, but do tend to be too thin and don't quite offer the same depth of flavour or texture.

Method Cut 100g (4oz) of very small broccoli florets from the large heads. Quickly blanch in boiling salted water for just 30 seconds to 1 minute, then refresh in iced water. Drain and keep to one side for garnish.

To make the soup, cut the flower heads from the broccoli stalks and roughly chop the florets. Thinly slice the stalks and keep them separate.

Melt the knob of butter in a large saucepan. Add the chopped onion and potato. Cook for 12–15 minutes without colouring, until beginning to soften. Add the broccoli stalks and cook for a further few minutes. Add 600ml (1pint) of hot stock and bring to a simmer. Cook for 5–6 minutes until all the vegetables are cooked. Season with salt and pepper, then bring to the boil and add the chopped broccoli heads. Cook for a further 2–3 minutes, then liquidize to a smooth purée. If the soup is too thick, add the remaining vegetable stock. For the smoothest of finishes, strain through a sieve, then add the cream, if using, and season with salt and pepper.

Now warm the broccoli florets in the finished soup or reheat in a few tablespoons of hot water. If heating them separately, they can be sprinkled into the soup just before spooning over the almonds.

Melt the 25g (1oz) of butter in a frying pan and add the almond slices. Fry on a gentle heat until just colouring.

Ladle the soup into soup plates and place a warm poached egg in the centre. Increase the heat under the butter and almonds and, when just approaching its nutty brown stage, add a squeeze of lemon juice, salt, pepper and the chopped parsley. The butter and almonds will now be bubbling, almost soufflèing, in the pan. If using the olive oil, it can be added to the almonds now, before spooning them over the poached eggs and soup.

- *The almonds can first be toasted to a golden brown, then added to the butter as it becomes nutbrown.*

Serves 4 as a starter

- 8 large sardines (16 fillets), scaled and filleted
- 2 small-to-medium aubergines
- salt and pepper
- 4 tablespoons olive oil, plus more for brushing and warming
- 5 tablespoons white wine vinegar
- 1 heaped tablespoon clear honey
- butter, for frying (optional)
- 1 heaped teaspoon chopped chives

For the lemon marinade

- 1 shallot, finely chopped
- juice of 2 lemons
- ½ teaspoon caster sugar
- ¼ teaspoon salt
- ¼ teaspoon freshly ground black pepper

For the tomato and basil mayonnaise (optional)

- 125ml (4fl oz) *Mayonnaise* (page 180), or bought variety
- 3 tomatoes, preferably plum
- iced water
- 6 basil leaves, snipped into small pieces

Grilled honeyed aubergines with lemon-marinated sardine fillets

Both the main components of this dish can be prepared 24 hours in advance. For the aubergines it's not essential, but they do need several hours for the honey-sweet, almost pickle-like, flavour to become infused. The sardines, however, do need the 24 hours, basically because they are not going to be cooked. Instead they are marinated and 'cooked' by the citrus acidity of the lemon juice, in what is almost a curing process.

The aubergines will be served hot from the pan, which works well with the cold fish. I've also included a tomato and basil mayonnaise; this is purely optional, but does offer something creamy to finish this combination.

The fresh sardines need to be scaled, gutted and filleted. Your fishmonger can do this, but it's reasonably easy to do at home. Run the fish under cold water while you push the scales off and away. Remove the head, which will then show you exactly where to sit the blade of a sharp filleting knife. Cut along the bone confidently and the fillet will come away in one movement. Turn the fish over and repeat the same cut. Scrape away the innards and any little bones, rinse and pat dry. Any fine pin bones will virtually disintegrate during the curing, becoming tender enough to eat.

Method To make the lemon marinade, mix the chopped shallot with the juice from one of the lemons, the caster sugar, salt and pepper. Pour into a dish and place the sardines on top, filleted-sides down. Cover with cling film and refrigerate for 24 hours, turning once or twice to ensure even marinating.

Trim the stalks from the aubergines then cut them lengthwise into 5mm (¼in) slices. Lightly salt and leave to stand in a colander for 30 minutes, to draw out the excess moisture. Rinse and pat dry. Brush each slice with olive oil and place on a very hot griddle plate or frying pan. Cook for 2 minutes to colour well, then turn and cook for a further 2–3 minutes until tender.

Meanwhile, prepare the tomatoes for the mayonnaise, if using. Remove the eyes from the tomatoes with a sharp knife, cut a cross at the base and blanch in boiling water for 10 seconds. Plunge into iced water and, once cold, peel the tomatoes. Halve them and scoop out the seeds and discard. Cut into 5mm (¼in) dice.

While the aubergines are cooking, mix together the vinegar and honey with 150ml (¼pint) of warm water. Once all the aubergines are coloured, steep them in the sweet sharp liquor for several hours, up to 24. To reheat simply remove from the liquor and pan-fry in butter or brush with olive oil and place under a preheated grill until warmed through. Season with salt and pepper.

The aubergines can now be kept in their slices or cut diagonally to form triangular pieces, presenting them on plates with a fan of sardine fillets. To finish, whisk the juice of the remaining lemon with the 4 tablespoons of olive oil and salt, pepper and chopped chives. Spoon this over the sardines. If serving the tomato and basil mayonnaise, simply mix the three ingredients together.

- *For a more 'cocktail sauce' finish to the mayonnaise, add a tablespoon of tomato passata (sieved tomato) or a teaspoon of ketchup. A splash of brandy can also be added for extra cocktail bite.*

Serves 4 as a generous starter or main course

For the gnocchi
- 450g (1lb) large potatoes
- small knob of butter (approximately 10g/⅓oz), plus 2 knobs
- 2 tablespoons chopped mixed herbs, such as tarragon, parsley, basil, chervil, chives
- 75g (3oz) plain flour, sifted, plus more for dusting
- 1 egg, plus 1 extra yolk
- salt and pepper
- freshly grated nutmeg
- iced water
- cooking oil, for frying

For the asparagus and sauce
- 20–24 medium asparagus spears
- knob of butter
- 200ml (7fl oz) *Vegetable stock (page 177)* or water
- 1 heaped tablespoon curly parsley
- 50g (2oz) spinach leaves
- 5–7 tablespoons double cream
- squeeze of lime juice (optional)
- olive oil, to serve (optional)

Fresh herb gnocchi with warm asparagus sauce

The gnocchi for this recipe are potato-based, providing a meaty but light texture. They can be made several hours in advance, taking them to their poached stage, ready to fry to order. The asparagus, crossing over the seasons and still in abundance now, makes a flavoursome sauce, using a percentage of the spear bases cooked and creamed with fresh parsley and spinach.

Method To prepare the gnocchi, boil the potatoes in salted water until cooked and tender. Peel the warm potatoes and mash to a smooth texture. Add the measured butter and herbs, then fold in 50g (2oz) of the flour and the egg and extra egg yolk. Season with salt, pepper and nutmeg. The mixture should feel moist but not sticky, with a workable texture. If too wet, add the remaining flour.

Now mould the gnocchi (this is easily achieved while the mixture is still warm) on a floured surface or in floured hands into 2cm (¾in) balls. Place in batches into simmering salted water. The gnocchi will sink and, when cooked, rise to the surface. The cooking time is generally 3–4 minutes, five maximum. It is important that the dough balls are firm to the touch. Refresh in iced water and, once cold, allow to dry on a kitchen cloth. The gnocchi can now be refrigerated until needed.

To prepare the asparagus, trim the pointy ears from the spears and snap or cut away the root base stalk and discard. Cut a third of each spear away at the base. Chop the cut-off thirds roughly into small pieces. Melt a knob of butter in a saucepan and add these. Cook for 2 minutes, then pour in the stock or water. Bring to the boil and add the parsley and spinach leaves. Cook for 4–5 minutes, then remove from the heat. Blitz in a liquidizer until smooth. Season with salt and pepper, and add the double cream. Strain through a sieve and leave to one side.

To finish, heat 2–3 tablespoons of cooking oil in a large frying pan. When medium hot, fry the gnocchi to a golden brown, turning them carefully as they colour. Finish with a small knob of butter.

Meanwhile, cook the asparagus spears for a few minutes in boiling salted water until tender. Arrange them in a fan towards the front of the plate. Spoon the gnocchi at the base of the stalks, then add a squeeze of lime juice, if using, to the sauce and spoon it across the asparagus. A little olive oil can now be dotted around the plate.

● *If an electric hand blender is available, blitz the sauce just before serving to create a frothy finish.*

● *The gnocchi can be served without the asparagus as a complete starter or vegetarian main course. Fresh Parmesan shavings melted across them help complete a flavoursome dish.*

Makes 6 small side dishes
- 2 cos lettuces

For the dressing
- 100ml (3½fl oz) good-quality mayonnaise
- 1–2 tablespoons lemon juice
- 2 garlic cloves, crushed
- 1 teaspoon Dijon mustard
- 2 anchovy fillets

- 1 teaspoon capers (optional)
- dash of Tabasco sauce (optional)
- dash of Worcestershire sauce (optional)
- 2 tablespoons grated Parmesan or 50g (2oz) Parmesan shavings

Creamy Caesar salad

Caesar salad is thought to have been invented in Mexico, by a chef called Caesar Cardini, in the 1920s and since then this dish has spread across the world. Its now-classic combination of flavours lives on, with often one or two extras finding their way into the bowl.

There's nothing particularly seasonal in this recipe, but it was put together to to accompany the *Crispy red mullet, shrimps and tomatoes* (page 128). It is a quick variation of a *Caesar salad*, omitting the garnish of whole anchovy fillets and bread croutons, although please add these if you wish. Instead it's purely the highly flavoured creamy dressing that gently coats the leaves, with the addition of the freshly grated or shaved Parmesan to finish.

Method To make the dressing, place the mayonnaise, lemon juice, garlic, mustard and anchovy fillets in a liquidizer or small food processor. Add the optional ingredients, if using – they will help create a more piquant finish. Blitz to a smooth purée. A rich double-cream consistency is all that is needed simply to coat the leaves. If too thick, loosen with water until the right balance is found. This dressing can now be used as it is, or pushed through a fine sieve for the smoothest of finishes. Salt and pepper have not been used as seasoning should be provided by the anchovies and Tabasco, if using.

Shake off any excess water from the lettuce leaves and tear them into bite-size pieces. Toss the leaves together with the dressing to coat all pieces well and add the grated or shaved Parmesan. Serve immediately.

● *This salad will serve four as a light lunch or supper dish.*

Serves 4

- 8 sardines (16 fillets), scaled and filleted
- butter, for greasing
- salt and pepper
- 1 tablespoon olive oil, plus more for brushing
- rock salt
- cracked black pepper
- 4 medium courgettes
- 1 lemon, peeled and segmented
- pinch of caster sugar
- 2 tomatoes, preferably plum
- iced water
- 1 large or 2 small shallots, finely chopped
- 150ml (¼pint) crème fraîche (or reduced-fat crème fraîche)
- sorrel leaves (optional)

Rock-salt-and-pepper sardines in bitter lemon, tomato courgette linguine

Sardines are available all year round, but during the summer months can be found at their plumpest. This dish also eats very well using herring or mackerel fillets. The fresh courgettes, cut into long, thin strips, are in fact the linguine in this recipe, without a string of pasta in sight. I've just used the name to describe the shape of these vegetables.

This recipe makes a good starter, lunch or supper dish, so four sardine fillets and one medium courgette per portion will be plenty. The sauce is literally just crème fraîche with a hint of finely chopped shallot and sweet tomatoes. Sorrel leaves are also included, but not essential. However, they are around at this time of year and will work well, so why not include them?

Method Lay the sardine fillets on a buttered and seasoned baking tray and brush each with olive oil. Sprinkle a few flakes of rock salt and pinch of cracked black pepper over each fillet. These can now be refrigerated ready to cook at the last minute.

To make the courgette linguine, cut them into long, spaghetti-like strips on a mandolin or vegetable cutter. If these are unavailable, then cut them with a sharp knife into long slices approximately 3mm (⅛in) thick.

Dry the lemon segments on kitchen paper, sprinkle with the caster sugar and either sear them quickly in a hot dry frying pan, or colour them under a preheated grill or using a gas gun (page 11). Once coloured each segment can be cut into two or three small pieces.

Bring a large pan of salted water to the boil. Remove the eyes of the tomatoes with the point of a knife and blanch in the boiling water for 10 seconds, then refresh in iced water. Peel, quarter, seed and cut into approximately 1cm (½in) dice. Heat the tablespoon of olive oil in a large saucepan, add the chopped shallots and cook for 3–4 minutes, without allowing them to colour until beginning to soften. While cooking the shallots, blanch the courgette linguine for 15 seconds in the large pan of rapidly boiling salted water, then drain in a colander and add to the saucepan with the shallots. Fry on a high heat for a minute, then season with salt and pepper. Add the crème fraîche and bring to a simmer. Add the chopped lemon and diced tomatoes, and check the seasoning again.

At the same time, cook the sardines under a preheated hot grill. These will take between 2–5 minutes, depending on their size, cooking to a crisp finish.

If using sorrel leaves, dice or shred two or three and add them to the linguine (four small leaves can be used as an optional garnish). Now spoon the courgette linguine onto plates or into bowls, placing the sardine fillets on top or beside it and trickle with any juices. Garnish with the small sorrel leaves, if using.

- *The tomatoes and lemon pieces can be kept separate from the linguine, adding a few tablespoons of olive oil to create a dressing, and be spooned over and around the sardines and linguine just before serving. The crème fraîche can be warmed separately and trickled over the courgettes.*

- *Basil or marjoram can be used in place of sorrel.*

Serves 4 as a starter
- 4 small fresh herrings, filleted and trimmed
- 1 dessertspoon salt

For the marinade
- 100ml (3½fl oz) white wine
- 3 tablespoons white wine vinegar
- 1 level tablespoon demerara sugar
- 1 teaspoon pickling spices (optional)
- 2 shallots, sliced, or ½ onion
- 1 bay leaf

For the salad
- 2 medium potatoes
- 6 tablespoons olive oil
- 3 teaspoons lemon juice
- salt and pepper
- ½ small cucumber
- 2–3 medium beetroots, cooked (method, page 132)
- 4 tablespoons soured cream
- 2 teaspoons chopped chives

Sweet soused herrings with potato, beetroot and cucumber salad

In late summer beetroots and cucumbers both reach their prime, and herrings are in the middle of a very generous season. The herrings in this recipe are cured from raw, the acidity and sweetness both playing their part in the 'no-stove' cooking process.

As curing or sousing of fresh fish takes anything from just a few hours to a few days, you need to plan ahead. Here, at least 24 hours notice is needed, and the finished flavour will hold and still eat well for up to four or five days.

The salad, particularly the potatoes, is best served at room temperature. When cooked, peeled, crushed or sliced, they maintain their moist crumbly smoothness. Once refrigerated, potatoes do tend to change texture, becoming too firm – almost brittle – to eat.

Method Sprinkle the prepared herring fillets with the salt and leave to drain in a colander for a few hours. Once salted, rinse and dry on a kitchen cloth or paper.

While the fish are draining, place all the marinade ingredients in a saucepan with 150ml (¼pint) of water and bring to a simmer, then cook on a gentle heat for 15 minutes. Remove from the heat and leave to cool.

Place the rinsed herring fillets in a suitable dish, and pour the marinade liquor over. Cover and refrigerate for at least 24 hours, to allow the flavours to permeate.

To make the salad, boil the potatoes in their skins for 20 minutes or until completely cooked through. Remove from the water and allow to cool slightly, then peel and crush loosely with a fork. While the potatoes are still warm, mix 2 tablespoons of the olive oil with 2 teaspoons of the lemon juice. Stir the dressing into the potatoes and season with salt and pepper. Leave to cool, but do not refrigerate.

Peel the cucumber and halve into two shorter lengths. Slice each lengthwise into 5mm (¼in) thick slices. Slice these into 3mm (⅛in) thick sticks, discarding any central seeds. Place in a colander, sprinkle and mix with half a teaspoon of salt, and allow to drain for 20–30 minutes.

Peel and slice the beetroots into 5mm (¼in) thick rounds, then season with salt and pepper. Add 2 tablespoons of the soured cream to the potatoes, along with 1 teaspoon of the chopped chives.

Remove the herring fillets from the marinade and place them to one side. Strain the marinade through a fine sieve, then whisk 4 tablespoons of it into the remaining olive oil with the last teaspoon of lemon juice. Season with salt and pepper. A little of this dressing can now be used to flavour the beetroot slices.

There are many ways of finishing this dish, keeping all items separate on the plate before finishing with dressing being one. Another is to 'tower' the soured cream potatoes with the beetroots, interlayering the two: offer three slices of beetroot to three spoons of potatoes, then place the herring fillets on top and finally the cucumber sticks. Add the remaining teaspoon of chives to the oil dressing and spoon this over and around the serving plate, with drizzles of soured cream.

- *The herring skins can be left on or removed.*

- *A few salad leaves can be added to the finished dish.*

**Serves 4 as a generous
starter or main course**
- 2 × 675–900kg (1½–2lb) John Dory, filleted and skinned
- 2 oranges
- 50g (2oz) caster sugar
- 2 oranges, peeled and segmented
- 2 tablespoons hazelnuts, peeled
- drop of oil for frying (optional)

- flour, for dusting
- butter, for brushing
- 2 tablespoons olive oil
- 225–350g (8–12oz) mixed green leaves
- bunch of watercress, picked into sprigs
- 1 tablespoon chopped chives
- 1 heaped teaspoon chopped tarragon

For the dressing
- 3 tablespoons white wine vinegar
- 1 level tablespoon caster sugar
- 5 tablespoons orange juice
- 1 tablespoon Grand Marnier (optional)
- 100ml (3½fl oz) hazelnut oil
- squeeze of lemon juice
- salt and pepper

Pan-fried John Dory with an orange and hazelnut salad

John Dory is available year-round, particularly when sourced from Morocco. When sourced from our Devon coast it can be found between the months of May and November. This dish will be just perfect for the summer months, with so many salad leaves and herbs ready and waiting. To the salad, I've added an optional extra, with a confit of orange zest lending its bitter-sweet touch to the overall flavour.

Method The John Dory fillets consist of three fillet fingers per portion. These can now be separated or left as a complete fillet.

To make the orange confit, peel the rind from the two oranges, cutting away any pith and then slice it into thin strips (you could use an orange zester). Place in 150ml (¼pint) of cold water and bring to the boil. Strain and refresh in cold water, then repeat the same process twice more. This reduces the bitter edge from the zest. Juice the 2 oranges and pour the juice into a saucepan with the caster sugar and orange strips. Bring to the simmer and cook on a very low heat for 20–25 minutes, until the orange strips are tender. If the sweet orange juice has not reached a loose syrupy consistency, strain and reduce for a few minutes until it just coats a spoon. The strips can now be kept in the syrup in an airtight jar for up to a week or more.

To make the dressing, boil together the white wine vinegar and sugar, and add the orange juice and Grand Marnier, if using. Return to the boil and reduce by half. Allow to cool slightly, then whisk in the hazelnut oil and a squeeze of lemon juice. Season with salt and pepper.

To prepare the garnishes, the orange segments can be left whole or cut into two or three pieces. They can also be seared quickly (first patting them dry on kitchen paper) in a hot frying pan or coloured with a gas gun (page 11), creating a more bitter touch. The peeled hazelnuts can be toasted or quickly fried in a drop of oil to a rich, roasted, golden brown. Once coloured, roughly chop them into pieces.

To cook the fish, lightly dust the fillets with flour on the skinned sides, brushing each with butter and seasoning with salt. Heat the olive oil in a frying pan. Place the fillets carefully in the hot pan and season the upper side of the fillets. Fry on a moderate heat for a few minutes until golden brown. Turn the fish, removing the pan from the heat. The residual warmth in the pan will finish the cooking of the fish while the salad is being created.

Place all of the salad leaves and watercress in a large bowl, and drizzle with 2 tablespoons of the dressing. Add a little of the orange confit, if using, along with the orange segments and hazelnuts. The salad can now be arranged on plates. Add the chopped herbs to 4–5 tablespoons of the hazelnut dressing. Place the John Dory on top of the salad and drizzle the remaining dressing over and around.

- *Any remaining dressing will keep in an airtight jar for several days.*

- *Cooked beetroot slices or wedges can be added to this salad, or perhaps warm slices of new potatoes crushed and used as a base to the total salad. The salad is also a perfect accompaniment to duck and chicken.*

Serves 6–8 as a starter or 4 as a main course

- 175g (6oz) *Shortcrust pastry* (page 184) or *Puff pastry* (page 185)
- flour, for dusting
- 4 tomatoes
- iced water
- 350g (12oz) cooked unpeeled North Atlantic prawns
- knob of butter
- 6 spring onions, finely shredded
- 2 eggs, plus 1 extra yolk
- 150ml (¼pint) crème fraîche
- salt and pepper
- 75g (3oz) grated Gruyère or Cheddar cheese
- 1 tablespoon chopped chives (about 1cm /½in long)
- 1 *Prawn dressing* (page 118), using shells from the prawns
- 350g (12oz) samphire

Prawn and crème fraîche tart with samphire and tomato salad

The prawns used in this recipe are the North Atlantic variety, and are fairly easy to obtain cooked but unpeeled. Some of the shells will be used to make the dressing for the samphire salad. Samphire comes on the culinary scene during the last month of spring and goes on into summer. It is certainly not the easiest of ingredients to hunt down, mostly found growing on the salt marshes along the north coast of Norfolk. If unavailable, the prawn tart will survive on its own or with blanched French beans making a good substitute.

Method Roll out the pastry on a lightly floured surface and use to line an 18cm (7in) flan tin or ring set on a baking tray. Any overhanging pastry can be left (once cooked, this can be carefully cut away to give an even finish). Refrigerate and allow to rest for 30 minutes.

Preheat the oven to 190ºC/375ºF/Gas 5. Line the base of the pastry with greaseproof paper and fill with baking beans or rice. Bake blind for 20 minutes. Remove the beans and paper and return to the oven for a further 6 minutes. Then trim off excess pastry and leave to cool. Reduce the oven temperature to 160ºC/325ºF/Gas 3.

Blanch the tomatoes (this can be done up to 24 hours in advance). Using the point of a small, sharp knife cut around the edges of the tomato eyes until they become completely free and cut a small cross at the base of each. Plunge the tomatoes into rapidly boiling water, leaving firm tomatoes in the water for 8–10 seconds, very ripe ones for 6–8, then transfer to iced water. The tomatoes are now ready to peel, with the skin pulling away easily. To prepare the tomatoes for the salad,

quarter them, remove the seeds and discard, and place the flesh on kitchen paper. This will absorb the excess water, leaving a firmer texture. The flesh can then be diced into 1cm (½in) pieces.

Peel the prawns, saving 50g (2oz) of the shells for the prawn dressing. Melt the butter and, when bubbling, add the spring onions. Turn in the pan just once or twice to remove their rawness, but retain their texture. Remove from the pan and leave to cool.

Beat together the eggs and egg yolk, then whisk in the crème fraîche and season with salt and pepper. Stir in the grated cheese, along with the chives.

Mix together the peeled prawns and spring onions, season lightly and sprinkle into the tart case. Pour the crème fraîche mixture over the prawns and bake for 40–45 minutes until the flan has just set. The flan is now best left to rest for 15–20 minutes before removing from the tin and serving. This not only allows the flan to cool slightly to a warm temperature, eating at its best, but also allows the cream filling to relax, giving a softer finish.

While the flan is cooking, prepare the dressing and salad. For the dressing, use the reserved prawn shells and follow the recipe on page 118.

For the salad, cut the woody roots from the samphire and wash well, then blanch in rapidly boiling salted water for 30–60 seconds. This will still leave it with a crisp texture. Refresh in iced water and drain. Add the tomato dice and season with a twist of pepper (salt is not really necessary due to the saltiness of the samphire).

Add enough prawn dressing to bind the salad before serving with the tart.

Serves 4 as a generous starter

- 20 large raw prawns (or 350g/12oz cooked unpeeled North Atlantic prawns)
- salt and pepper
- 12–16 small new potatoes, scrubbed
- 175g (6oz) podded fresh peas
- 25g (1oz) butter
- 2 handfuls of green salad leaves
- 8–10 picked tarragon leaves

For the prawn dressing

- 100–150ml (3½fl oz–¼pint) olive oil
- 2 strips of lemon peel
- 4 black peppercorns
- 1 bay leaf
- juice of 1 lemon
- cube of brown or white sugar

For the cream dressing

- 2 dessertspoons sherry vinegar
- 1 teaspoon soft brown sugar
- 4 tablespoons single cream
- 2 tablespoons walnut oil
- squeeze of lemon juice
- 1 tablespoon chopped chives

Buttered prawns with a warm potato and fresh pea salad

It's best to buy large raw prawns for this dish. You are then in total control of their cooking time. If unavailable, then cooked prawns still in the shell should be your next choice.

The prawn dressing is really quite unique, almost creating its own prawn bisque flavour to lift the taste of the shellfish. The other dressing, with a single-cream base, gives the salad a buttery feel without any being added.

I've suggested new potatoes in the salad as there are so many good varieties in season, including the classic Jersey Royals, Pink Fir Apple and Charlotte.

Method If using raw prawns, first plunge them into boiling salted water for 30 seconds. Remove and leave to cool. These can now be carefully peeled, removing the heads along with all of the tail shells, reserving 50g (2oz) of the shells for the prawn dressing. Make a fine cut along the back of each prawn and remove the black intestine. The prawns can now be kept refrigerated until needed.

To make the prawn dressing, heat 2 tablespoons of the olive oil with the reserved shells, lemon peel, peppercorns and bay leaf. Cook gently for a few minutes but don't fry. This will draw the flavour and colour from the shells. Add the lemon juice and sugar cube and continue to cook until the cube has dissolved. Add 100ml (3½fl oz) of the remaining oil, bring to a simmer, remove from the heat and leave to infuse for 8–10 minutes.

Remove the bay leaf and blitz the dressing in a liquidizer until almost completely blended. Check for seasoning at this point. Add a pinch of salt, and more olive oil if needed to calm the lemon flavour. Strain through a fine sieve or tea strainer and the dressing is ready. This can now be kept in a jar or squeezy bottle for up to 24 hours. However, this dressing eats at its best as soon as possible after making.

To make the cream dressing, whisk together the sherry vinegar, sugar and cream, then add the walnut oil. Add a squeeze of lemon juice and season with salt and pepper. This can also be kept refrigerated, adding the chives just before serving.

To cook the new potatoes, plunge them into boiling salted water and boil until almost overcooked – this will create a soft creamy finish. New potatoes do come in all shapes and sizes, consequently the cooking time will vary from 15–25 minutes. Once cooked, drain and, when cool enough to handle, cut into rounds between 5mm–1cm (¼–½in) thick or simply quarter lengthwise. Season with salt and pepper and keep warm.

While cutting the potatoes, the peas can be cooked in boiling salted water. Good fresh young peas should literally take only as long as their frozen friends, about 3 minutes. However, it is best to check continually after the 3 minutes until they are completely tender. Once cooked, drain and add to the potatoes.

Heat the butter in a frying pan. Once melted and bubbling, add the peeled prawns. Simmer gently for just 2–3 minutes until the prawns have cooked through.

While frying the prawns, add the chopped chives to the cream dressing and spoon it over the potatoes and peas. Add the salad leaves and torn tarragon, and fold them in along with the prawns. Divide between four plates, drizzle liberally with the prawn dressing and serve.

Serves 4 as a main course
- 12 × 50–65g (2–2½oz) medallions (mini round steaks) of monkfish fillet taken from 1kg (2¼lb) fish (for preparing the whole fish, see page 35)
- flour, for dusting
- salt and pepper
- 2 tablespoons olive or groundnut oil
- knob of butter

For the fennel marmalade
- 4 shallots, thinly sliced
- 6 tablespoons cider vinegar or white wine vinegar
- sprig of thyme
- 1 star anise
- 2–3 bulbs of Florence fennel
- ½ teaspoon finely grated lemon zest
- large knob of butter
- 2 heaped tablespoons caster sugar
- twist of cracked white pepper
- good pinch of coarse sea salt
- ½ teaspoon picked thyme leaves

For the salad (optional)
- juice of 1 lime
- pinch of caster sugar
- 4 tablespoons single cream or crème fraîche
- 2 tablespoons walnut oil
- salt and pepper
- 175–225g (6–8oz) baby spinach leaves
- 50g (2oz) sorrel leaves

Pan-fried monkfish medallions with fennel and thyme marmalade

The marmalade is not quite the consistency of the jellied orange variety with which we are all so familiar. This particular marmalade holds a soft sweet-and-sour flavour, with the aniseed of the fennel, and the thyme, both predominant. The recipe can be doubled and, once made, it will keep in sterilized airtight jars (page 11) for up to one week. I've also included an optional accompanying salad of sorrel and baby spinach with a lime crème-fraîche dressing. It is not essential, but does lend a fresh crisp bite to the complete dish.

Method To prepare the marmalade, place the shallots, vinegar, thyme and star anise in a saucepan. Bring to a simmer on a low heat and cook for several minutes, until the liquid is almost completely reduced and the shallots are just moist. Place to one side. Trim the tops and base from the fennel, split the bulbs in half and cut the stalk from each half. Finely shred the fennel pieces and mix with the lemon zest.

Melt the knob of butter over a moderate heat and add the sliced fennel along with the caster sugar and 2 tablespoons of water. Cook gently for 15–20 minutes until tender. Add the shallots and bring back to a simmer, stirring all of the ingredients together well, and seasoning with the cracked pepper and sea salt. The sprig of thyme and star anise can now be removed. The picked thyme leaves are best added just before you serve it, to introduce a fresh flavour to the marmalade. The marmalade can be kept (see above) or allowed to cool until just warm before adding the fresh thyme and

serving. The marmalade can be served chilled, or rewarmed when needed.

If made 24 hours in advance all of the ingredients get a chance to blend and mature, for a more distinctive flavour.

To make the dressing for the salad, if using, whisk together the lime juice and sugar, then add the cream or crème fraîche followed by the walnut oil. Season with salt and pepper. This can be kept refrigerated in a screw-top jar or squeezy bottle, ready to drizzle over the mixed spinach and sorrel leaves.

To finish the dish, lightly flour the monkfish medallions and season with salt and pepper. Heat the oil in a large frying pan and, when very hot, place in the medallions. Cook for 2 minutes, then add a knob of butter, turning the fish pieces and continuing to cook for a further 2 minutes.

The monkfish is now ready to serve, offering three medallions per portion, along with the salad, if using, and the fennel marmalade.

Serves 4 as a starter or a lunch or supper dish
- 175–225g (6–8oz) *Puff pastry* (page 185), or bought variety
- flour, for dusting
- oil, for greasing
- 2 bulbs of Florence fennel
- juice of 1 lemon
- large knob of butter
- 1 onion, thinly sliced
- ½ teaspoon caster sugar
- salt and pepper
- 4 × 100g (4oz) slices of halibut fillet, skinned

For the dressing
- 225g (8oz) rhubarb, washed
- 1 level teaspoon caster sugar, plus an extra pinch
- large knob of butter
- ¼ teaspoon sea salt
- 1 tablespoon Pernod
- 2 tablespoons groundnut oil (optional)
- 2 tablespoons hazelnut oil (optional)

Steamed halibut and soft fennel tarts with rhubarb and Pernod dressing

Although this dish has quite an elaborate title, it is filled with reasonably simple but robust flavours. The tart is made of just four very thin, crisp, puff pastry discs, topped with softened fennel and enhanced with the help of onion and snipped fennel tops. The unforced garden rhubarb, abundant in summer, carries an acidic sharp bite that does blend well with the aniseed touch of Pernod. All of this is topped with the almost pure white of lightly steamed halibut.

Method Roll out the puff pastry very thinly on a lightly floured surface, refrigerate and allow to rest for 10 minutes, then cut out four 9–10cm (3½–4in) discs. Place these on a lightly greased baking tray (or one topped with parchment paper), prick with a fork and leave to rest in the refrigerator for 30 minutes.

Preheat the oven to 200°C/400°F/Gas 6. Once the pastry has rested, bake in the preheated oven for 10–15 minutes until crisp. For a completely flat finish, it's best to cover the pastries with parchment paper and top them with another baking tray while baking. This will keep the discs completely flat.

To make the dressing, cut 50g (2oz) of the rhubarb into small 3mm (⅛in) dice. Place in a sieve and sprinkle with the pinch of caster sugar. I prefer to leave these pieces of rhubarb raw, so the sugar will help to calm their tartness. Cut the remaining rhubarb into rough 1cm (½in) dice. Melt the knob of butter in a saucepan and add this rhubarb, the sea salt and the teaspoon of sugar. Cook for 5–6 minutes until beginning to soften. Add 4 tablespoons of water and the Pernod. Cook for

a further 5 minutes, then liquidize to a purée. Strain through a sieve. To finish, whisk in the two oils (using 4 tablespoons of groundnut if hazelnut is unavailable). The oiled finish is an optional extra, creating more of a dressing than a sauce. It's not essential and can be left to personal choice. This dressing is best served warm, adding the uncooked diced rhubarb just before serving.

To prepare the fennel, remove any green tops, cutting enough of the fronds to make about 1 teaspoon when snipped, for adding to the fennel just before serving. Split the fennel bulbs through the centre and remove the base stalks. Thinly slice and place the cut fennel in a bowl, adding a little of the lemon juice to prevent the slices from discolouring.

Melt the large knob of butter in a saucepan and, once bubbling, add the sliced onion. Cook for 5–6 minutes until beginning to soften. Add the fennel, with the remaining lemon juice and caster sugar. Continue to cook for 10–12 minutes until the fennel has also softened. Season with salt and pepper.

Place the halibut slices on buttered and seasoned pieces of greaseproof paper. Lightly salt the fish and place in a steamer over a pan of simmering water. Cover with a lid and steam for just a few minutes, 4–5 maximum, until only just firm, and tender to the touch.

While the fish is cooking, place the warm pastry discs on plates. Add the snipped fennel fronds to the cooked shredded bulbs. Divide the soft fennel between the four tarts and spoon the rhubarb dressing or sauce around. Remove the halibut fillets from the steamer and grease-proof paper and present the slices over the fennel tarts.

Serves 4 as a starter

- 8 asparagus spears
- salt and pepper
- iced water
- 50–75g (2–3oz) podded peas
- 50–75g (2–3oz) podded broad beans
- 150ml (¼pint) white wine
- 200ml (7fl oz) *Vegetable stock* (page 177), *Instant stock* (page 175) or water
- 2 sprigs of tarragon
- 2 sprigs of chervil
- few flatleaf parsley leaves
- 2 sorrel leaves
- 4 × 100g (4oz) portions of sea trout fillet, pin-boned (page 11) and skinned
- 50g (2oz) butter, plus more for the sea trout
- 1 level teaspoon flour (optional)
- 4 spring onions, cut into 4mm (⅛in) slices

Green vegetable 'casserole' with buttered sea trout

During the month of June, English asparagus has just a few weeks to run, while broad beans and fresh peas still have a couple of months left in them. It's with all of this in mind that we should take advantage of their flavours during this first official summer month.

Also added are the fresh herbs that are available, not missing the lemony bite of sorrel and piquant touch of tarragon. The sea trout (salmon can also be used) is so softly cooked in butter, it is almost like poaching it so that it takes on the faintest of golden finishes.

Method Each of the vegetables can be prepared and cooked in advance. Most asparagus spears don't need to be peeled. For this dish, however, I suggest they are. This will then leave a paler green spear to counter the colour of the deep green beans and peas. Simply peel, leaving about 4cm (1½in) of the tips as they are. The woody base can now be broken or cut away. Cook the spears in boiling salted water for just a minute or two, 3–4 maximum, until tender, then refresh in iced water.

Bring the salted water back to the boil and add the peas, cooking for just 3 minutes before refreshing in iced water. Bring the water back to the boil again and cook the broad beans for just 2 minutes, up to a maximum of 5 minutes if large. Also refresh these in iced water, then peel away the protective skin to reveal the green beans.

Once all the vegetables are drained, cut the cooked asparagus into 3cm (1¼in) sticks and refrigerate all of the vegetables until needed.

Bring the white wine to the boil and reduce by three-quarters. Add 200ml (7fl oz) of your chosen stock or water, bring to the boil and reduce by half. Leave to one side.

Tear or gently chop all the herbs, finely shredding the sorrel.

To cook the sea trout, first season with salt and then place, skinned-side down, in a frying pan of gently bubbling melted butter. Cook on a low heat for 4 minutes, allowing the fish to colour just a little. Season with pepper, then turn the fish in the pan. Remove from the heat and allow the fish to finish cooking in the pan while the casserole is completed.

Heat the reserved, reduced wine mixture. To finish the sauce, if a slightly thicker finish is preferred, first add the flour to the measured butter. As this is whisked in the liquor will begin to thicken, but stay loose enough not to become a sauce. If finishing in this way, simply simmer for a few minutes once the flour is added, to cook out its flavour. For a looser consistency, simply whisk the butter into the wine mixture.

Add the vegetables and spring onions to the liquor. Simmer for 1–2 minutes to heat them through, then add the herbs and season with salt and pepper. Spoon the casserole into suitable bowls then place in the buttered sea trout fillets.

Serves 4 as a main course

- 1 small cucumber
- 1 teaspoon salt
- 4 × 175–225g (6–8oz) portions of sea trout fillet, pin-boned (page 11), with skin on
- flour, for dusting
- 4 tablespoons olive oil
- salt and pepper
- 4 tablespoons crème fraîche
- ½ teaspoon English mustard
- squeeze of lime juice
- 2–3 *cornichons* (gherkins) cut into small dice, plus 1 tablespoon *cornichon* vinegar
- 1 teaspoon caster sugar
- 1 large shallot, sliced into thin rings
- 1 teaspoon chopped tarragon

Pan-roasted sea trout with cucumber and cornichon salad

English cucumbers will be with us from late spring to mid-autumn, the sea trout more or less staying with them. *Cornichon* is French for gherkin, the small tart pickles made from tiny gherkin cucumbers. The acidity they hold creates an almost instant dressing with which to bind the salted cucumber. To accompany both the fish and cucumber, there's a warm English mustard crème-fraîche cream to drizzle around the plate, adding a soft warmth to the complete flavour. The experience of warm crispy fish and the cold cucumber salad with a bite leaves a very fresh and lively finish on the palate.

Method Peel the cucumber and slice into approximately 3mm (⅛in) slices. Add the teaspoon of salt and mix in well. Place in a colander over a bowl and leave for 20–30 minutes. During this salting period, a quantity of liquid will be drawn from the flesh. This will remove the rawness from the cucumber, leaving a more pliable texture but still preserving its bite.

After this time the cucumber can be rinsed of any excess salt, however I'm not so keen on this practice as water can then be reabsorbed by the cucumber. Taste the slices and, if not over-salty, then just pat dry with a cloth. The salt content of this salad may then be complete.

Lightly dust the skin side of the sea trout fillets with the flour. Warm 2 tablespoons of the olive oil in a large frying pan to medium hot. Place the fillets in, skin-sides down, leaving them undisturbed to fry, and not shaking the pan, for 4–5 minutes. (If portions are taken from a particularly thick fillet, 6 minutes may be needed.)

Season the flesh side of the fish with salt and pepper and turn over in the pan, then turn the heat off. The residual warmth of the pan will be enough to continue the frying without drying the flesh. This will leave you with a few minutes to complete the garnishes, it being almost impossible to overcook the fish.

Warm together the crème fraîche, mustard and lime juice, whisking to a smooth emulsion. Season with salt and pepper, adding a touch more mustard if preferred.

In a bowl, whisk together the remaining olive oil with the *cornichon* vinegar and caster sugar. Season with salt and pepper, then mix in the cucumber slices, shallot rings, chopped *cornichons* and tarragon. Divide between the top ends of four plates, then place the sea trout in front and drizzle the warm crème-fraîche mustard cream around each.

● *The sea trout can be scored with the sharp point of a knife to create parallel lines across each fillet. This will produce a slightly different presentation to the fish.*

● *Hot buttered new potatoes are the perfect accompaniment to this dish.*

● *The cucumber and* cornichon *salad also eats well with pan-fried or barbecue-grilled chicken breasts.*

Serves 4 as a main course

- 4 × 175–200g (6–7oz) portions of wild salmon fillet, pin-boned (page 11), with skin on (scaled)
- flour, for dusting
- 1 tablespoon olive oil
- knob of butter

For the gazpacho salad
- ½ cucumber, peeled, seeded and cut into 8–10mm (⅛in) dice

- 1 tablespoon olive oil
- knob of butter
- 1 bulb of Florence fennel, cut into 8–10mm (⅛in) dice
- 1 garlic clove, halved
- 1 small red pepper, cut into 8–10mm (⅛in) dice
- 1 small yellow pepper, cut into 8–10mm (⅛in) dice
- 1 courgette, cut into 8–10mm (⅛in) dice

- 1 teaspoon wild marjoram (oregano) leaves
- 4 basil leaves, torn

For the sauce
- knob of butter
- 225g (8oz) tomatoes, quartered
- 1 teaspoon caster sugar
- 2 tablespoons double cream
- salt and pepper
- 1 tablespoon port

Wild salmon with warm gazpacho salad and fresh tomato sauce

These ingredients, so many of which are home-grown, are coming into their own, reaching a peak in mid-summer. The gazpacho consists of sweet pepper, cucumber, courgette and fennel. Fresh herbs are also added, featuring basil and wild marjoram. Wild marjoram holds a completely different flavour to that of basic marjoram and, in fact, is also known as oregano. The tomatoes, usually found in the classic gazpacho, join the dish as a fresh sauce.

Method Score the skin of the salmon fillets with a sharp knife (four or five cuts will be plenty), leaving a 1cm (½in) border around the edge of each. Refrigerate until needed.

To make the sauce, melt the knob of butter in a saucepan, add the tomatoes and sugar and cook for 10–15 minutes until most of the tomato liquid has evaporated. Liquidize to a purée and then push through a fine sieve. Return to the pan and add the cream. Cook for a minute or two and then season with salt and pepper.

For the gazpacho salad, lightly salt the diced cucumber, then leave it for 15–20 minutes in a sieve to drain off the excess liquid. Heat the olive oil with a knob of butter in a saucepan. Once bubbling, add the diced fennel and garlic halves, cover with a lid and cook for 6–7 minutes on a low-to-medium heat, until just tender. Add the red and yellow peppers along with the courgette and cook for a further 2 minutes. The rawness will now just come off the vegetables, leaving a slight bite. Place to one side.

To cook the salmon, season the skin with salt and lightly dust with flour. Heat the olive oil (a little extra may be needed). Place the fillets skin-side down in the pan and season with salt and pepper. Cook on a moderate heat for 6–7 minutes without shaking the pan or moving the fish (this will only take heat from the pan). Add a knob of butter and, once bubbling, turn the salmon and switch off the heat. The residual heat of the pan will finish the cooking process, the fish needing just a minute or two more.

While the fish finishes, add the drained cucumber and herbs to the gazpacho salad vegetables. When ready to serve, add the port to the sauce and stir well. The dish can now be presented on plates, either placing the salmon on top of the gazpacho and spooning the sauce around, or setting these two main ingredients side by side and drizzling with the sauce.

● *For a richer tomato sauce simply increase the fresh tomato quantity to 350g (12oz).*

● *Mixed salad leaves, or perhaps just rocket, can be added to this dish, along with some* Lemon oil *(page 183).*

● *The gazpacho salad and sauce will also eat very well with grilled chicken breasts.*

Serves 4 as a main course
- 24–28 medium asparagus spears
- 4 × 175g (6oz) portions of wild salmon fillet, pin-boned (page 11) with skin on (scaled)
- salt and pepper
- flour, for dusting
- 2 tablespoons cooking oil
- knob of butter, plus more for brushing
- coarse sea salt (optional)

For the mayonnaise
- 120ml (4fl oz) sunflower or groundnut oil
- 3 tablespoons extra virgin olive oil
- 2 egg yolks
- juice of ½ lemon
- salt and cayenne pepper
- 1 heaped teaspoon chopped tarragon

Crispy wild salmon with warm lemon and tarragon mayonnaise

It has been with us for a few months now, but the wild salmon is at its best during these summer months, with a richer flavour and at its most competitive price. The crispy edge is provided by the skin, which, when not cooked too rapidly, becomes a crackling to top the moist flakes.

Buttering asparagus is without doubt the simplest, and one of the best, ways to enjoy this vegetable. English asparagus has a fairly short season, but imported varieties are available all year.

The third and final component to this dish is really an optional extra as the marriage of salmon and asparagus is one that is, in itself, so outstanding. However, this particular sauce recipe is one I have borrowed from a very good friend, a Mr Rick Stein. It's a combination of two recipes, the base a hollandaise sauce, using the oils from a mayonnaise to finish. As Rick showed me, it's well worth making, as it offers a creamy finish to the salmon and asparagus, both old friends of the two sauces this recipe combines.

Method First make the sauce, which can then be kept warm while completing the dish. Put the sunflower or groundnut oil and the olive oil in a small saucepan and place on a very low heat just to warm through. Mix the egg yolks and lemon juice with 2 tablespoons of water. Place over a pan of simmering water, making sure the water is not touching the base of the bowl. Whisk the yolk mixture vigorously until thick and frothy, then continue to whisk until the frothy consistency becomes almost creamy. Remove the bowl from the heat and gradually whisk in the warmed oils. Once all the oil has

been added, whisk in 2–3 tablespoons of warm water to loosen the thick sauce. This addition of extra water will prevent the oils and eggs from separating. If the sauce continues to thicken as it sets, simply add a little more water. Season with salt and cayenne pepper adding the tarragon and setting aside to keep warm while cooking the salmon and asparagus.

Trim the spiky ears from along the asparagus stalks and break or cut the grey-white base stalk away, keeping the spears a uniform length. Season the salmon fillets with salt and pepper and lightly flour the skin sides only. Put a large pan of salted water on to heat.

Heat the cooking oil in a large frying pan and place the fillets in skin-side down. Fry on a medium-hot heat for 6–7 minutes, not shaking or moving the fish, just allowing the skins to fry and crisp. Turn the fillets, add the knob of butter and remove the pan from the heat. The remaining residual heat will continue to cook the fish for a further few minutes, keeping the flesh moist and buttery.

After turning the salmon, plunge the asparagus tips into the large saucepan of rapidly boiling salted water. Cook for just 2–3 minutes until tender, 4 minutes should be the maximum. Lift the spears from the pan, drain well and brush with butter to add more flavour and create a shine.

Place the spears side by side on plates and season with a sprinkle of coarse sea salt, if using. Sit the crispy salmon on top, offering the warm lemon and tarragon sauce separately.

- *This dish works equally well with almost any fish.*

Serves 4

- 4 red mullet fillets (see below)
- 1 kg (2¼lb) ripe tomatoes
- iced water
- *Caesar salad* (page 111, optional)
- salt and pepper, plus coarse sea salt
- 6–8 tablespoons olive oil
- flour, for dusting
- butter, for greasing
- 175g (6oz) peeled, cooked shrimps or prawns (250g/9oz if only available in shell)
- 1 large garlic clove, finely chopped (optional)
- 4 tablespoons chopped mixed herbs (such as tarragon, basil, chervil, chives, flatleaf parsley)
- juice of 1 lemon

Crispy red mullet and shrimps with tomatoes and herbs

The shrimps are a pure delight in this recipe, simply added and warmed through at the last moment. Having said that, they can also become an optional extra. The flavour of red mullet, with lots of our summer tomatoes and almost every fresh herb available, brings pleasure enough.

The *Caesar salad* to accompany this dish is a quick and light salad, made using just the cos lettuce leaves coated with a creamy-style Caesar dressing, making a complete summer meal.

This recipe offers supper or main course portions if the fillets are from large 675g (1½lb) mullets. Smaller starter portions from 400g (14oz) fish can also be used, reducing the quantity of the other ingredients.

It is not essential to chop the herbs, all bar the chives can be torn. This prevents any bruising, discolouration and change of flavour. However, a good sharp knife can be used to cut carefully and neatly, rather than a rough chop.

Method There are several stages to this recipe that can be made well in advance. The mullet fillets should have all pin bones removed with tweezers (page 11) and their scales scraped and rinsed away.

Using the point of a small, sharp knife, cut around the tomato eyes to free them and cut a small cross at the base of each. Plunge the tomatoes into rapidly boiling water, leaving firm ones in the water for 8–10 seconds, very ripe ones for 6–8. Transfer to iced water, then peel and quarter and discard the seeds. Place the flesh on kitchen paper to absorb all excess juice and refrigerate until needed. When ready to use, cut each quarter into neatish 1cm (½in) dice, not wasting any trimmings.

If serving the Caesar salad with this dish, the dressing can be made well in advance and the cos lettuce leaves rinsed ready to tear or cut.

Preheat the oven to 190ºC/375ºF/Gas 5. Season the mullet fillets flesh-sides up, with salt and pepper, only salting the presentation skin-sides to keep them clean of pepper dots. Using one large (or two smaller) frying pans, heat 2–3 tablespoons of the olive oil. Once hot but certainly not smoking, lightly flour the skin sides of the fillets and place floured-sides down in the pan. Cook on a medium heat for 5–6 minutes. During this time the skin will have crisped, but the fillets will be a few minutes short of being cooked. At this stage, remove each from the pan and place skin-side up on a buttered baking tray. Finish the cooking in the preheated oven for a further 2–3 minutes. This will keep the fish very moist and only just cooked through.

While the fish is in the oven, add the shrimps or prawns and tomatoes to the oil in the pan along with the garlic, if using. Bring to a soft simmer. Add a further 3 tablespoons of olive oil, all the chopped herbs and lemon juice to taste, and season with coarse sea salt and pepper. If a looser finish is preferred, add the remaining oil. The tomatoes and shrimps can now be spooned onto a serving dish or plates before placing the red mullet fillets on top, and offering with the Caesar salad, if using.

Serves 4 as a main course

- 4 × 175–200g (6–7oz) portions of cod fillet, pin-boned (page 11), with skin on (scaled)
- 175g (6oz) coarse sea salt
- 4 tablespoons olive oil
- 550g (1¼lb) onions, sliced
- sprig of thyme
- salt and pepper
- 8 rashers of streaky bacon
- knob of butter

For the pea sauce

- 125ml (4fl oz) *Fish stock* (page 176) or *Instant stock* (page 175)
- 100g (4oz) podded peas
- bowl of ice
- knob of butter

Crackling cod on stewed onions with bacon and a fresh pea sauce

The crispy crackling topping needs some planning ahead, but nothing to feel too stressed about. The skin takes on this texture through pre-salting up to an hour before cooking. This brief salting prevents the fish fillets from becoming over-salty, and doesn't change their flavour or texture. Instead all moisture is drawn from the skin which, while cooking, crisps in the pan.

While the fish is being salted, the onions can be stewed, cooking them for 30 minutes to a soft, almost mush-like, consistency. With peas probably at their sweetest this time of the year, the sauce shows them off at their best. The bacon completes this garnish, creating an almost '*petit pois à la francaise*' touch alongside the onions and peas.

Method Score 4–5 short lines in the cod skin across the length of each fillet, leaving at least 1cm (½in) unscored around the edge. Sprinkle the sea salt on a tray and place the fillets skin-side down on it and leave to sit for at least 45 minutes to 1 hour.

While the cod is salting, heat 2 tablespoons of the olive oil in a flameproof casserole or large saucepan. Add the onions and thyme, and cook for 2 minutes, then cover with a lid and stew, stirring from time to time, for 30 minutes over a low heat. Season with salt and pepper. The onions can be cooked in advance, ready just to reheat when needed.

The bacon can be cooked in either of the following ways. The rashers can be placed in an oven, preheated to 200°C/400°F/Gas 6, between two baking sheets for 30 minutes to guarantee a flat and crisp finish. Alternatively, slowly fry or grill, releasing all the fats for a more rustic finish.

All stages of this dish can be cooked in advance, the sauce included. Boil the stock, add the peas and cook rapidly for 2 minutes then liquidize to a smooth finish. Strain through a sieve and cool over a bowl of ice. This will maintain the rich green colour of the vegetables, ready to reheat.

To cook the fish, wipe all salt from the skin. Heat the remaining olive oil in a large frying pan. When very hot, lay the fillets skin-sides down in the pan, season the flesh sides with a twist of pepper and cook for 5–6 minutes until the skins are crispy. Add a knob of butter to the pan, turn the fillets and turn off the heat. The residual warmth of the pan will finish the cooking process, the fillets needing just another minute or two.

The pea sauce can now be reheated, adding a knob of butter and checking for seasoning. Spoon the onions onto plates, top them with the crisp bacon rashers and finish with the cod fillets. Pour the pea sauce around.

● *When making the pea sauce, 2–3 mint leaves can be added.*

- 2 × 350g (12oz) Dover soles, filleted and skinned, head, bones and trimmings reserved
- 2 jacket potatoes or 10 new potatoes
- salt and pepper
- 2 large or 3 cooked medium globe artichokes (page 96), or bought marinated artichokes
- 50g (2oz) butter, plus 2–3 knobs for frying
- flour, for dusting
- 1–2 tablespoons groundnut or vegetable oil
- 1–1½ tablespoons lemon juice
- 1 tablespoon chopped mixed curly and flatleaf parsley

Fried Dover sole with artichokes, potatoes and parsley

Dover sole is a fish that holds top position alongside turbot in the flat-fish premier league. Being very firm in texture and rich in flavour also keeps it pretty high up in the cost league too.

The fish has a spring/summer season in Britain's waters, but can be obtained more or less throughout the year. This recipe is a French classic called *sole Murat* after one of Napoleon's generals. The fillets are cut into finger strips, then fried in butter, the artichokes and potatoes following suit. Classically they were finished with *beurre noisette* – nutbrown butter flavoured with lemon and parsley. Here the recipe is not too dissimilar, just replacing the *beurre noisette* with a trickle of parsley butter; the nutbrown flavour being found amongst the artichokes and fish themselves. The quantities here are for starter portions, but can easily be doubled for use as a main course.

Method Two whole sole will provide four fillets. Split each of these into two pieces, making a total of eight. Each piece can now be cut at an angle into strips or fingers 1cm (½in) thick and 7–8cm (3in) long. Refrigerate until needed.

If using jacket potatoes, peel and cut into 1cm (½in) dice. Cook in boiling salted water until tender, for approximately 6–8 minutes. Drain, season and keep warm to one side. If using new potatoes, simply cook in boiling salted water for approximately 20 minutes until tender. Drain, quarter and keep warm to one side.

Cut the artichokes in halves, then cut each of these halves into six wedges. Fry the pieces in a knob of

butter, allowing them to take on a golden brown edge. Season with salt and pepper and keep warm.

Season and roll the sole strips lightly in flour. Heat a tablespoon of the oil in a large frying pan and, once hot, add the sole fingers (this may need to be carried out in two batches).

Cook on a high heat for just 1–2 minutes, adding a knob of butter. Remove the fish, repeating the same process if necessary. Once all the strips are coloured, squeeze a tablespoon of lemon juice into the frying pan. This will immediately lift all of the juices and solids from the pan. Follow with 4 tablespoons of water and, once bubbling, add the 50g (2oz) of butter and whisk it in well. Check for seasoning and lemon flavour and adding more lemon juice if necessary, then strain through a fine sieve (or tea strainer) or muslin.

Carefully mix the sole fingers, artichokes and potatoes, dividing them between serving plates. Add the chopped parsley to the lemon butter and spoon it over each portion.

● *Sole bones and trimmings (like those of the turbot) make the best fish stock. It's always best to freeze any available, saving them until you have the right quantity to create a stock.*

● *The sole fillets can also be steamed for a few minutes, leaving them an almost pure white against the sautéed vegetables (lemon sole fillets also steam very well).*

Serves 4 as a main course

- 4 × 450g (1lb) gurnard, filleted and trimmed (skin removed or left on)
- salt and pepper
- flour, for dusting
- cooking oil
- knob of butter

For the salad

- 100g (4oz) dried white beans, preferably cannellini, plus 1 onion, 1 carrot, 1 stick of celery, 1 sprig of thyme and 1 bay leaf (or 400g (14oz) tin of haricot beans)
- 6 small-to-medium fresh uncooked beetroots
- 2 oranges, segmented (save any juice, optional)

- small knob of butter (optional)
- 1 tablespoon chopped chives
- 1 quantity *Citrus dressing* (page 182)
- 225g (8oz) mixed green leaves (such as rocket, baby spinach, watercress, etc.)

Roast gurnard with beetroot, white bean and orange salad

So often this fish is used purely for soups and stews, but it really should not be ignored that this strong red-armoured fish will eat equally well as a tender fillet. The fish are mostly found relatively small, as little as 175–225g (6–8oz). However, larger ones can be found, some up to 2kg (4½lb). The best for this recipe will be about 450g (1lb) each, providing two good fillets per portion.

Fresh, young beetroots are also around and, if possible, go for those about 4–5cm (1½–2in) in diameter as these tend to have a richer and sweeter flavour. The *Citrus dressing* is a St Clement's combination of orange and lemon working together.

Dried white beans are best for this recipe. For this particular dish it's not essential to cook your own, but if you wish to use tinned beans choose a good quality product, as cheap tinned ones are very bitter. If cooking your own beans, it will be the job to attack first.

Method If using dried white beans for the salad, place them in a pan and cover with cold water. Bring to the boil and cook for 10 minutes. Remove the pan from the heat, cover with a lid and leave to cool. Drain. Return the beans to the pan with the onion, carrot, celery stick, thyme and bay leaf and cover with water to 4–5 times the depth of the beans. Bring to the boil and simmer gently for 2–2½ hours or until tender. When ready, remove the cooked vegetables and herbs and keep the beans to one side.

Trim off the beetroot stalks, making sure not to cut into the bulbs themselves as they will then bleed during cooking. Place in a saucepan and cover with water, then bring to the boil. Reduce the heat to a rapid simmer and cook for 20–30 minutes. Depending on size, the beetroots may be tender at this stage. If not, continue to cook, testing every 10 minutes. The most they should take is 1 hour. Once cooked, remove from the water and leave to cool slightly before peeling away the skins with the thumb. Keep warm to one side.

Season and lightly flour the gurnard fillets. Heat 2 tablespoons of cooking oil in a large frying pan. Once hot, place the fillets skinned- or skin-side down in the pan and fry on a medium-to-hot heat for 4–5 minutes. Add a knob of butter, turn the fillets over and remove from the heat. The residual heat of the pan will be sufficient to finish the cooking of the fish.

While the fillets are cooking, boil any orange juice saved from the segmenting to reduce by two-thirds. Remove from the heat and add and shake in the small knob of butter. This glossy orange reduction is totally optional, but does provide a glaze to brush the fillets or roll them in before serving.

If using tinned beans, warm them in their liquid.

To finish the salad, cut the cooked beetroots into 6–8 segments, adding the orange segments. Mix the chopped chives with the citrus dressing and spoon a third over the beetroots and orange. Season with salt and pepper. The warm white beans can now be drained before flavouring them with a little of the dressing. Spoon the beetroots, orange segments and beans across four plates, scattering each with salad leaves. Drizzle the remaining dressing between each portion. The fillets of gurnard can now be presented on top of the salads and served.

Serves 4 as a starter
- 2 small or 1 large red peppers
- 225g (8oz) runner beans
- salt and pepper
- 4 × 100g (4oz) skate wing fillets, skinned
- knob of butter, plus more for greasing
- salt and pepper

- 175–225g (6–8oz) chanterelles, cleaned as below, ceps or chestnut mushrooms
- 3 teaspoons balsamic vinegar
- 6 tablespoons *Red pepper oil* (page 183, or the alternative mentioned in the introduction)
- 1 tablespoon chopped chives

For the *beurre blanc* sauce (optional)
- 1 tablespoon white wine vinegar
- 2 tablespoons white wine
- 2 tablespoons single cream
- 50g (2oz) butter
- squeeze of lemon juice
- salt and pepper

Steamed skate with runner beans, chanterelles and sweet red pepper dressing

All of the ingredients mentioned in this recipe title are available during the month of August. The chanterelle wild mushrooms arrive in July and go through to the frosty winter days. With an appealing egg-yolk-yellow colour, when very fresh they almost give off a similar aroma to that of fresh apricots. To clean the chanterelles it's best to scrape the stalks before trimming the base. If possible, I would suggest wiping the mushrooms clean rather than washing them. If they are particularly grubby, then wash gently in a large bowl of water 2–3 times, changing the water each time, and allow to drain well on a kitchen cloth.

The *Red pepper oil* will give you the maximum flavour, but a quick olive oil and balsamic dressing can replace it: simply add 1 teaspoon of the vinegar to 2 tablespoons of olive oil (or multiply these quantities to your required quantity).

Skate is normally cooked on the bone, but for this recipe it's filleted.

Method If you are using the *beurre blanc* sauce, boil the white wine vinegar and white wine together until reduced by two-thirds. Add 3 tablespoons of water and the single cream. Bring to a simmer, then whisk in the butter, adding a squeeze of lemon juice and seasoning with salt and pepper. If making the sauce in advance, follow the method only to the cream stage, adding the remaining ingredients when needed.

The red peppers will eat at their best when skinned. To achieve this, place under a preheated grill, keeping the peppers as close to the heat as possible and cooking until almost burnt. This will ensure the peppers become tender

and their skins will pull away readily. As the peppers colour, turn until completely coloured and tender. Remove from the heat and leave to one side until just warm enough to handle. The skins can now be easily removed, then split the peppers in half lengthwise. Remove the stalk and seeds then cut into 1cm (½in) dice. Save any pepper juices to add them to the finished dressing.

Top and tail the runner beans, pulling away any side strings attached. Cut the beans at an angle into 7–8cm (3in) long thin strips. Pre-cook in boiling salted water. Once brought back to the boil, the beans will take just a minute to cook. If they are coarser runner beans rather than the flat variety, however, they may well take 2–3 minutes. Strain and leave to one side. For this particular dish it's best to serve them just warm.

Place the skate fillets on buttered and seasoned greaseproof paper. Season the fillets with a pinch of salt then place in a steamer over rapidly simmering water. Cover with a lid and cook for 6–8 minutes until tender to the touch.

While the fish is cooking, melt the knob of butter in a large frying pan. Once bubbling, add the chanterelles. These will now just take a few minutes to fry. Season with salt and pepper.

Place the warm runner beans and chanterelles in a bowl with the sweet peppers. Mix the balsamic vinegar and red pepper oil and add 2–3 tablespoons to the beans. Stir together carefully then spoon onto plates and drizzle the remaining dressing around. Place the skate on top. Sprinkle the chopped chives over or add to the warmed *beurre blanc* sauce and spoon over the fish to serve.

Serves 4 as a main course

- 4 × 175g (6oz) skinless chicken breast fillets
- 175g (6oz) podded broad beans
- salt and pepper
- iced water
- 100g (4oz) piece of streaky bacon or diced pancetta
- 2 tablespoons olive oil, plus more for brushing
- 2–3 tablespoons red wine vinegar
- knob of butter
- 100–175g (4–6oz) washed mixed salad leaves, preferably including a bunch of dandelion leaves
- 1 tablespoon chopped chives (optional)

Grilled chicken with a warm bacon and broad bean salad

I often wonder whether old school-dinner memories of trying (and usually being forced) to eat broad beans, still within their grey shells, is the reason so many of us are not so keen on them today. Available from late spring to late summer, when cooked and completely peeled they are a pure sensation to eat.

This salad of broad beans and bacon is a perfect summer accompaniment to chicken. There are many salad leaves available throughout the late spring and summer months; one in particular I do like to include in this recipe is dandelion. Known as *piss-en-lit* in France, its long thin leaves, ranging in colour from white to yellow and green, have a similar flavour to rocket, and do seem to work and eat so well with bacon.

Method Place the chicken breasts between sheets of cling film and flatten a little. These will now hold their shape while cooking. Refrigerate until needed.

To cook the broad beans, plunge them into a pan of rapidly boiling salted water and cook for 1–2 minutes if small and up to 5 minutes for larger ones. Once tender, lift them from the pan and drop into iced water. When cold, drain and remove their shells. The beans can be prepared to this stage a few hours in advance and refrigerated until needed.

If using bacon, cut it into 5mm (¼in) strips and then again into slices. Heat a dry frying pan or wok and add the bacon or cubes of pancetta. Cook, tossing from time to time, until light golden brown, crispy and rendered of all fat. Strain through a colander, saving the fat. Add the 2 tablespoons of olive oil, and red wine vinegar to taste,

to the fat. Season this dressing with a twist of pepper.

Brush the chicken breasts with olive oil and season with salt and pepper. These can now be cooked either under a hot grill or on a barbecue, or in a hot frying pan, for just a few minutes on each side. Grilling will obviously produce grill lines, adding an extra bite to the flavour.

While the chicken is cooking, warm the broad beans in a saucepan with the knob of butter and 2 tablespoons of water. Once warm, season with salt and pepper. Mix the broad beans and bacon or pancetta with the salad leaves, adding 2 tablespoons of the dressing. Then either place the chicken breasts on plates and top with the leaves or vice versa. Finish by adding the chopped chives, if using, to the dressing and drizzling it over and around the salad.

- *It's not essential to serve the broad beans rewarmed. They will eat very well just at room temperature.*

- *Soured cream can also be drizzled into and around the salad for a creamier and more piquant finish.*

- *The chicken breasts can be flattened into very thin escalopes for an even quicker cooking time.*

Serves 4 as a main course

- 1 × 1.75kg (4lb) free-range chicken, cut into pieces as below
- salt and pepper, plus a few peppercorns
- 2 tablespoons olive oil
- 1 onion, chopped (optional)
- 1 carrot, chopped (optional)
- 300ml (½pint) white wine
- sprig of thyme (optional)
- 150ml (¼pint) double or whipping cream
- squeeze of lemon juice
- 1 heaped tablespoon mixed chopped herbs (such as chives, parsley, marjoram, tarragon)
- 12 fresh almonds, shelled and split in half (page 156, optional)

For the summer vegetables and herbs

- 100g (4oz) podded peas
- 100g (4oz) podded broad beans
- iced water
- 8 asparagus spears, trimmed of spiky ears and base of stalk
- 12 baby onions, peeled
- pinch of sugar
- 12 baby carrots, peeled leaving 1–2cm (½–¾in) of stalk attached
- 2 knobs of butter

Fricassee of chicken with summer vegetables and fresh almonds

A fricassee is a stew, usually of chicken pieces, cooked in stock with the sauce finished with a touch of cream or butter. This sounds quite rich, and that it can be, but only if the sauce is so reduced and creamy that it becomes sticky and coating, rather than a loose soft finish. The cooking liquor can be a chicken stock, but with this recipe a basic tap stock called water is the one we shall be using, cooking the chicken carcass with the pieces.

Summer vegetables are so sweet in flavour, and here asparagus, broad beans, peas, baby carrots and onions all take part. All of these can be cooked well in advance and added to the dish later. The fresh almonds are a luxury extra, not essential to this dish, but if available do treat yourself to their quite amazing soft sweet bite, so different to the hard dried variety we're used to. And, as I'm sure you've noticed, fresh herbs are also a part of this complete meal. The ingredients list may look extensive, but read on and you'll see it is all quite simple. (Pre-cut chicken pieces can also be used.)

To prepare the chicken for the fricassee is quite a simple operation. The first step is to remove the legs, then separate the drumsticks from the thighs. The breasts can now be removed from the carcass and each split into two pieces.

The carcass can now be cut into four pieces, ready to cook with the meat to create the stock.

Method Season the chicken pieces with salt and pepper. Heat the olive oil in a large flameproof braising pot and fry the chicken pieces on all sides until golden brown. Remove them from the pot and add the chopped carcass, trimmings, onion and carrot, if using. Fry on a medium heat until golden, then add the white wine, thyme, if using, and peppercorns. Bring to the boil and reduce by half. Return the chicken pieces and their juices to the pan, then add 300ml (½pint) of water. Bring to a simmer and cover with a lid. Cook gently on top of the stove, or in an oven preheated to 190°C/375°F/Gas 5 for 20 minutes.

Remove the chicken and carcass pieces from the pot discarding the carcass bones, and keeping the chicken pieces warm to one side. Bring the liquor to the simmer then add the cream and cook for 5–6 minutes before straining through a fine sieve. Check the sauce for seasoning.

The summer vegetables can all be cooked well before cooking the chicken, or while it is braising. Each will be cooked individually to ensure their even tenderness. The peas and beans can simply be cooked separately in boiling salted water, both needing just a few minutes until tender. When cooking either of these vegetables it is best to check as they cook. If not absolutely 'just picked fresh', they may need a little longer in the pan. It is also important to make sure no lid is placed on the pan as they cook, to maintain their rich green colour. Once tender, refresh in iced water. Cut the asparagus spears in half and cook for 2–3 minutes, with 4–5 the absolute maximum, then refresh in iced water.

Place the onions in a saucepan of cold water, bring to the simmer and cook for 10–12 minutes until tender. Strain and keep to one side. Place the baby carrots in a saucepan only just covering with water. Add a pinch of salt, sugar and a knob of butter. Bring to a simmer and cook until tender. Depending on the size of the carrots, this can take 3–10 minutes. Once cooked, lift the carrots from the pan and keep to one side. Boil and reduce the cooking liquor by half. This can be kept and used to reheat the vegetables.

Once the chicken sauce has been finished and the pieces of bird are being kept warm in the oven – pouring any juices collected into the sauce – the vegetables can be warmed. The quickest route is to place all of them in a glass or china dish, season them with salt and pepper, add a knob of butter and then microwave them. The alternative is first to warm the baby onions and carrots in a large pan with the reduced carrot liquor. Place a lid on the pan to create a steam. Once warmed, add the peas, beans and the cut asparagus spears. After a few minutes all will be ready, then add the seasoning and knob of butter.

Arrange the chicken pieces, vegetables and almonds on a large plate or bowl and sprinkle with the chopped herbs. Add a squeeze of lemon juice to the sauce then spoon it over the chicken to complete the dish.

● *It is not essential to feature all of these summer vegetables. The basic fricassee recipe can be made on its own, adding only what's available.*

● *The cream can be totally omitted from this recipe, adding 50g (2oz) of butter to enrich the cooking liquor instead. This will provide you with a loose finish rather than the creamy touch.*

Serves 4 as a main course
- 1 × 1.75kg (4lb) chicken
- salt and twist of pepper
- 2 lemons, halved
- 2–3 sprigs of thyme
- 25g (1oz) butter, plus a knob to finish (optional)
- 2 tablespoons cooking oil

For the pickled aubergines
- 2 medium aubergines
- 2 tablespoons groundnut oil
- 3 tablespoons olive oil
- 2–3 spring onions, thinly sliced
- 3 tablespoons white wine vinegar
- 1 tablespoon caster sugar
- 1 tablespoon soy sauce

For the dressing
- 2 plum tomatoes
- iced water
- 6–8 tablespoons *Red pepper oil* (page 183)
- 1 small red pepper, cut into 5mm (¼in) dice
- 1 tablespoon chopped mixed herbs (such as tarragon, basil, chives, chervil, parsley)

Roast lemon and thyme chicken with pickled aubergines and sweet red pepper dressing

Home-grown aubergines and red peppers are at their best this time of the year. The pickled aubergines can be served hot, warm or cold, each temperature giving them a slightly different flavour.

The roast chicken is just simply roasted, but first stuffed with a summery twist of lemon halves and thyme. As the bird roasts, it is perfumed with the flavours.

Method Preheat the oven to 200°C/400°F/Gas 6. Rinse the insides of the chicken and dry well, also removing any excess fat. Season the insides with salt and pepper, placing the lemon halves and thyme inside.

It is best now to fasten the cavity with cocktail sticks to help the flavour stay within the bird. Brush the outside of the bird with the 25g (1oz) of butter, season with salt and pepper and tie the legs together.

Heat the cooking oil in a roasting tray and lay the bird on its side. Fry on a medium heat for a few minutes until beginning to colour. Turn the bird over on its other side and also colour. Place in the preheated oven and roast for 20 minutes, turn the bird over onto the other breast and continue to roast for another 20 minutes.

The chicken can now be turned onto its back, basted well and roasted for a further 30 minutes. The total cooking time is 1 hour 10 minutes. This will be plenty of cooking time, guaranteeing a succulent finish. Remove from the oven and leave to rest for 10–15 minutes.

While the chicken is roasting, prepare the aubergines. Cut them into 2cm (¾in) dice. Heat the grountnut and olive oils together and, when hot, fry the aubergines until well coloured and only just becoming tender. Stir in the spring onions and remove from the heat. In a large bowl, whisk together the vinegar, sugar and soy sauce. Add the aubergines, mix in well and season with salt and pepper. The pickled aubergines are ready, eating at their best when just warm.

To make the dressing, remove the stalks from the tomatoes, cutting around the edge of the eyes with a small knife until completely free. Blanch the tomatoes in boiling water for 8–10 seconds and refresh in iced water. The skin will now peel away easily. Quarter and seed, pat the wedges dry and cut into 5mm (¼in) dice.

Heat 2 tablespoons of the red pepper oil and gently simmer the diced pepper in this for a few minutes until tender. Remove from the heat and add four more tablespoons of the oil, followed by the diced tomato. Season with salt and pepper. The dressing will now be at room temperature and ready to add the chopped herbs, and remaining oil if a looser consistency is preferred.

Portion the chicken, removing the legs and breasts. Halve each piece, offering half a breast with a thigh or drumstick per portion. Serve with the pickled aubergines, spooning the sweet red pepper dressing over the chicken. A cooked lemon half and sprig of thyme, removed from the bird, can also be used as a garnish. Strain any juices from the roasting tray and carcass into a saucepan and warm through. These can now be finished with the knob of butter, if using, and spooned over or around the chicken.

Serves 4 as a starter or supper dish
- 8 chicken livers
- milk, to cover
- 2 garlic cloves, thinly sliced
- 4 thick slices of granary, brown or white bread
- 2 knobs of butter, plus more for spreading
- 1 tablespoon groundnut or cooking oil
- salt and pepper
- 225g (8oz) chanterelles, cleaned as described on page 134
- 100g (4oz) spinach leaves, torn
- 1 quantity *Basic butter sauce* (page 179, optional)
- 4–6 tablespoons *Sweet port red wine dressing* (page 182, optional)

Sautéed chicken livers with garlic chanterelles and spinach

These wild mushrooms are just very quickly fried in butter with garlic, then served on toast to make quite a memorable starter, lunch snack or supper dish.

The addition of just a few chicken livers cooked to a medium-rare stage – eating almost like *foie gras* if soaked well in milk – creates a fuller dish.

An optional extra to this dish is a spoonful or two of *Sweet port red wine dressing*. This adds a robust red wine punch, sweetened by the port addition. Two flavours that will certainly eat well with both the livers and the chanterelles.

Method This dish is best planned 1–2 days in advance, to provide time in which to soak the livers in milk. I would always suggest a minimum of 24 hours, but 48 hours will help remove more blood from the livers, taking away any bitter flavour and leaving a sweeter and more foie-gras-like texture and taste. Once soaked, drain and rinse the livers under cold water and dry well before cooking.

The sliced garlic cloves can be used in their completely raw state, but to make their flavour a little more mellow, place the slices in cold water and bring to a simmer, then refresh under cold water and repeat the process twice more. Drain and dry on kitchen paper. The garlic flavour will now not overpower the dish or make you unsociable.

Spread the slices of your chosen bread with butter on both sides, then fry them over a moderate heat until golden brown and crisp on each side. Keep warm to one side.

Add the oil to the same pan. Once very hot, add the chicken livers and sauté for 1–2 minutes on each side, keeping them slightly pink. It is important that the pan is very hot for this stage; the livers will then colour and sauté well, and not just poach and stew. When almost cooked, add a small knob of butter and season with salt and pepper. Remove from the pan and keep warm.

After quickly wiping the pan clean, reheat it again, adding another knob of butter. Quickly fry the chanterelles for 1–2 minutes, adding the garlic slices and torn spinach leaves. Season with salt and pepper.

Slice the livers and place on the toasts. Spoon over and around with the garlic chanterelles and the spinach. If including the butter sauce, spoon this over the livers. If using the sweet port red wine dressing, spoon a trickle over and around each portion.

● *If you are not using the dressing or butter sauce, add extra butter to the mushrooms before spooning over the livers.*

● *Wild ceps and chestnut mushrooms can be used instead of the chanterelles.*

Serves 4 as a main course
- 4 large duck breasts
- 2 tablespoons cooking oil

For the compote
- knob of butter
- 2 large (or 3 small) red onions, chopped
- strip of orange peel and juice of 1 orange

- 500g (1¼lb) juicy cherries, halved and pitted
- 2 tablespoons kirsch (optional)
- 100ml (3½fl oz) red wine
- 1 heaped tablespoon morello cherry jam
- salt and pepper

For the vegetables
- 20–24 baby turnips, peeled or scraped, but leaving 1.5cm (½in) stalk attached
- 1 teaspoon white wine vinegar
- squeeze of lemon juice
- 50g (2oz) butter
- 1 teaspoon snipped tarragon leaves

Roast duck breasts with cherry compote and summer turnips

Cherries begin their British season in June, with summer turnips joining them. The two work very well side by side, with the sweet fruit countering the bitter turnips. If available, the duck breasts I suggest for this recipe are the French *magret*, which are quite large and plump. If unavailable, try to buy large breasts as, when off the bone and cooked, they do tend to shrink.

Method To make the compote, melt the knob of butter in a shallow pan. Once bubbling, add the red onions and cook on a reasonably fast heat for 4–5 minutes, until the onions have taken on a slight colour and are softening. Add the orange peel and juice. Continue to cook until almost dry. Add the cherries and, after just 30 seconds, flambé with the kirsch, if using. Add the red wine and cook for 2 minutes until the cherries have softened. Strain over a clean saucepan. Reduce the strained red wine liquor by two-thirds, then add the cherry jam, which will sweeten and thicken the liquor. Return the cherries and red onions to the pan and season with salt and pepper, stirring well. Remove from the heat until needed. The compote should now have a loose jam-like consistency, with the cherries still maintaining their shape.

Preheat the oven to 200°C/400°F/Gas 6. To cook the duck breasts, score the skin sides with a sharp knife in close lines from side to side to help release excess fat and produce a crispier skin. Season with salt and pepper on both sides of the breasts. Heat the cooking oil in an ovenproof frying pan or roasting tin. Once just warm, place the breasts in the pan, skin-side down.

Fry slowly for 8–10 minutes. During this time a lot of excess fat will be released, with the skin itself becoming crispy. If possible, pour away the fat before turning the breasts in the pan and finishing them in the preheated oven for a further 5–6 minutes for a pink finish or 10–12 for well done. Remove the breasts from the pan and allow to relax for 6–7 minutes.

The turnips can be cooked while the duck is frying. Place them in boiling salted water and cook uncovered, until tender. This will depend on the size of the vegetables: if they are small baby ones as listed, 6–7 minutes with a maximum of 12–15 will be plenty. To finish the turnips, in another pan boil together 4 tablespoons of water and the white wine vinegar, and reduce by just a third. Add a squeeze of lemon juice, and whisk in the butter. Season with salt and pepper, then add the tarragon just before serving.

To serve the dish, carve the duck breasts into 5mm (¼in) slices. Spoon the cherry compote onto plates and top each portion with a duck breast. Place five or six turnips next to the duck and spoon the tarragon butter sauce over before serving.

Serves 4

- 2 oven-ready ducklings, each approximately 1.5kg (3¼lb)
- salt and pepper, plus coarse sea salt
- 450g–675g (1–1½lb) new potatoes
- 1 tablespoon roughly chopped parsley

For the gooseberry and marjoram onions

- knob of butter
- 225g (8oz) onions, finely chopped
- 225g (8oz) gooseberries, topped and tailed
- juice and finely grated zest of 1 lime
- 1 tablespoon caster sugar
- 1 heaped teaspoon marjoram

For the salad

- 2–3 medium beetroots (or 6 baby beetroots), cooked and peeled (method, page 132)
- 4 tablespoons olive oil
- 2 tablespoons red wine vinegar
- 1 teaspoon clear honey
- 1 tablespoon finely chopped shallot
- 100–175g (4–6oz) mixed salad leaves
- 2 tablespoons soured cream (optional)

Duckling with gooseberry and marjoram onions and beetroot salad

This recipe produces two courses. The first consists of the roast duck breasts with gooseberries, accompanied by duck-fried new potatoes. The second course is a beetroot salad, topped with the twice-roasted duck legs. This way of serving duck is quite classic in France, the breasts cooked beautifully pink with the legs returned to the oven for a well-done finish. Here the duck breasts are more well done, with the moist fresh gooseberry and marjoram onions to accompany them. You'll notice that two ducks are needed for four portions, but these are the smaller ducklings rather than the usual 'six-pounders'.

Method For the first course, preheat the oven to 220°C/425°F/Gas 7. To help release the excess fat from the ducks, score each breast five or six times with a sharp knife. Season with coarse sea salt and pepper. If possible, place a roasting rack in a large roasting tray and sit the ducks on top. Place in the preheated oven and roast for 30 minutes. Reduce the oven temperature to 180°C/350°F/Gas 4 and continue to roast for 2 hours. During the cooking time, a lot of duck fat will collect in the pan.

Every 45 minutes, remove the ducks from the oven, lift off the rack and pour the excess fat into a bowl. This will be used to fry the potatoes.

To cook the gooseberries, melt the knob of butter and add the chopped onions. Cook for 7–8 minutes until beginning to soften. Add the gooseberries along with the lime zest, juice and sugar. Cook for 10–15 minutes, until the fruits begin to soften. The fruits can now be stirred and broken. Remove from the heat, add the marjoram and season with salt and pepper. The gooseberries are best served warm and can be reheated when needed.

Once the ducks are cooked, remove them from the oven and leave to rest for 15–20 minutes. The last of the fat from the duck roasting tray can be strained.

To cook the new potatoes, place them in a pan of boiling salted water and simmer for 20 minutes until tender, then drain. (These can be cooked in advance, while the duck is roasting, allowing them to cool naturally out of the cooking water.) Peel the potatoes, cutting any of the larger ones in half. Shallow-fry in 2–3 tablespoons of the saved duck fat until light golden brown. Season with salt and pepper and finish with the chopped parsley.

Remove the duck breasts from the carcasses and return the legs, still attached, to the oven. (During the first course, the legs will reheat and continue to roast, ready for the salad.) The breasts can now be presented with the warm gooseberries and duck-fried new potatoes.

For the second-course salad, the beetroots can be cut into wedges, diced or coarsely grated.

To make the dressing, whisk together the olive oil, red wine vinegar and honey. Raw shallots, when added to dressings, are best first rinsed under cold water to release their acidity. Now add them to the dressing and season with salt and pepper. Spoon some of the dressing over the beetroots and mixed salad leaves.

Present the leaves and beetroots on plates and, if using, drizzle with a drop or two of soured cream before finishing with the remaining honey dressing. Remove the duck legs from the carcasses and place one on top of each salad.

Serves 4 as a starter or supper dish

- 4 wood pigeons
- salt and pepper
- 25g (1oz) butter, plus a knob for frying
- 4 chicory heads
- 2 teaspoons caster sugar
- 100g (4oz) spinach leaves, torn into bite-size pieces
- juice of ½ lemon
- 20 cherries, halved and pitted
- 2 tablespoons walnut oil (optional)

For the cherry dressing

- knob of butter
- 3 juniper berries, lightly crushed
- 2 strips of orange peel
- 12 cherries, halved and pitted
- few black peppercorns
- 1 bottle of red wine, preferably claret
- 4 sugar cubes (white or brown)
- splash of red wine vinegar

Caramelized lemon-shredded chicory with roast pigeon and cherry dressing

Slowly caramelized half or whole chicory heads are so good – the finished bitter-sweet, tender flavour eating well with many fish and meats. This caramelizing method is going to be a lot quicker, the chicory first being finely shredded. I've introduced spinach leaves, although they are not essential they do go well with the chicory.

Cherries begin their season in June and have quite a classic relationship with duck dishes, working equally well with smaller birds, such as pigeons. The dressing is an almost sauce-like consistency, made by cooking the pigeon legs and carcasses in lots of red wine with juniper, orange and cherries.

Method Preheat the oven to 200°C/400°F/Gas 6. Remove the legs from the pigeons. The back carcasses beneath the breasts can now be cut away. Trim off the wings. The breasts now sit proudly on the bone ready to be roasted. Refrigerate until needed.

To make the cherry dressing, roughly chop the pigeon legs, back carcasses and wings (it's from these that the dressing will capture its gamey flavour). Melt the knob of butter in a saucepan and add the chopped pigeon pieces. Fry on a fairly rapid heat until well coloured. Add the juniper berries, orange peel, cherry halves, and the black peppercorns. Continue to cook for 5–6 minutes, then add the red wine. Bring to a simmer and allow to reduce to just 300ml (½pint). Strain the wine liquor through a fine sieve or muslin cloth, squeezing all juice from the bones and cherries. Bring back to the boil and reduce to 150ml (¼pint), then add the sugar cubes and stir until dissolved. The gamey wine liquor will now have thickened to a sauce-like syrupy consistency. Now add a little splash of red wine vinegar to add a piquancy to the sweet sauce.

To cook the pigeons, season the breasts with salt and pepper. Melt a knob of butter in a frying or roasting pan. Once bubbling, place the pigeons in, breast-side down, and cook for a few minutes until golden brown. Turn and colour the breasts on the other sides then finish in the preheated oven, breast-sides up, for 10–12 minutes. This will keep the pigeons pink. Remove from the oven and allow to rest for 5–6 minutes.

While the pigeons are cooking, prepare the chicory. Remove any bruised outside leaves and split the heads lengthwise, cutting away any base stalk. Shred the halves very finely. Melt the remaining butter in a frying pan. Once bubbling, add the shredded chicory. Cook on a fast heat for a minute then add the caster sugar. Continue to cook for a further 2–3 minutes until the sugar has dissolved and the chicory is beginning to caramelize gently. Add the spinach leaves. These will be tender within 30 seconds to a minute. Squeeze over the lemon juice and season with salt and pepper.

The cherries should be lightly warmed in a saucepan with just 2 tablespoons of the dressing, to lightly soften just before serving.

Remove the pigeon breasts from the bone, also removing the skins to reveal the moist meat. Divide the chicory between four plates or bowls. The pigeon breasts can now each be cut into two or three slices or left whole before placing on top of the chicory. Spoon the softened cherry halves over and around, finishing with the warm cherry dressing. If using, drizzle with a little walnut oil.

Serves 4 as a generous main course
- 1 short-cut saddle of lamb, weighing approximately 2kg (4½lb)
- salt and pepper
- 2 tablespoons cooking oil

For the beans
- 450g–675g (1–1½lb) young runner beans
- 100g (4oz) piece of streaky bacon or diced pancetta
- 1 onion, finely chopped or sliced
- 100–150ml (3½–7fl oz) crème fraîche or double cream
- knob of butter
- 1 quantity *Sweet port red wine dressing* (page 182)

Roast saddle of lamb with creamed runner beans and bacon

Although we associate lamb with spring, it's wonderful in summer too. The saddle of lamb, along with the best end racks, is among the best prime cuts. The two fillets sitting along the backbone cook beautifully and are so tender they almost melt in the mouth. Short-cut saddles can be bought from the butcher, trimmed and oven-ready. 'Short-cut' means that it is minus the chump end that usually makes a full saddle and so weighs less, is cheaper and has less wastage through trimmings.

The summer's runner beans are cooked and bound in cream with sautéed onion and bacon pieces.

Method Preheat the oven to 200°C/400°F/Gas 6. Season the saddle with salt and pepper. Heat the cooking oil in a roasting tray and lay the saddle on its back in the tray. Cook on a medium heat for at least 8–10 minutes to release the fat and give a crisper finish. Once well coloured, turn the lamb on its side and fry for a further 6–8 minutes until golden, repeating this process and cooking time until completely turned and coloured. At this point there will be a reasonable amount of fat in the tray. Remove the saddle and pour away 90 per cent of the fat. Return the lamb and lay base-side down, then place in the preheated oven and roast for 18–20 minutes for a medium-rare to medium finish (for a very pink medium-rare, cook for only 15 minutes). Remove from the oven and roasting tray, and leave to rest for a minimum of 15 minutes.

While the saddle is cooking, prepare the beans and bacon or pancetta. The actual cooking can be performed while the saddle relaxes, providing the perfect timing for the vegetables to be ready just before serving.

Top and tail the beans, pulling away the strings on either side. Cut the beans at an angle into strips – these can be very fine or 5–10mm (¼–½in) thick.

Cut the bacon pieces into 5mm (¼in) thick slices and then into 5mm (¼in) thick strips. Place the bacon or pancetta in a heated wok or frying pan and cook on a fairly high heat for a few minutes until golden brown. Remove the bacon, leaving in the excess fat. Add the chopped onion to the pan and cook on a moderate heat until softened and beginning to colour. Strain through a sieve to remove any remaining fat.

While the bacon and onions are being fried, plunge the beans into boiling salted water. If cut very fine, once reboiling they will take as little as 1 minute to cook: 2, 3 or a maximum of 5 minutes for thicker cut beans. Drain.

Return the bacon and onion to the pan. Add the cooked beans and season with salt and pepper. Add 100ml (3½fl oz) of crème fraîche or cream for 450g (1lb) of beans or 150ml (¼pint) for 625g (1½lb), along with the knob of butter. Bring to a simmer, stirring in well. Check the seasoning.

Untie the saddle and cut along either side and under the central bone so that the loins simply fall away. You will now have beautiful relaxed loins of lamb ready to be sliced. The two smaller tenderloin fillets found beneath the bone can also be cut away. Slice the loins and present alongside spoonfuls of the creamy runner beans. Drizzle the lamb with a little of the sweet port red wine dressing, which is best served just warm – its flavour cutting the creamy richness of the beans.

Serves 4 as a starter
- ½ large (or 1 small) cauliflower, divided into small florets
- salt (or coarse sea salt) and pepper
- 2–3 tablespoons olive oil
- knob of butter, plus more for the beans
- 175g (6oz) runner beans, finely shredded
- iced water
- 4 × 100–150g (4–5oz) slices of calf's liver
- flour, for dusting
- 175g (6oz) mixed salad leaves
- 1 heaped tablespoon picked mixed herbs (such as sorrel, parsley, wild marjoram, tarragon, basil, etc., optional)

For the dressing
- ½ teaspoon caster sugar
- 1–2 tablespoons balsamic vinegar
- 1 heaped teaspoon Dijon or wholegrain mustard
- 4 tablespoons crème fraîche (or reduced-fat crème fraîche)
- squeeze of lemon juice

Seared calf's liver with roast cauliflower and runner bean salad

This recipe makes four starter portions, providing a good dish to precede a fish main course. Cauliflower and runner beans, in abundance right now, are lifted by the coating of a creamy mustard and balsamic vinegar dressing that also carries a hint of lemon. Lots of herbs can be added, but they are optional.

Method Cook the cauliflower florets in boiling salted water for 3–4 minutes until just tender. Drain and leave to cool naturally, allowing residual moisture to steam off.

Fry the florets in a tablespoon of olive oil until golden brown, finishing by adding a knob of butter to enrich the flavour. Alternatively, cut the raw cauliflower florets into 5mm (¼in) thick slices and fry in the same measures of olive oil and butter for 4–5 minutes on each side. These become beautiful crunchy bite-size pieces that fit into the salad very comfortably amongst the green beans and salad leaves.

To make the dressing, whisk the sugar, vinegar and mustard together, then add the crème fraîche and lemon juice. Season with salt and pepper.

The runner beans can be pre-cooked, blanching them in boiling salted water for 1–3 minutes, depending on their thickness of cut. As with most green vegetables, unless serving them immediately it is best to refresh them in iced water. This will instantly stop the cooking process and retain the maximum colour. The beans can now be served cold or quickly warmed in a little water and butter, or microwaved.

To cook the calf's liver, lightly flour the pieces on both sides and place in a very hot frying pan with a tablespoon or two of olive oil. Sear and cook for just 1–2 minutes on each side for a good pink finish. Season with salt and pepper on both sides.

The salad leaves, runner beans, cauliflower and herbs, if using, can now be mixed with the dressing, presented on plates and topped with the slices of calf's liver.

● *Pan-fried chicken livers, cooked for just 2 minutes on each side, are a good alternative to calf's liver.*

Serves 4 as a main course
- 4 × 175–225g (6–8oz) pork loin fillets, free of all fat and sinew
- salt and pepper
- 25g (1oz) butter, plus a knob for vegetables

- 600ml (1pint) milk
- 2 sprigs of sage
- 2 large onions, sliced
- 225g (8oz) podded broad beans
- 225g (8oz) podded peas
- iced water

For the dressing
- 6 tablespoons olive oil
- 2 tablespoons lemon juice
- finely grated zest of ½ lemon
- 2 teaspoons English mustard powder (heaped teaspoons for a stronger finish)
- pinch of caster sugar
- pinch of salt

Pork loin in milk with soft sage onions, broad beans and peas

The two green vegetables, both available from late spring to late summer, go together so well. Whether it be a hot dish like this or in a good tossed green salad, the soft delicate sweetness of the pea and the meatiness of the broad bean working as one are irresistible.

The pork loin cooked in milk does give the meat a soft, warm finish. Preliminary gentle frying in butter before adding the pork to the warm milk helps give it a tender touch in contrast to the quickly, hot-seared golden brown edge we're used to.

The 'sauce' to accompany this dish is put together with fried onions and some of the milk blitzed to a loose purée, almost a French *soubise*. The peas and beans are finished with a lemon mustard dressing.

Method Season the pork loin fillets with salt and pepper. Melt the measured butter in a frying pan and, once bubbling, add the pork pieces. Cook on a low-to-medium heat, only allowing the pork to take on a little colour. The fillets will almost be poaching. Continue until sealed on all sides, saving the butter in the pan.

While the pork is frying, warm the milk to just below simmering point. Tear four sage leaves from the sprigs and keep to one side. Place the remaining sage, including the stalks, in the milk.

Put the pork loin fillets in the milk, maintaining the same temperature. After 6 minutes, check the pork. If too 'soft' in texture, continue to poach for a further 2–4 minutes for a medium finish. If you prefer pork well done, simply poach for 15–20 minutes.

While the pork is cooking, fry the onions in the fried pork butter. Cook on a medium heat for 6–8 minutes until completely softened and golden brown. Season with salt and pepper.

Once cooked, remove the pork from the milk and keep warm, allowing it to rest for 4–5 minutes. Add 3 tablespoons of the milk to the onions and liquidize to a soft purée. If too thick, add a further 2 tablespoons of milk to soften. This should now be a thick purée sauce consistency. Chop the reserved sage leaves and add to the onions, checking for seasoning with salt and pepper.

The broad beans and peas, if both young and small, can be cooked together in boiling salted water for just 2–3 minutes, then refreshed in iced water, before peeling the broad beans. Should you not be so lucky, I suggest cooking them separately: the beans will take 2–5 minutes, depending on size, and the peas also 2–5 minutes but, if late in their season, they can take up to 12–15 minutes before they are completely tender. To reheat, the two can either be microwaved with a knob of butter, or warmed in a few tablespoons of water, also with a knob of butter, seasoning just before serving.

To make the dressing, mix all of the ingredients together. Once all components are ready, spoon 2–3 tablespoons of the onion purée onto each plate. The pork loins can now be cut into 5–6 slices and laid beside or on top of the purée. Spoon the beans and peas onto the plates, drizzling with the lemon and mustard dressing. This dish is now ready to serve.

**Serves 4–6 as a main course,
8–10 as a starter**

- 4 × pork knuckles (hocks)
- 100g (4oz) streaky bacon
- 1 pig's trotter, split in two
  (optional)
- 1 carrot, peeled
- 2 celery sticks
- 1 onion
- sprig of thyme, plus a sprig for
  garnish (optional)

- sprig of sage
- 1 bay leaf, plus a leaf for garnish
  (optional)
- 6 black peppercorns
- 1.2litres (2pints) *Chicken stock*
  (page 175) or water to cover
- bowl of ice
- ½ packet powdered gelatine or
  2 leaves of gelatine (optional)

For the gooseberry relish
- 1 onion, finely chopped
- 3 strips of lime peel and juice of
  1 lime
- 1 tablespoon white (yellow)
  mustard seeds, lightly crushed
- 1 teaspoon mixed spice
- 200ml (7fl oz) white wine vinegar
- 175g (6oz) caster sugar
- 900g (2lb) gooseberries, topped
  and tailed
- pinch of salt

Jellied knuckle of pork with gooseberry relish

This makes a wonderful al fresco summer dish. It does take several hours of cooking, but needs very little preparation time, and can be made several days in advance.

Gooseberries often join us in late spring and stay with us until mid-summer. This relish recipe is not quite a chutney, but pretty close. I prefer to cook the fruits until very tender, but not classic chutney style to a complete pulp. The touch of mustard seed does lift the flavour, providing a warm fragrant bite, with a nice lime background.

The relish quantities will produce approximately 1kg (2¼lb) of finished relish and, if stored in sterilized jars (page 11), will keep for several weeks. The pig's trotter, as you can see, is purely an optional extra, simply adding extra jelly to the finished dish.

Method Place the pork knuckles, bacon and split pig's trotter, if using, in a large saucepan along with the carrot, celery, onion, thyme, sage, bay leaf and peppercorns and add the chicken stock. (This stock is not essential, but does lift and enhance the overall flavour and jelly finish of the dish.) Now just top up to cover with water. If not using the stock, simply cover completely with water. Place on the heat and bring to a gentle simmer, skimming away any impurities. Partially cover with a lid and continue to cook at this soft simmer for 3 hours.

Once cooked, remove from the heat and allow to stand for 20 minutes, then remove the knuckles and bacon. Strain the stock through a fine sieve, preferably lined with a muslin cloth. Skim away any excess floating fat. This stock can now be reboiled and reduced to approximately 900ml (1½pints). Check a few spoonfuls

in a bowl over ice for setting point. If it does not set, gelatine can be added following the packet instructions.

While the stock is reducing and the pork is still warm, remove and discard the skin. The meat can now be broken into chunky flakes, removing any sinews. The bacon pieces can be broken and added to the pork, but this is purely a matter of personal taste. The bacon can also be eaten separately, broken into a salad to accompany the pork or discarded. Place the meat in a suitable deep dish. Pour over the stock and leave to cool, then cover with cling film and refrigerate until needed. This will now keep well for up to 1 week.

To prepare the relish, place the chopped onion and 6 tablespoons of water in a saucepan and bring to a simmer. Cook gently for 10 minutes until the onion has softened. Add the lime peel and juice, the mustard seeds, mixed spice, vinegar and sugar, and return to a simmer. Cook for a further 5 minutes, then add the gooseberries. Stir the fruits to take on all of the flavours and simmer for 15 minutes until they have become well softened but not totally puréed. Strain the gooseberries, remove and discard the lime peel. Reboil the liquor and reduce by at least three-quarters to a thick syrupy consistency. Lightly press the gooseberries and add any collected juices to the strained liquor pan as it reduces.

Once reduced, add the gooseberries, seasoning with a pinch of salt. The relish can now be served warm or cold, to accompany the jellied knuckles, or many other cold meats and poultry.

A sprig of thyme can be set on top of the jellied knuckles with a fresh bay leaf, as garnish, to serve.

Serves 12 as a starter
- 900g (2lb) pork belly, coarsely minced
- 100g (4oz) pork kidney, coarsely minced
- 175g (6oz) pork fat, coarsely minced
- 12 juniper berries
- 12 black peppercorns
- 1 teaspoon salt
- ¼ teaspoon ground cinnamon
- ¼ teaspoon allspice
- ¼ teaspoon ground mace
- 1¼ teaspoons ground ginger
- 1 teaspoon chopped sage
- 1 teaspoon chopped thyme
- finely grated zest of 1 orange
- 2 garlic cloves, crushed
- 50g (2oz) chopped pistachio nuts (optional)
- 5 tablespoons brandy
- 5 tablespoons whisky
- lard, for greasing, and sealing (optional)

For the cherries and beetroots
- 75g (3oz) dark soft brown sugar
- 2 tablespoons honey
- 175ml (6fl oz) red wine vinegar
- 150ml (¼pint) port or water
- 8 juniper berries (optional)
- 8 black peppercorns (optional)
- ½ stick of cinnamon (optional)
- 450g (1lb) cherries, pitted
- 350g (12oz) fresh uncooked beetroots

Coarse pork pâté with sweet-and-sour cherries and beetroot

This recipe requires some thinking ahead. It's best to order the meats from your butcher ready minced, and if you prefer a fine finish to your pâté ask for fine-cut mince. It is all pork involved here, and although the list does look quite long most of the other ingredients are dry and only need measuring, with no preparation involved. This is a perfect dish for a summer picnic or family gathering, offering at least twelve generous portions. For real fullness of flavour, it is best if allowed to mature for a minimum of two days, preferably three, in advance.

The sweet-and-sour cherries are a separate recipe, with cooked beetroots added when ready to serve. This balances the rich flavour of the liquor as the beets take it on while not being overpowered.

Method If ready-minced meat isn't available, either mince the meats and fat through a medium blade or pass in stages through a food processor until roughly chopped. Place all the meats and pork fat in a large bowl. Crush the juniper berries and peppercorns reasonably finely, then add to the meats along with the salt. Mix all together well, then add all of the spices, chopped herbs, orange zest, garlic and the pistachios, if using. Mix well again throughout the meats, then add the brandy and whisky. Turn a few times more, then cover and leave to stand for 2–3 hours. This will help the flavours to develop.

Preheat the oven to 160°C/325°F/Gas 3. Grease a 450g (1lb) loaf tin or terrine, or a 25 × 8 × 8-cm (10 × 3 × 3-in) earthenware terrine with lard, then spoon and press in the pâté mix. Cover with a lid and place in a roasting tray. Fill with enough hot water to reach at least halfway to three-quarters of the way up the sides of the container. Bake in the preheated oven for 1½–1¾ hours. Check after 1½ hours, piercing with a skewer; it should come out hot, not just warm. If done, remove from the oven or return for the extra 15 minutes if needed. Remove the terrine from the roasting tray and leave to cool – don't pour away any of the juices. At this point, lay a foil- or cling-film-wrapped piece of wood or cardboard on the pâté and sit a suitable weight on top. This will press the mixture together, preventing too crumbly a finish.

After 1 hour of pressing, pour any escaped juices over the pâté and replace the weight. If possible, it is best to leave the pressed pâté to refrigerate for several hours or overnight. Once completely set, remove the weight and replace the lid and cling-film the terrine until ready to use. To ensure a longer shelf life, lard can be melted and poured across the pâté. Once set, this prevents any air from entering. Chilled, the fat will pull away easily.

The cherries can be cooked a few days in advance or simply cooked on the day. To prepare them, place the soft brown sugar, honey, red wine vinegar and port or water (the port is not essential but will leave a richer flavour) into a saucepan. If using the juniper berries and peppercorns lightly crush both and tie in muslin cloth. Add to the pan along with the cinnamon, if using. Bring to a simmer and allow to cook gently for 15 minutes. Bring to the boil and add the cherries. After 2 minutes remove from the heat. Strain the cherries from the liquor along with the cinnamon and muslin bag (which can now be discarded). The juices can now be returned to the boil and reduced to a syrup consistency then poured over the cherries. Leave to cool. The cherries can be served cold, but are best at room temperature, or just warmed with the beetroots before serving.

Boil the beetroots until tender. This can take up to an hour, depending on their size. To check, lift a beet from the pan: the skin should pull away easily with the thumb when the beetroots are ready; if not, return to the pan until tender. It's best not to test with a knife as this will only encourage the vegetable to bleed its rich juices. Once cooked, remove the beetroots from the pan and leave to cool before peeling. They can now be cut into 1cm (½in) dice and added to the cherries.

To turn out the terrine, submerge the tin in hot water. This will slightly melt the setting jellies and the pâté should now fall easily onto a chopping board or serving dish. Cut into portions, offering the sweet-and-sour cherries and beetroot apart.

● *The pâté will eat very well with just-pickled gherkins, onions and crusty bread.*

● *Soured cream can be served with the sweet-and-sour cherries and beetroots, drizzling the cream around the pâté along with a flavoured walnut or hazelnut oil. For a hotter finish, add a level teaspoon of Dijon or English mustard to every 4–5 tablespoons of soured cream.*

● *The sweet-and-sour cherry and beetroot flavours make a very nice accompaniment to cheese.*

fruit and puddings

Serves 6 generously
- butter, for greasing
- 175–225g (6–8oz) *Puff pastry* (page 185), or *Simple puff pastry* (page 185) or bought variety
- flour, for dusting
- 1 egg, beaten
- 1 heaped teaspoon icing sugar, plus more for dusting
- 450g (1lb) mixed soft summer fruits (such as strawberries, raspberries, blackberries, blackcurrants, blueberries, redcurrants)
- 2 heaped tablespoons caster sugar
- 200ml (7fl oz) *Pastry cream* (page 188)
- 100–150ml (3¼fl oz–¼pint) double cream
- seeds from 1 vanilla pod (optional)

Summer fruit family slice

This summer dessert offers so much for so little. It is simply a combination of baked pastry slices, with lots of our traditional summer berries, creamed together with a soft vanilla spread. The quantities of fruit and pastry cream spread are quite generous, more than will be needed to fill this sweet crispy sandwich. Any extra can be offered separately.

The basic *Pastry cream* recipe will make a larger quantity than required here. The remainder can be kept refrigerated for a few days, finding its way into many more puddings.

The puff pastry used here can be either the *Puff pastry* or *Simple puff pastry* featured on page 185. Bought, frozen puff pastry can also be used.

Method Preheat the oven to 220ºC/425ºF/Gas 7 and lightly butter a large baking tray or line it with baking parchment. Roll out the pastry on a lightly floured surface into a 30 × 24cm (12 × 9½in) rectangle. Carefully roll the pastry around the rolling pin and then unroll it onto the prepared baking tray. Refrigerate, to allow to rest for 20–30 minutes.

Prick the rested pastry with a fork and brush with the beaten egg. Place towards the top of the preheated oven and bake for 20–25 minutes, until lightly risen and golden brown. If still too pale, brush again with egg and bake for an extra minute or two.

Remove the pastry from the oven and carefully cut it lengthwise into two rectangles. For a rich glazed finish, dust each liberally with icing sugar and, very quickly and carefully, lightly caramelize and glaze under a preheated grill. Once coloured, turn the rectangles over and repeat the same process. The crispy pastry strips can now be transferred to a cooling rack.

Place 75g (3oz) of the fruits in a small saucepan with the caster sugar and 3 tablespoons of water. Bring to a simmer and cook for a few minutes, then gently mash with a fork to help release the juices. Strain through a sieve squeezing all flavours from the fruits. (Discard the fruit pulp.) If the juices are too thin, return to a rapid simmer and cook to a syrupy consistency. Keep to one side.

Beat the pastry cream to a smooth consistency then whip the double cream with the vanilla seeds, if using, and the heaped teaspoon of icing sugar to a soft peak consistency. Fold the cream into the softened pastry cream, to taste.

To assemble the slice, place a pastry rectangle on a suitable serving plate or board. Spoon half of the pastry cream or pipe it (using a 1cm/½in plain tube and piping bag) onto the slice. Spoon the remaining fruits on top, without being over-generous and overspreading the cream. Now drizzle a tablespoon or two of syrup over the fruits and top with a little more cream. Place the remaining slice of glazed pastry on top. The summer fruit family slice is now ready to serve. As mentioned above, any fruits and pastry cream left over can be offered separately.

- *An extra dusting of icing sugar can be sprinkled over the top before serving.*

Serves 6

- butter, for greasing
- 225g (8oz) *Sweet shortcrust pastry* (page 184)
- flour, for dusting
- 275g (10oz) blackcurrants, plus more sprigs for garnish (optional)
- 75g (3oz) caster sugar, plus a tablespoon or so for the juice (optional)
- 300ml (½pint) double cream
- 3 eggs
- 100g (4oz) clear honey
- 50g (2oz) ground almonds
- 2 tablespoons ground rice
- icing sugar, for dusting
- 12–16 fresh almonds, for garnish (optional)

Blackcurrant, honey and almond tart

This rich black fruit joins us in June and holds its own throughout the three summer months, often surviving into September. With this tart there is a choice as far as finished presentation is concerned. There's an element of surprise if the fruits are spooned into the pastry case and then topped with the honey almond cream. The alternative is to pre-cook the cream in the case and then top that with the poached fruits. Although the latter shows off the fruits, I do enjoy cooking this dessert with the blackcurrants waiting to be discovered. The tart can then be garnished with sprigs of blackcurrants and, if available, a dozen or more freshly peeled almonds. (These are both optional choices.)

During the summer months, imported fresh almonds are available. These fresh nuts will be found encased in a green velvet jacket. When very young, no inner shell has formed and consequently when cutting through the almond it's purely the kernel that you find. Later in the season the hard shell forms and the nuts need cracking before revealing their kernels. Whichever the case, it's important to blanch and steep the kernels in boiling water for a few minutes, and peel or squeeze away their skins before use. When peeled and eaten raw, the flavour is so totally different from the dried variety we all know. Fresh almonds contain more of the almond oil, giving them a moist soft, almost sweet, finish. They are well worth trying, if available.

Method Preheat the oven to 220°C/425°F/Gas 7 and butter a 20 × 4-cm (8 × 1½-in) flan ring set on a baking sheet. Roll out the pastry on a lightly floured surface into a disc large enough to line the flan ring. The excess pastry can be left hanging over the edge. Prick the base with a fork and refrigerate for at least 30 minutes.

Line the pastry case with greaseproof paper and fill with baking beans or rice and bake blind for 15–20 minutes in the preheated oven. Remove the tart case from the oven and remove the paper and beans. Leave to cool before trimming away the excess pastry.

Place the blackcurrants and 1 tablespoon of the caster sugar in a large saucepan with 2 tablespoons of water. Cook on a low heat for a few minutes until the fruits are only just beginning to soften. Remove from the stove and pour the blackcurrants carefully into a colander. Leave to drain, saving all of the syrupy juices.

Lightly whisk together the double cream, eggs, honey, remaining caster sugar and ground almonds. Sprinkle the ground rice across the base of the tart and then spoon the blackcurrants across the tart base. Pour over the honey and almond cream, and bake in the preheated oven for 25–30 minutes until golden brown and just set. Remove from the oven and leave to rest for 10–15 minutes before removing the flan ring. Dust with icing sugar.

While the tart is baking, boil the blackcurrant juices until reduced to a syrupy consistency, adding more caster sugar if needed. This juice can be drizzled over or around the warm tart portions when served. If using the whole fresh almonds and sprigs of blackcurrants, place these on top of the tart to garnish.

● *Blueberries or blackberries can replace the blackcurrants in this recipe.*

Serves 8–10 generously

- 50g (2oz) butter, melted, plus more for greasing
- 350g (12oz) *Sweet shortcrust pastry* (page 184)
- flour, for dusting
- 100g (4oz) digestive biscuits, crushed to crumbs
- 1 kg (2¼lb) greengages
- 100g (4oz) light soft brown sugar

For the sabayon cream

- 3 egg yolks
- 60g (2¼oz) caster sugar
- seeds from 1 vanilla pod
- 125ml (4fl oz) sweet white wine
- 125ml (4fl oz) double cream

Greengage biscuit tart with wine and vanilla cream

These yellow and green plummy fruits are generally with us for just two months of the year, August and September. I personally feel we just don't see, or use, enough of them. After all, they offer a fuller, juicier and sweeter flavour than almost any of their counterparts. The fruits featured here are baked in a pastry case sprinkled with broken digestive biscuits (ginger snaps can also be used for a spicier finish), hence the recipe title. As the fruits bake gently, caramelizing with the sugar, any juices are collected by the biscuits, preventing the pastry from becoming soggy. The sabayon cream is very much like the Italian zabaglione, but once whisked to its fluffy thick stage it is then continually whisked until cold. It is at this point that whipped cream is added, allowing you then to keep this light 'custard' refrigerated (for up to 24–48 hours) without collapsing.

Method Preheat the oven to 200°C/400°F/Gas 6 and lightly butter a 25-cm (10-in) flan ring set on a baking sheet. Roll out the pastry to approximately 3mm (⅛in) thick on a lightly floured surface and line the flan ring with it, leaving any excess hanging over the edge. Prick the base of the tart case with a fork and refrigerate for 30 minutes.

Before baking, line the chilled pastry case with greaseproof paper and fill with baking beans or rice. Cook in the preheated oven for 20–25 minutes. Remove the paper and beans, return the pastry case to the oven and bake for a further 6–8 minutes. Remove from the oven, leaving the oven switched on. Allow the pastry to cool. Carefully trim off any overhanging edges,

before sprinkling with the biscuit crumbs to cover the base.

Halve and stone the greengages. Place the halves, skin-side up and overlapping, in the tart case, starting with an outside border and continuing, circle by circle, until the centre is reached. Trickle the melted butter over the fruits and then sprinkle with the soft brown sugar. Bake towards the top of the preheated oven for 55–60 minutes. At this point the fruits should be beginning to slightly caramelize, with the pastry also becoming a rich golden brown. Remove from the oven and leave to cool to just a warm stage before removing the ring.

While the tart is baking, make the sabayon cream. Place all the ingredients, except the double cream, in a bowl sitting over a pan of simmering water. Whisk vigorously (this can be made very simple using an electric hand whisk) until at least doubled in volume and holding thick ribbons. This sabayon can now be used as it is, but to turn it into a sabayon cream, and for speed, transfer it to an electric mixer bowl and continue to whisk until cold. The double cream can now be quickly whisked by hand to a soft peak stage, and folded into the cold sabayon. The cream is now ready to serve as an accompaniment to the tart.

● *The biscuit quantity can be halved and replaced with ground almonds for a rich nutty finish. The sweet white wine can also be halved, or completely replaced with amaretto. If using ground almonds in the tart, this becomes the perfect accompaniment.*

Serves 8-10
- 100g (4oz) butter, melted
- 225g (8oz) digestive biscuits, crushed (preferably savoury or wholemeal)

For the filling
- 3 tablespoons cornflour
- 50–100g (2–4oz) caster sugar (less for a more savoury finish)
- 450g (1lb) full-fat soft cream cheese, softened
- 225g (8oz) Stilton or other blue cheese, rind removed and crumbled
- 2 eggs
- 150ml (¼pint) crème fraîche
- 150ml (¼pint) whipping cream

For the compote
- 1kg (2¼lb) greengages, halved and stoned
- finely grated zest of ½ lemon
- 4 tablespoons icing sugar
- juice of 1 lemon
- 1 heaped teaspoon picked thyme leaves

Baked blue cheesecake with warm lemon-and-thyme greengage compote

The blue cheese featured here is the British classic Stilton. There are many others available on the market – Beenleigh Blue, Blue Vinney, Wensleydale and Cashel Blue to name just a few. All of these will work well in this recipe. The greengages become available from August, taking us through to mid autumn. This particular fruit is part of the plum family, regarded by many as the finest of all gages. The touch of lemon and savoury thyme blends with the flavour of the rich fruit, as a perfect accompaniment to the blue cheese. The cheesecake can be served as an alternative dessert.

Method Preheat the oven to 180°C/350°F/Gas 4 and butter a 25-cm (10-in) loose-bottomed cake tin, then line the base with parchment paper. Mix together the crushed digestive biscuits and melted butter. Spoon and press the mix into the prepared cake tin, creating a base for the cheesecake.

To make the filling, mix together the cornflour and caster sugar, then beat in the cream cheese and Stilton. Add and stir in the eggs, followed by the crème fraîche and whipping cream, beating constantly to produce a thick, creamy consistency. Spoon and spread the mix into the biscuit-lined cake tin.

Cover the outside base of the tin with foil and place in a baking tray, filled with 3mm (⅛in) of warm water to help create steam during cooking. Place in the preheated oven and bake for 50 minutes to 1 hour, until the top is just firm to the touch and golden brown.

If not quite ready, continue to bake for a further 10–15 minutes (the cooked cheesecake can be finished under the grill for a deeper colour).

Remove from the oven and leave to cool until just warm before lifting from the tin. It is at this, or room temperature, that the cheesecake will eat at its best. It can, of course, be refrigerated, but then does take on a more solid 'cakey' texture, rather than its warm creamy finish. Increase the oven setting to 190°C/375°F/Gas 5.

While the cheesecake is cooling, make the compote. Place the greengages in a large ovenproof dish or tray, cut-side up. Sprinkle with the lemon zest and icing sugar. Place in the preheated oven and bake for 10–12 minutes. During this cooking time the fruits will become tender (if not very ripe, they may take 12–15, or even 20, minutes), releasing their natural juices which will combine with the sugar to create a greengage syrup. The greengage halves will be soft and tender, still holding their shape.

Remove the fruits from the pan, pouring any syrup into another saucepan. Add the lemon juice to the syrup and bring to the simmer. This acidity will counter the sweetness of the fruits. Add the thyme leaves to the greengages, stirring well, then pour the lemony syrup over the fruits. Mix well and the warm compote is ready to serve with the cheesecake.

Serves 4

- 6 slices of thin-cut white bread (preferably 2–3 days old)
- icing sugar, for dusting
- 20–24 raspberries per portion
- 1 quantity *White chocolate mousse* (page 74)

For the raspberry coulis (optional)

- 100g (4oz) fresh raspberries
- 50g (2oz) icing sugar
- 4 tablespoons of water
- 1–2 teaspoons raspberry jam (optional)

Grilled raspberry Melba stack

This dish is a variation on the French classic, *millefeuille* (thousand leaves), using very thin Melba toasts rather than puff pastry. Melba toast was created by one of the greatest culinary artists known, Auguste Escoffier, who was for many years Executive Chef at the Savoy Hotel, London. A regular visitor to the hotel's restaurant was the great Australian opera singer Dame Nellie Melba. She requested thin toast and the classic Melba toast was born.

The Melba toast featured here takes on a new identity, not being allowed to curl (one of the distinctive features of Melba toast). Instead it is caramelized and crisped between icing sugar and baking trays. Virtually all summer fruits can be used here, but the beauty of raspberries with this particular dish is not only their wonderful texture and flavour, but also that they are so uniform in size the stack stands upright. Raspberries are at their best from July to early September, particularly during August when the Scottish raspberry is probably the best you'll ever taste.

Method Preheat the oven to 180°C/350°F/Gas 4 and line a baking tray with greaseproof paper. Toast the slices of bread, remove the crusts and cut through the width, splitting each into two very thin squares. Scrape away any excess crumbs from the untoasted sides, then cut each slice into a 7–8½cm (3–3½in) disc. Place untoasted-side up on the baking tray, each spot on the tray first being dusted well with icing sugar. Now dust the top of the discs generously. Cover with another sheet of paper and top with a second baking tray. This will prevent the natural curl of Melba toasts when exposed to heat.

Place in the oven and bake for approximately 12 minutes, until dried and with a crisp golden finish. Remove from the oven and transfer the toasts to a cooling rack. These can be made several hours in advance and kept in an airtight container to maintain their crispness. Dust four of the Melba toasts with icing sugar and grill-mark with a heated skewer to create four or five lines, before doing this again at a different angle for a crisscross finish.

To make the raspberry coulis, if using, chop the raspberries and place in a saucepan with the icing sugar and water. Bring to a simmer and cook for 2–3 minutes before liquidizing and pushing through a sieve. A teaspoon or two of raspberry jam can also be added while simmering. This will give the sauce a richer flavour.

Now place the raspberries on the remaining eight Melba toasts, all around the edges, leaving the centres to be generously filled with the chocolate mousse. For this recipe the mousse does not need to be refrigerated until set. Once the double cream has been whipped in, it will be just the right consistency. Spoon a tablespoon or two into each raspberry-surrounded toast. If using the raspberry coulis, this can be spooned into pools on plates, 2 tablespoons per portion, before building the stacks on top, or just offer the sauce separately. If you're not saucing the plates, spoon a teaspoon of the white chocolate mousse onto the centre of each plate. (This creamy base will prevent the stacked dessert from sliding on the plates and quickly becoming the leaning tower of Pisa!) Now place the base layer on top and finish with the remaining layer and marked top.

- *Sweet whipped cream is an option to the mousse.*

Serves 6–8 portions

- 50g (2oz) butter, plus more for greasing and a knob for the gooseberries
- 350g (12oz) *Sweet shortcrust pastry* (page 184)
- flour, for dusting
- 50g (2oz) caster sugar, plus 3 tablespoons for the gooseberries
- finely grated zest and juice of 2 limes
- 2 eggs
- 675g (1½lb) gooseberries, topped and tailed
- icing sugar, for dusting
- whipped or pouring cream (optional)

Gooseberry and lime pastry plate

This is simply a sweet shortcrust pastry disc baked until crispy, spread with fresh lime curd and sweet, softened gooseberries. The pastry base is the plate in the recipe title. It can be cut to a perfect 30cm (12in) circle or left as rolled, in a more rustic fashion. The lime curd can quite easily be omitted from the recipe, leaving just the cooked base and fruits. This would then become a sort of upside-down 'Old English' gooseberry pie.

The lime curd can also be mixed with whipped cream (100ml–150ml/3½ fl oz–¼pint) and offered as an accompaniment.

Method Preheat the oven to 180°C/350°F/Gas 4 and very lightly butter a baking tray or line it with grease-proof paper. Roll out the pastry on a lightly floured surface to a 30cm (12in) circle. Roll the pastry around the rolling pin and transfer it to the prepared baking tray. Prick with a fork and refrigerate for 30 minutes. Bake the pastry for 20–25 minutes, until golden brown. Remove from the oven and allow to cool on a wire rack.

In a small saucepan, warm the 50g (2oz) of butter until softened. Add the 50g (2oz) of caster sugar, lime zest, lime juice and eggs and mix all together well. Place on a moderate heat and whisk continuously until approaching a soft simmer and thickened to a lime curd. Remove the pan from the heat and pour the curd into a chilled bowl. Cover and leave to cool.

Melt the knob of butter in a large saucepan, add the gooseberries and the remaining 3 tablespoons of caster sugar, warming and stirring gently so as to not break the fruits. Cook for a few minutes then add a tablespoon of

water and continue to cook for a further minute or two, until the gooseberries are becoming tender but not breaking down. Remove from the heat and leave to cool.

Carefully spoon the soft fruits into a colander and allow the syrup juices to drain. Once drained, the syrup can be boiled for a few minutes and reduced to a thicker coating consistency.

Spread the lime curd on the pastry plate base, leaving a 1–2cm (½–¾in) border all round. Place the gooseberries on top of the curd, keeping them close together. Before brushing with the syrup, a few burnt baked tinges can be made on the fruits. To achieve this, dust the gooseberries with icing sugar and glaze and colour with a gas gun (page 11). Once coloured, brush with the sweet syrup to glaze, and dust the exposed pastry border with icing sugar.

Whipped or pouring cream make a lovely optional extra to this sharp sweet plate.

- *A teaspoon of elderflower cordial can be added to the gooseberries once they are softened. When boiled and reduced with the natural syrup, this offers that classic combination of the two that's so familiar to so many gooseberry recipes, the elderflower lifting the gooseberry wonderfully.*

- *A really safe method for making the lime curd, without it curdling, is to place all the ingredients – butter, sugar, zest and juice of the limes, and the eggs – into a bowl over simmering water. Stir and cook for 20–30 minutes until thickened, then cool.*

Serves 6

For the gooseberries
- knob of butter
- 900g (2lb) gooseberries, topped and tailed
- 3 heaped tablespoons caster or demerara sugar

For the sabayon
- 3 large egg yolks
- 100ml (3½fl oz) sweet white wine or calvados
- 75g (3oz) caster sugar
- 150ml (¼pint) double cream, lightly whipped

Sabayon-glazed gooseberries

Sweet white wine has been chosen to flavour the sabayon. However, calvados also blends very well offering its appley bite to the small green gooseberries.

Method To prepare the gooseberries, melt the knob of butter in a large saucepan and add the gooseberries and the sugar. Add 2 tablespoons of water and cook for a few minutes until the gooseberries have become tender, but are not totally breaking down. Remove the gooseberries from the pan and drain, collecting any juices. Boil and reduce these to a sweet syrup.

To make the sabayon, place the egg yolks, sweet white wine or calvados and sugar in a bowl and whisk together. Place over a pan of simmering water and whisk vigorously and continuously until the sabayon is thick, creamy and quadrupled in quantity. This can be made much easier by using an electric hand whisk.

Remove the bowl from the heat and continue to whisk until cool. Gently fold in the whipped cream. Spoon the gooseberries into a dish or dishes, then top with the creamy sabayon.

Glaze under a preheated grill to a golden brown. If available, drizzle the dessert with the saved gooseberry syrup. The dessert is best served while the gooseberries are just warm.

● *The sabayon recipe can be used to glaze almost any fruit. Soft summer fruits and fresh apricots, peaches, etc., eat particularly well once glazed.*

- 225g (8oz) gooseberries, topped and tailed
- 1 dessertspoon caster sugar, or more if required
- approximately 150g (5oz) mixed salad leaves
- 4 teaspoons olive oil

For the dressing

- 50g (2oz) Roquefort cheese
- 4 tablespoons single cream
- 2 tablespoons lemon juice
- twist of pepper

Soft gooseberry and Roquefort salad

This recipe is literally a tossed salad consisting of the two main ingredients – gooseberries and Roquefort – held together by mixed leaves and one or two helping hands within the dressing. As an accompaniment to a summer salad table or a sweet-and-savoury dessert, these distinctive flavours blend very well. Freshly carved ham welcomes this recipe to its plate, or perhaps mix tender Parma ham or crisply grilled strips of bacon into the salad as an alternative.

Method Place the gooseberries in a saucepan, with 3 tablespoons of water and the dessertspoon of sugar. Cook gently over a low heat until the fruits have become tender but not puréed. Taste for sweetness. One dessertspoon of sugar may well have been enough; if the fruits are still too tart, add a little more, stirring it in to dissolve until the preferred flavour is obtained. Leave to cool. The gooseberries are best served at room temperature.

To make the dressing, mash or blitz the Roquefort in a small food processor, adding the cream, lemon juice and a good twist of pepper. Salt will not be needed in this recipe; the salty Roquefort provides this part of the seasoning.

To finish the salad, mix the leaves with some of the softened berries, binding all of the flavours with the Roquefort cream. Divide between plates or bowls and serve, drizzling each with a teaspoon of olive oil.

Alternatively, spoon the softened gooseberries between the plates or bowls, mix the salad leaves with the Roquefort cream and sit them on top of the fruit. The olive oil can now be drizzled around each serving.

Serves 4

- 8–10 fresh figs
- 40g (1½oz) butter
- 1 vanilla pod, split in two
- ½ teaspoon freshly grated nutmeg
- 2 tablespoons caster sugar
- 4 small sprigs of rosemary (optional)
- 2–3 tablespoons olive oil
- 4 thick oval slices of French stick (approximately 10cm/4in long)
- 175–225g (6–8oz) triple-cream cheese (either Brillat Savarin, Explorateur or Boursin), cut into 8 slices and at room temperature

Roast figs on toast with triple-cream cheese

For this dish, which serves as a starter or a pudding, the triple-cream cheeses listed are nothing like the soft cream cheeses used making cheesecakes. All of the cheeses suggested are rich French cheeses with a fat content of at least 75 per cent, mostly found all year round, and many are available from delicatessens and supermarkets. Brillat Savarin has a buttery texture with a milky slightly sour flavour. Explorateur, although soft, has quite a firm texture with a mild but very creamy taste. Boursin can be found plain or with a variety of savoury flavourings. Soft Brie can also be used in this recipe.

Method Preheat the oven to 200°C/400°F/Gas 6. Trim the stalks from the figs and split each fig in two. Grease an ovenproof dish with half the butter. Place the figs in the dish, cut-sides up. Scrape the vanilla seeds from the split vanilla pod and mix them with the remaining butter. Dot the spiced butter over the figs and sprinkle with the grated nutmeg followed by the sugar. Split each of the empty vanilla pod halves into two strips, lengthwise, and keep to one side.

If including the rosemary, place the sprigs in a small pan with the olive oil and bring to a simmer. Remove from the heat and leave to infuse.

Bake the figs in the preheated oven for 15–20 minutes, until softened and syrupy. Remove from the oven.

Brush the French bread slices with some of the rosemary-infused or natural olive oil on both sides. These can now be baked in the oven along with the figs until golden brown, or can be simply toasted.

To serve, preheat the grill. The warm figs can be presented on the toasts, offering 4–5 halves per portion. Drizzle each portion with any remaining fig syrup juices. Place the cheese slices on top of the figs. These can be served as they are, the warmth of the fruits softening the cheese even more. Alternatively, very lightly melt the cheese over the figs under the preheated grill.

To finish, decorate each serving with a strip of vanilla pod and an infused rosemary sprig, if using, and trickle with olive oil.

- *You can also grill this dish, placing the sliced figs on top of oil-brushed toasts, topping with the sugar and nutmeg, and adding the cheese when the sugar is bubbling and the figs have taken on a little colour. Melt the cheese, as above, and drizzle with olive oil.*

Serves 4–6

- 100g (4oz) caster sugar
- 550g (1¼lb) dark red cherries, pitted
- 100ml (3½fl oz) kirsch

For the vanilla cream
- 150ml (¼pint) double cream
- 25g (1oz) icing sugar
- 1 vanilla pod, split and seeds scraped out

For the pancake variation (makes 10–12 × 15cm/6in pancakes)
- 100g (4oz) plain flour, sifted
- pinch of salt
- 1 egg
- 300ml (½pint) milk
- knob of butter, melted, plus butter for greasing
- vegetable oil
- icing sugar, for dusting

For the lemon syrup (optional)
- finely grated zest of 2 lemons
- juice of 4 lemons
- 75g (3oz) caster sugar

For the vanilla soufflé variation
- 4 large egg whites
- 4 heaped tablespoons caster sugar
- 8 tablespoons *Pastry cream* (page 188)

Stewed kirsch cherries with vanilla cream or vanilla soufflé pancakes

Fresh cherries – or almost any fruit for that matter – simmered in syrup until tender, allowed to cool and served with thick vanilla cream, are a pure summer delight.

Serving the deep red syrupy fruit with a vanilla soufflé or soufflé pancakes is another experience altogether. Such experiences don't come cheap – you will find yourself spending a little more, time that is, than perhaps you had originally bargained for. But the results are worth every moment.

Should you choose to make the pancakes, the vanilla soufflé recipe will fill 10–12 small pancakes, making two per portion and offering an interesting twist to the recipe. If you don't want the pancakes, the soufflé mix will fill four size-1 ramekins (see notes opposite).

Method Boil 150ml (¼pint) of water with the caster sugar for 5 minutes. Add the pitted cherries and bring the syrup back to the boil and remove from the heat. If the cherries are under-ripe and over-firm, simmer for a minute or two before removing from the heat. Add the kirsch and leave to cool.

Once cold, the cherry syrup can be thickened with some of the fruits. This is not essential, but does add more depth to the overall taste. To do this, strain the cherries through a sieve and pour the syrup into a liquidizer. Add 2–3 tablespoons of the fruits and blend to a purée. For the smoothest of finishes, strain through a fine sieve, then pour back over the fruits. Divide the cherries between glasses and serve; or chill, or even warm them, before offering to your friends.

To make the vanilla cream (*crème Chantilly*), whisk together the cream, icing sugar and vanilla seeds to a thick soft-peak stage. Spoon the cream on top of the cherries or serve separately.

The vanilla pod, rather than being wasted, can be placed in a container of caster sugar. The pod will now infuse its rich flavour into the sugar, giving the granules a vanilla flavour for use in many dishes. The pod halves can also be cut into ultra-thin strips – this can be made easy by simply using a sharp knife and ruler – then laid flat in the sugar. Not only will they infuse it with vanilla, but they will also dry to crisp black sticks for use as a garnish. One stick sitting on top of each portion of cream looks quite stunning and different.

Method for the variation For the pancake alternative, first make the pancakes. Place the flour and a pinch of salt in a bowl and whisk in the egg, milk and melted butter. This batter is quite loose, its consistency helping to make the pancakes thin. Heat a 15-cm (6-in) non-stick pancake pan and trickle in a drop or two of oil. Ladle a thin layer of the batter into the pan and cook on a medium heat for approximately 45–60 seconds, until golden brown. Turn the pancake over and cook for a further minute. Remove the pancake from the pan and place on a greaseproof paper square. Repeat the process, stacking the pancakes between paper squares. Leave to cool. This batter quantity will make 10–12 pancakes.

If making the lemon syrup, bring all the ingredients to a rapid simmer and cook to a syrupy consistency. Strain through a sieve or tea strainer and the syrup is ready. This doesn't make an awful lot, but it is quite powerful so not a lot is needed and just a little drizzle over each pancake gives the dish a new kick.

Preheat the oven to 220°C/425)F/Gas 7. To make the soufflé mix, whisk the egg whites until reaching a soft peak stage. At this point, continually sprinkle in the caster sugar, until just a tablespoon is left. Fold the last spoonful into the stiff-peak meringue. Whisk a third of the meringue into the pastry cream then carefully fold in the rest.

Lay the pancakes on a buttered or greaseproof-prepared baking tray (two trays may be needed). Spoon 2 dessertspoons of soufflé mix onto each pancake, placing the mix slightly towards one side to leave room for the pancake to be carefully folded over. It is important, when folding, to leave the pancake sitting lightly on the soufflé mix. Bake in the preheated oven for 6–8 minutes. The soufflé will now have risen, leaving a soft creamy texture in the centre.

Lift the pancakes carefully with a large spatula or fish slice onto warmed plates, then spoon the stewed cherries (best served warm with this dish) around, drizzling each pancake with lemon syrup, if using. A dusting of icing sugar also adds a nice finishing touch to the pancakes.

● *If making four small ramekin soufflés with no pancakes, as mentioned in the introduction, the ramekins should first have a double layer of greaseproof paper taped around the outside. This will now provide the guide and shape for when the soufflé rises above the rims. It is also important, once the ramekins are surrounded with paper, to butter the insides of the ramekins and the paper collars liberally, dusting well with caster sugar. This will prevent the soufflé from sticking as it rises.*

- butter, for greasing
- flour, for dusting
- 100g (4oz) caster sugar
- 3 tablespoons vegetable oil
- finely grated zest of 2 lemons
- 4 eggs

- 225g (8oz) semolina
- 2 teaspoons baking powder
- 100g (4oz) ground almonds
- 7 tablespoons milk

For the lemon syrup
- 100g (4oz) caster sugar
- juice of 3 lemons

For the blueberries
- 225g (8oz) blueberries
- 50–75g (2–3oz) icing sugar

Soaked lemon semolina wedge with warm blueberries

The soaking process is achieved by spooning a warm lemon syrup over and into the cake. The dense, soft texture happily absorbs the flavour and moistness, producing a very rich result.

Blueberries tend to be with us from July into mid-autumn. Cooked in sugar, lemon juice and water, they soften nicely, becoming very tender partners to this dessert (the cake on its own eats very well with a cup of hot British tea). To finish, extra-thick cream could be served as a first choice with whipped or pouring cream close behind.

Method Preheat the oven to 160°C/325°F/Gas 3 and butter and flour a 20 × 2.5–4-cm (8 × 1–1½-in) cake tin. Mix together the sugar, oil and lemon zest. Beat the eggs together and then pour and whisk into the sugar mixture. Add the semolina and baking powder, mix in well and then add the ground almonds and milk. Pour into the prepared cake tin and bake in the preheated oven for 30–35 minutes until just set. Remove from the oven and leave to rest.

While the cake is baking, make the lemon syrup. Boil together the sugar and 200ml (7fl oz) water for 8–10 minutes. At this point a syrupy consistency should have been reached. Add the lemon juice, return to a rapid simmer and cook for a further few minutes.

Once the warm cake has been allowed to rest for 15 minutes, prick with a knife or fork and spoon the warm syrup over, a little at a time, until all of the syrup has been absorbed. This cake is best served at warm to room temperature.

To prepare the blueberries, place them in a pan with 50g (2oz) of the sugar and 3 tablespoons of water. Warm until the sugar dissolves and the blueberries begin to soften. At this point, if the berries are too tart, add more icing sugar until the right flavour is achieved. If the syrup is too thin, remove the blueberries, return the syrup to the stove and simmer rapidly until reduced to a thicker consistency. Pour back over the blueberries and they are ready to serve with the warm cake.

● *Almost any soft summer fruit or a summer pudding mixture can be used in this recipe.*

● *If available, a splash or two of blueberry liqueur, crème de myrtilles, or crème de cassis (blackcurrant), can be added to the warm fruits or simply used in place of the water for a richer finish.*

Serves 6

- 450g (1lb) mixed soft summer fruits (such as strawberries, raspberries, blackberries, loganberries, redcurrants, blackcurrants etc.)
- 1 tablespoon icing sugar, plus more for dusting
- 225g (8oz) caster sugar
- 4 egg whites
- pinch of salt
- 300g (10½oz) crème fraîche
- fruits for garnish – say a mixture of 1 or 2 strawberry halves, whole raspberries, blackberries, blueberries, plus sprigs of redcurrants and blackcurrants (optional)
- few mint leaves (optional)

Ice summer fruit soufflés

This soufflé cannot fail. It is almost like eating an ice-cream set in soufflé ramekin moulds, but with a much lighter texture. July and August are the best months for this dessert, particularly August, with every soft summer fruit available.

This recipe will fill six 150ml (¼pint) ramekins. To create the risen soufflé effect, cut six strips of parchment paper, long enough to completely wrap around the ramekin moulds with a slight overlap and wide enough to stand 2.5–3cm (1–1¼in) above the rim. The strips can be secured in place with elastic bands or sticky tape. Place the moulds in the freezer, to chill, ready for filling.

Method Wash the 450g (1lb) of fruit and pick over the currants and hull the strawberries. In a liquidizer, blend the fruits to a purée with the tablespoon of icing sugar. For a smooth seedless purée, pass the fruits through a fine sieve. Refrigerate the strained fruit purée.

Place the caster sugar in a saucepan with 8 tablespoons of water and cook over a fairly high heat. The sugar will dissolve, creating a syrup with the water and this needs to be cooked to 120°C/250°F. The easiest way to check the temperature is with a sugar thermometer. If unavailable, once the syrup is producing large bubbles, take a teaspoon and spoon a little of the syrup into a bowl of iced water. If the iced syrup can easily be formed into a small soft ball, the syrup is ready.

While the syrup is boiling, place the egg whites and a pinch of salt in a very clean electric-mixer bowl. Begin to whisk (making sure the whisk is also spotless) at a reasonable speed, increasing the speed when the whites begin to foam. At a firm peak stage, and when the syrup has just reached the required temperature, begin to pour the syrup into the whisking egg whites very steadily and slowly. Once all the syrup is added, continue to whisk until this meringue mixture has cooled.

Mix the fruit purée into the crème fraîche, then fold in the meringue. Spoon the soufflé mix into the frozen moulds, levelling the tops if possible. The soufflés will now need to be frozen for at least 2–3 hours to freeze completely and set. The frozen soufflés are best eaten within 24–48 hours. After this, the fruit flavour will become less pronounced. It is always best to transfer frozen desserts to the fridge for 1–1½ hours before serving. This allows the deep-frozen texture to soften slightly, making the dessert more pleasant to eat.

Before serving, carefully remove the paper and dust each soufflé with icing sugar through a tea strainer. The garnishing fruits can now be arranged on top, along with a small mint leaf or two (whole or finely shredded), if using, dusting once again with just a little more icing sugar. The soufflés are ready to serve.

● *Almond or pistachio* Tuile biscuits *(page 189) make nice accompaniments to offer with the soufflés.*

Serves 4
- 2 × 410g tins of peach halves or slices in syrup
- 32–40 fresh raspberries

For the sorbet
- 200ml (7fl oz) *Stock syrup* (page 187)
- 225g (8oz) raspberries (frozen raspberries are perfect)
- 2–4 tablespoons *crème de framboise* (raspberry liqueur, optional)
- juice of ½ lemon

Peach soup with raspberry sorbet and fruits

Fresh Spanish peaches will normally be with us from the month of May, all through the summer. They will often start quite small, growing to a larger sweet orange-pink ball as summer moves on.

For this recipe, however, I'm using tinned peaches. Tinned fruits, particularly peaches and apricots, should not be ignored. Their soft syruped texture will often adapt to some recipes better than that of fresh fruits.

Peach halves or slices can be used for this recipe; a 410g tin will provide enough fruit and syrup for two portions. Should you ever come across white peaches tinned or in a jar, although more expensive, don't deprive yourself of the experience of their distinctive flavour.

The sorbet recipe will work well with all red and soft fruits. When making an apple or pear sorbet, the fruit quantity is best doubled to appreciate their full flavours. The sorbet recipe can also be doubled.

Method To make the sorbet, bring the stock syrup to the boil and pour it over the 225g (8oz) raspberries. Liquidize to a smooth purée then strain through a sieve to remove all seeds. Leave to cool. If using the *crème de framboise* (if not, no extra syrup is required), add as much as you like, to taste, just before placing the sorbet mix, along with the lemon juice, in an ice-cream machine. Churn for approximately 20 minutes, then transfer to a suitable container and freeze until completely set.

To make the soup, simply liquidize the tinned peaches, including all the syrup, until smooth. To guarantee the smoothest of finishes, push through a fine sieve. The soup can be served chilled or at room temperature.

To serve, divide the soup between four soup plates. Scoop the raspberry sorbet into balls, or scroll it with a warm tablespoon, and place a portion in the centre of each soup. Scatter the fresh raspberries around the sorbet, offering 8–10 fruits per portion, and serve.

- *Freshly shredded mint leaves, one or two per portion, can be sprinkled on top of the fruits and soup before serving.*

- *As an accompaniment, almond* Tuile biscuits *(page 189) offer a crispy nutty bite to enjoy with the sorbet and soup.*

Serves 4

- 450g (1lb) raspberries
- 1 level teaspoon finely grated orange zest
- 3–4 tablespoons champagne
- 1 tablespoon icing sugar, plus more for sprinkling
- 2 tablespoons cointreau

For the vanilla whipped cream

- 1 vanilla pod
- 150ml (¼pint) double or whipping cream, chilled
- 1 heaped tablespoon icing sugar

Cointreau champagne raspberries

These flavoured raspberries, served almost iced, on a hot day provide probably one of the 'coolest' and easiest of desserts.

A spoonful of sweet vanilla whipped cream, made here, or the *Vanilla whipped pastry cream* (page 189), is all that is needed to complete the dish.

Method Blend 100g (4oz) of the raspberries with the orange zest, 3 tablespoons of the champagne and the tablespoon of icing sugar, then strain through a fine sieve. This should now have a fairly loose raspberry-sauce consistency. The extra tablespoon of champagne can now be added for a stronger flavour, if needed. Chill until ready to serve.

Separate the remaining raspberries between four dessert glasses or bowls, then sprinkle each portion with icing sugar and the cointreau. These can now also be refrigerated until needed.

To make the vanilla whipped cream, split the vanilla pod, scraping the seeds from each half. Add the seeds to the cream in a chilled bowl, along with the icing sugar. Whisk to a thick soft-peak stage and the cream is ready to serve. The addition of the icing sugar to the cream will help maintain the creamy consistency for up to 1 hour comfortably, providing it is kept refrigerated.

Just before serving, spoon the champagne raspberry sauce over each bowl of raspberries, offering them with the flavoured whipped cream.

● *Extra icing sugar can be added to the champagne raspberry sauce for a sweeter finish.*

Serves 4
- 4 large oranges
- 450g (1lb) fresh strawberries
- 1 quantity *Cocoa sorbet* (page 78, optional)

For the sorrel syrup
- 300ml (½pint) orange juice
- 100g (4oz) caster sugar
- 10 sorrel leaves

Orange and strawberry salad with sorrel syrup

In summer, fresh oranges have joined us from abroad and British strawberries are in abundance. The two help one another so well, both also eating deliciously with chocolate.

Fresh sorrel syrup is an optional extra: the lemony herb can be omitted from the syrup recipe, perhaps even replacing it with a few mint leaves – another herb that will complement. Fresh sorrel can be used in a lot of dessert recipes. The herb's lemony flavour makes strawberries a perfect combination with orange and chocolate. It's not really important to include the *Cocoa sorbet* here; it's purely an extra idea to try. The fruit salad itself is clean, crisp and refreshing on its own.

Method With a sharp knife, top and tail the oranges, and peel, cutting away all the surrounding zest and pith to leave you with a clean fruit, ready to segment. Cut away the individual segments.

Remove the stems from the strawberries. These can now be halved, cut into quarters or sliced according to their size.

To make the syrup, pour the orange juice and caster sugar into a saucepan, along with 50–75g (2–3oz) of the strawberries and six shredded sorrel leaves. Bring to a simmer and cook for 15 minutes, until the strawberries are puréeing, and the syrup is reduced by a third. The syrup will now have reached a coating consistency. Push through a sieve for a smooth orangey-pink glossy finish.

The remaining strawberries and the orange segments can now be arranged in bowls casually, or overlapping in a circle, before spooning over the syrup. If serving the cocoa sorbet, or any particular ice-cream, scroll it with a warm tablespoon or scoop it into balls and place these in the centres of the bowls. The last remaining sorrel leaves can now also be finely shredded, and the strands sprinkled around the salad.

basics

Stocks

Instant stock

This stock can so easily become totally artificial and overpowering, spoiling the natural flavours of ingredients it is meant to be enhancing. A pinch of stock cube gives a rich cooking liquor, rather than a thick, totally artificial, deep brown gravy, and is very convenient when time is short.

This recipe can also be used simply to replace any stock required in a recipe, whether it be a soup, cream sauce or a stew. I would stress, however, that a fresh home-made stock cannot be beaten. The best stock cubes to use for this recipe, whether it be chicken, beef, lamb or fish, are those rectangular ones with a thicker paste-like texture, rather than the crumbly blocks.

Makes 300ml (½pint)
- 300ml (½pint) water (natural mineral water can be used if preferred)
- ⅛th stock cube

Method If using the stock immediately, boil the water in a saucepan and whisk in the stock cube piece. Simmer for a minute or two. This tends to clarify the liquor, leaving a clearer stock. Strain through a muslin cloth or fine tea strainer for the clearest of finishes. For roast gravies and cream sauces, just add the water when required, stirring in the broken cube piece. Once the gravy or sauce is complete, strain and serve.

Chicken stock

Chicken stock is one of the most important bases in the professional and domestic kitchen. It is used for most soups and white cream sauces. There are two methods for making this recipe, each offering a different finish: one is a clear white stock, used in most soups and cream sauces; and the other a dark chicken stock, which is preferred when making stews, casseroles, sautés and fricassees. If making the dark variety the chicken wings and carcasses should first be cut relatively small then fried or roasted to a rich deep golden brown. While the chicken is colouring, the vegetables are also coloured in the stock pan, frying them in a knob of butter. The golden touch will offer again a different taste to the end result.

Chicken wings and carcasses are listed in the ingredients. Chicken wings would be my first choice, as these obviously contain a quantity of meat to give the stock more flavour. They are, at the same time, more expensive, so a combination of both, bones included, will still work very well. An alternative method to making a good white stock is to use a whole boiling fowl, cooked with all of the vegetables. After 2–3 hours of boiling/poaching, the chicken has flavoured the water, also carrying the bonus of being able to be eaten. This recipe produces large quantities, but these can be halved to make approximately 1.25 litres (2pints) of finished stock. However, bearing in mind the cooking time required, making one large pot provides enough finished stock to freeze, saving a lot of time with future recipes.

Makes 2.25 litres (4pints)
- 2 onions, chopped
- 2 celery sticks, chopped
- 2 leeks, chopped
- 25g (1oz) butter
- 1 garlic clove, crushed
- 1 bay leaf
- sprig of thyme
- few black peppercorns
- 1.75kg (4lb) chicken wings and carcasses, chopped
- 3.4 litres (6pints) water

Method In a large stock pot (minimum 5.5 litre/10pint capacity), lightly soften the vegetables in butter, without allowing them to colour. Add the garlic, bay leaf, thyme, peppercorns and chopped wings and carcasses. Cover with the 3.4 litres (6pints) of cold water and bring to a simmer. Allow the stock to simmer, skimming from time to time to remove impurities, for 2 hours, then strain through a fine sieve.

The stock is now ready to use, or allow to cool and refrigerate until needed. The stock can also be frozen in quantities, and will keep frozen for 3 months.

Court-bouillon

This may seem quite a large recipe, but this quantity will be needed if making the *Warm spider crab linguine* (page 52), for example. As well as most shellfish, lobsters, langoustines, mussels, etc., court-bouillon can also be used for poaching – fish, salmon and trout being the most usual.

The quantities listed can easily be halved or even quartered for just 900ml–1.25litres (1½–2pints) of finished liquor.

Makes about 4 litres (7 pints)
- 2 carrots, sliced
- 2 onions, halved and sliced
- 2 celery sticks, sliced
- 2 garlic cloves, sliced
- 25g (1oz) peeled fresh root ginger, roughly sliced
- 1 teaspoon fennel seeds
- 1 teaspoon white peppercorns
- 2 star anise
- 2 tablespoons sea salt
- generous bouquet garni of tarragon leaves, bay leaf and thyme, tied in muslin or a strip of leek
- juice of 2 lemons
- peeled zest of 1 orange
- 4 litres (7pints) water
- 500ml (18fl oz) white wine
- 150ml (¼pint) white wine vinegar

Method Place all of the ingredients, bar the white wine and white wine vinegar, in a large saucepan with 4 litres (7pints) of water. Bring to a simmer and cook for 20 minutes. (If the wine and vinegar are added before the vegetables have cooked, their acidity reacts with the vegetables, not allowing them to share and spread their flavours, and it takes almost double the cooking time to tenderize them.) After 20 minutes, add the wine and vinegar, return to a simmer and cook for a further 5 minutes. The court-bouillon is now ready to use.

● *The white wine vinegar can be omitted for a lighter and less piquant finish.*

Fish stock

To make a good fish stock, the bones of white fish – turbot and sole in particular – should always be used. These give a good flavour, a clear jelly-like finish and do not have an oily texture. A friendly fishmonger will help you out by providing the bones. This stock is perfect for poaching and for making fish soups and sauces. The quantities given here can be doubled, providing a larger quantity to freeze. Frozen stock has a 3-month shelf life.

Makes about 900ml–1.25 litres (1½–2pints)
- 1 small onion, sliced
- ½ leek, sliced
- 1 celery stick, sliced
- large knob of butter
- few parsley stalks (if available)
- 1 bay leaf
- 6 black peppercorns
- 450g (1lb) fish bones, preferably turbot or sole, washed
- 150ml (¼pint) white wine
- 1.25 litres (2pints) water

Method Sweat the sliced vegetables in the butter, without allowing them to colour. Add the parsley, bay leaf and peppercorns. Chop the fish bones, removing any blood clots left on them. Add to the vegetables and continue to cook for a few minutes. Add the wine and reduce until almost dry. Add the 1.25 litres (2pints) of water and bring to the simmer. Allow to simmer for 20 minutes, then strain through a fine sieve, followed by a muslin cloth, if available, for the clearest of finishes. The stock can now be left, making approximately 1.25 litres (2pints). If tasting a little shallow, reduce by a quarter to 900ml (1½pints) before use. The reduction will increase the overall depth of flavour. The stock is now ready to use, or be stored in the fridge for a few days. Freezing will provide a longer shelf life as mentioned earlier.

Salmon stock

This particular fish stock has its own distinctive flavour of salmon (sea trout also works in this recipe), helped by the natural sweetness of the tomatoes, and bite of the aniseed provided by the fennel and star anise.

Makes 900ml–1.25 litres (1½–2pints)
- 1 salmon carcass (including head and tail), rinsed and chopped
- 1 onion, sliced
- 1 small leek, sliced
- 2 garlic cloves, halved
- 225g (8oz) tomatoes, quartered
- 1 bulb of Florence fennel, sliced
- 150ml (¼pint) white wine
- 150ml (¼pint) dry vermouth, such as Noilly Prat (or more white wine if unavailable)
- sprig of thyme
- 1 celery stick, sliced
- 6 black peppercorns

- pinch of salt
- parsley stalks (if available)
- 1.8 litres (3pints) water

Method Place all the ingredients in a large saucepan and cover with the 1.8 litres (3pints) of water. Bring to a simmer and cook gently for 30 minutes. Strain through a fine sieve, and then through a muslin cloth, if available. Bring the stock to the boil and reduce by a third. If the flavour is a little shallow continue to reduce to approximately 900ml (1½pints). The stock will freeze very well in 150–300ml (¼–½pint) containers.

- *This stock can be used in place of basic* Fish stock *(see opposite) in virtually all fish recipes.*

Vegetable stock

This is a basic recipe, but it can be adapted in any number of ways: simply add or substitute other vegetables or herb flavours for a subtle difference. Never use root vegetables, however, as they will make the stock cloudy.

Makes about 1.25 litres (2pints)
- 225g (8oz) carrots (optional)
- 2 onions
- 4 celery sticks
- 2 leeks, white parts only
- 1 bulb of Florence fennel
- 1–2 courgettes
- 1 tablespoon vegetable oil
- 1 bay leaf
- sprig of thyme
- 1 teaspoon coriander seeds
- 1 teaspoon pink peppercorns
- ½ lemon, sliced
- 1.5 litres (2½pints) water
- pinch of salt

Method Cut all the vegetables roughly into 1cm (½in) dice. Warm the oil in a pan, then add all the diced vegetables, the herbs, coriander seeds, peppercorns and lemon slices. Cook, without colouring, for 8–10 minutes, allowing the vegetables to soften slightly. Add the water with a good pinch of salt and bring to a simmer, then cook without a lid for 30 minutes. The stock can now be strained through a sieve, leaving you with about 1.25 litres (2pints). If there is more, just boil rapidly to reduce.

Sauces

Simple hollandaise sauce

This is a simple version of the French classic, with acidity provided by lemon juice, which replaces the more usual vinegared hollandaise reduction.
This sauce is a real basic and has many variations, some of which I've added in the notes below.

Makes about 200ml (7fl oz)
- 175g (6oz) butter
- 2 egg yolks
- 2 tablespoons warm water
- juice of 1 lemon
- salt
- cayenne or ground white pepper

Method Clarify the butter by melting it until its solids have become separate from the rich yellow oil. Remove from the heat and leave to cool until just warm. The solids will now be at the base of the pan. Any excess solids on top can be skimmed away.

In a bowl, add the egg yolks to the warm water with half of the lemon juice. Whisk over a pan of simmering water to a ribbon stage, until at least doubled in volume, lighter in colour and almost the consistency of softly whipped cream. Remove from the heat and slowly add the clarified butter, whisking vigorously. This will emulsify the butter into the egg-yolk mixture. If the sauce seems too thick and almost sticky while adding the butter,

loosen slightly with another squeeze of lemon juice or water. Season with salt and cayenne or white pepper, and add the remaining lemon juice, if needed, to enrich the total flavour. The sauce is now ready to serve. For a guaranteed smooth, silky finish, strain through a sieve once seasoned.

Keep the sauce in a warm bowl and cover with cling film for up to 1 hour before use. If allowed to cool, the butter sets and the sauce separates when reheated.

Hollandaise sauce can take on a lot more flavours, so here are a few suggestions:
Sauce mousseline *Add 1 or 2 tablespoons of whipped cream before serving.*
Sauce moutarde *Add a teaspoon of Dijon mustard.*
Nutty hollandaise *(or sauce noisette) Melt the butter to a nutbrown stage before cooling slightly and continuing with the hollandaise recipe.*
Sauce maltaise *Replace the lemon juice with the juice of 2–3 blood oranges, reduced to a syrupy consistency, adding the finely grated zest of 1 blood orange to the juices while boiling to tenderize. Add this to a basic hollandaise, to create the sauce maltaise, perfect for serving with grilled duck, game or fish dishes.*

Béarnaise sauce

This French classic can accompany many dishes, such as grilled steaks, lamb chops, fish fillets and more.

Serves 4–6 (about 200ml/7fl oz)
- 2 shallots, finely chopped
- ½ teaspoon crushed black peppercorns
- 1 tablespoon snipped or broken tarragon leaves, with the stalks chopped separately
- 3 tablespoons white wine vinegar
- 2 egg yolks
- 175g (6oz) clarified butter (method for *Simple hollandaise sauce,* see left)
- squeeze of lemon juice
- salt and pepper

Method Combine the chopped shallots, crushed black peppercorns, chopped tarragon stalks and white wine vinegar in a small saucepan. Boil and reduce by half. Leave to cool.

Once cold, mix with the egg yolks and 3 tablespoons of cold water in a bowl over simmering water and whisk until a thick ribbon stage (sabayon) is achieved. Remove the bowl from the pan and ladle in the warm clarified butter slowly, whisking continuously until it has all been added. The mixture will emulsify and thicken.

Add a squeeze of lemon juice and season with salt and pepper before straining through a sieve. Add the snipped tarragon leaves and keep warm.

If *Béarnaise* sauce is allowed to cool, the butter will set, and when spooned on to anything hot the sauce will separate. For this reason, do not make the sauce more than 1 hour in advance. Keep it covered with butter paper or cling film and sit in a warm place so it retains its temperature.

Nutty Béarnaise sauce *To make a nutbrown version of the Béarnaise sauce, don't clarify the butter. Simply heat the unclarified butter to a nutbrown stage. Allow it to cool slightly and continue with the recipe above.*

● *Should the sauce become too thick when adding the clarified butter to the sabayon, slightly loosen with warm water before continuing. An extra egg yolk will give more body to the finished sauce.*

Basic butter sauce

This sauce is better known among chefs as *beurre blanc* (white butter). It is a simple and buttery sauce that works with many fish, meat or vegetarian dishes. The basic ingredients are normally white wine vinegar, water, chopped shallots and butter. I have added a few more to add a lot more flavour. I have also suggested alternative stocks to make this sauce with: your choice depends on which dish you are serving the sauce with.

Makes about 150ml (¼pint)
● 100g (4oz) cold butter, diced
● 1 shallot or ½ small onion, finely chopped
● 1 bay leaf
● ½ star anise (optional)
● 2 cardamom pods (optional)
● 4 tablespoons white wine vinegar
● 6 tablespoons *Chicken stock* (page 175), *Fish stock* (page 176), *Vegetable stock* (page 177), *Instant stock* (page 175) or water
● 2 tablespoons single cream
● salt and pepper
● few drops of lemon juice (optional)

Method Melt a small knob of the butter in a pan and add the shallot or onion, the bay leaf, the star anise and cardamom pods, if using, and a twist of black pepper. Cook for a few minutes, without colouring, until softened. Add the vinegar and reduce by three-quarters. Pour in the stock of your choice and reduce again by half. Add the single cream.

Bring the reduction to a simmer and whisk in the remaining butter a few pieces at a time. Season and strain through a sieve. If the sauce is too thick, loosen it with a few drops of water or lemon juice. The basic butter sauce is now ready to use.

Dressings

Mayonnaise

The basic recipe for mayonnaise is usually made purely with olive oil. However, for many recipes this can be overpowering with its rich finished flavour. For a less strong taste, mixing the olive oil half-and-half with vegetable oil helps balance its richness.

Makes about 300ml (½pint)
- 2 large egg yolks (3 yolks for a richer finish)
- 1 tablespoon white wine vinegar
- 1 teaspoon English or Dijon mustard (optional)
- 300ml (½pint) olive oil (or equal parts olive and vegetable oil)
- 1 teaspoon warm water
- few drops of lemon juice (optional)
- salt and pepper

Method Whisk together the egg yolks, vinegar and mustard. Very slowly add the oil in a steady trickle, whisking continuously. Once all the oil is added, it should have a good rich, thick consistency. If it becomes too thick, and almost gluey at any time, add a teaspoon or two of water to loosen before continuing. Add the teaspoon of warm water and the lemon juice, if using, to set a smooth consistency, then season with salt and pepper. If refrigerated, the mayonnaise will keep for up to 1 week, providing fresh egg yolks have been used.

Basic vinaigrette dressing

This particular dressing is very basic, but has lots of flavours, particularly from the infusion of the fresh basil, tarragon and thyme.

Makes about 600ml (1 pint)
- 300ml (½pint) extra virgin olive oil
- 300ml (½pint) groundnut oil
- 3 tablespoons balsamic vinegar
- bunch of fresh basil
- small bunch of fresh tarragon
- 3–4 sprigs of thyme
- 12 black peppercorns, lightly crushed
- 3 shallots, finely chopped
- 2 garlic cloves, roughly chopped
- 1 bay leaf
- 1 teaspoon coarse sea salt

Method Warm the olive and groundnut oils together. Place all the remaining ingredients in a 750ml (1¼pint) bottle. Pour the oil into the bottle and close with a cork or screw top. For the best results, leave to marinate for a week, which will allow all the flavours to enhance the oils. To help the dressing along, shake the bottle once a day. Taste for seasoning before using. Once marinated, this keeps for several months if refrigerated.

● *This recipe can have its acidity level increased with the addition of extra balsamic vinegar. When doing so, it's best to add a tablespoon at a time, until the required strength of flavour has been obtained. Red wine vinegar can be used in place of balsamic vinegar.*

Quick basic vinaigrette dressing

For a quick basic dressing, mix 1 teaspoon of balsamic vinegar with 2 tablespoons of olive oil. Season with salt and pepper, and the dressing is ready. This recipe can be increased accordingly to suit your recipes.

Vegetable vinaigrette

The vegetable vinaigrette dressing here can be used for most salads. Once all of the vegetables have been added it does take on a completely new character with their freshness and different strength of flavours. An alternative to this chunky oil is to cook everything together, vegetables included, before straining. This provides you with a very full-flavoured vegetable oil, again lending itself to potato, leaf and other salads.

Makes 300ml (½pint)
- 1 tablespoon neat finely diced carrots
- 1 tablespoon neat finely diced celery
- 1 tablespoon neat finely diced onion
- 1 tablespoon neat finely diced fennel
- 1 tablespoon neat finely diced leek
- 1 tablespoon neat finely diced red pepper

- 1–2 small knobs of butter
- 2 tablespoons olive oil (optional)
- salt and pepper

For the vegetable vinaigrette dressing
- 300ml (½pint) olive oil (if too strong, use equal parts olive oil and groundnut or grapeseed oil)
- 4 tablespoons white wine
- 4 tablespoons white wine vinegar
- sliver of orange peel (without pith)
- 1 bay leaf
- sprig of rosemary
- sprig of thyme
- sprig of tarragon
- sprig of parsley
- 1 teaspoon caster sugar
- 1 garlic clove, halved
- 6 black peppercorns
- pinch of salt

Method To make the vegetable vinaigrette dressing, mix all of the ingredients together and bring to a gentle simmer. Cook for 10–15 minutes, then remove from the heat and leave to cool. This dressing can now be refrigerated and left to infuse for several hours, even days, before straining or passing through a fine sieve.

To make the vegetables, blanch all of them, bar the red pepper, individually in boiling water for a minute or two until tender. Leave them to cool naturally once drained. Cook the red pepper in a small knob of butter until softened to help maintain its sweet pepper juices.

Alternatively, you can sauté the vegetables. To do so, warm the olive oil and butter together over a fairly gentle heat. Add the carrots, celery, onion and fennel, stirring, for a few minutes, until approaching tenderness. This can be helped by placing a lid on the pan to create a steamed rather than fried finish. Add the leek and continue to cook for a minute. Cook the red pepper separately in a small knob of butter. Remove the pans from the stove and leave to cool.

The vegetables and peppers can now be added to as much of the vinaigrette as you require. Check for seasoning and it is ready to use.

● *A squeeze of lemon juice can be added or a drop of balsamic vinegar for a more acidic finish. Fresh herbs can also become part of the finished vinaigrette.*

Red wine dressing

This dressing is a sharper, creamier dressing than the *Sweet port red wine dressing* (page 182). For this dressing, a Cabernet Sauvignon red wine vinegar is best as it has a rich, mature flavour. Consequently, less is needed to enhance the dressing. If using a basic red wine vinegar instead, it can be strengthened by adding a few tablespoons of reduced red wine, cooled and added as the last ingredient. White wine vinegar can be used, but I find a good-quality red wine variety works better. Adding the egg yolk

gives a creamy emulsion to the finished dressing, but be sure to refrigerate if using this. The egg yolk can be replaced by store-bought mayonnaise.

Makes about 150ml (¼pint)
- 2 teaspoons Dijon mustard
- 2 tablespoons red wine vinegar (if using Cabernet Sauvignon, add 1½ teaspoons, adding more once finished if preferred)
- 1 egg yolk or 1 tablespoon bought ready-made mayonnaise
- 4 tablespoons walnut oil
- 4 tablespoons groundnut oil
- salt and freshly ground black pepper

Whisk together the mustard, vinegar and egg yolk or mayonnaise. Mix together the two oils and slowly and gradually whisk them into the mustard and vinegar. The oil will emulsify with the base ingredients. Season with salt and pepper and the dressing is ready to use.

● *A simple version, mixing just the vinegar with the oils (pure groundnut or olive oil can be used instead of the walnut and groundnut oil combination offered), can be made omitting the mustard and egg yolk/mayonnaise.*

Sweet port red wine dressing

This dressing is featured in one or two recipes within this book, but I do hope you find other flavours for it to help and lift. Although a vegetarian dressing, it does hold quite a meaty full finish, the depth of the red wine vinegar marrying well with the sweet reduced port.

Finely chopped shallots can also be added to this recipe. If so, it's best first to sweat them in a drop of the oil until tender. This prevents a raw oniony flavour overwhelming everything else.

Makes about 200ml (7fl oz)
- 150ml (¼pint) ruby red port
- 2 tablespoons red wine vinegar
- pinch of icing sugar
- 5 tablespoons olive oil
- 5 tablespoons groundnut or grapeseed oil
- salt and pepper

Method Boil the port to reduce by two-thirds. Remove from the heat and add the red wine vinegar and icing sugar. Stir in the oils and season with salt and pepper. This can now be stored in an airtight jar and kept refrigerated until needed. To appreciate its full flavour, serve at room temperature.

Citrus dressing

This dressing works well with so many salad combinations, helping you through all four seasons.

A simple green salad, boiled beetroot, fennel, asparagus, fish and meat, particularly a duck salad, make great marriages.

Serves 4–6
- juice of 1 orange and finely grated zest of ½ orange
- juice of 1 lemon and finely grated zest of ½ lemon
- 1 tablespoon caster sugar
- 1 teaspoon Dijon mustard (optional)
- 6 tablespoons olive oil
- salt and pepper

Method Place the orange and lemon zest in a small saucepan with the orange juice. Bring to a simmer and allow to reduce by two-thirds. Remove from the heat and allow to cool. Whisk together the lemon juice, sugar and mustard, if using. Whisk the olive oil into the mixture and add the reduced orange juice and zests. Season with salt and pepper and the dressing is ready.

- *If stored in an airtight jar and refrigerated, this dressing will keep well for 2–3 days. This recipe can easily be doubled in volume. If trebling or quadrupling the recipe, only double the grated zests as any more will make it too bitter.*

Oils

Tarragon oil

This oil works well with many fish and chicken dishes, as well as being a good base for salad dressings. Once made, it will keep almost indefinitely if refrigerated. Bunches of tarragon, like most herbs, come in many different sizes. Obviously, a generous bunch, say 50g (2oz), will give you a stronger-flavoured oil.

Makes 150ml (¼pint)
- 150ml (¼pint) olive oil (one-third to a half can be replaced with groundnut oil for a softer flavour)
- bunch of tarragon

Method Tear the tarragon leaves and stalks and place in a small saucepan with the oil. Bring slowly to the simmer and cook for 1–2 minutes without allowing the tarragon to colour. Remove from the heat, place a lid on the pan and leave for several hours to cool and infuse. When ready, push through a sieve, squeezing every bit of flavour from the tarragon. The oil will have taken on a pale green colour with a rich tarragon flavour.

Chive and tarragon oil

This flavoured oil takes on not just the flavours of each herb, but also their rich green colour. For a more piquant finish add a squeeze of lime or lemon juice.

Makes 150ml (¼pint)

- bunch of tarragon
- bunch of chives, roughly chopped
- 100ml (3½fl oz) olive oil
- 3 tablespoons groundnut oil
- salt and pepper

Method Place the tarragon leaves and chopped chives in a liquidizer. Warm the two oils together to just above room temperature, then pour over the herbs. Liquidize then strain through a fine sieve or preferably a muslin cloth. The oil can now be kept in a screw-top jar in the refrigerator until needed. To enjoy the maximum flavour, season with salt and pepper, and serve at room temperature.

Lemon oil

Lemon juice and olive oil together can be the best basic dressing, with the citric acidity blending well and not masking other flavours. A plain green or mixed salad (and also asparagus salad) is perfect when lifted with this easy dressing.

- 2 tablespoons olive oil
- 2 teaspoons lemon juice
- salt and pepper

Mix the oil with the lemon juice and season to taste with salt and pepper. These quantities can be increased to almost any volume to suit your requirements.

Red pepper oil

Red peppers hold a natural sweet edge that is so pleasant as a main feature in a dish, or assisting other flavours.

This recipe provides the latter, a flavoured oil that can be used alone or quickly turned into a vinaigrette with a splash or two of balsamic, white wine or red wine vinegar.

British peppers are available during late summer and early autumn and are not to be missed, with the UK versions carrying a real sweet edge. As we all know, however, this recipe can be followed all year round, with so many other countries presenting peppers to us.

Makes about 175ml (6fl oz)

- 200ml (7fl oz) olive oil
- 2 shallots, finely chopped
- 1 garlic clove, chopped
- 2 red peppers
- 1 dessertspoon tomato purée
- 1 teaspoon caster sugar
- salt and pepper
- sprig of thyme
- sprig of rosemary

Method Warm 3 tablespoons of the olive oil and add the chopped shallots and garlic. Cook for 5–6 minutes, allowing them to begin to soften without allowing them to colour.

While these are cooking, split the red peppers lengthwise and remove the stalks and seeds. Cut the flesh into rough 1cm

(½in) dice and add to the shallots and garlic. Continue to cook for 8–10 minutes and tender.

Add the tomato purée, sugar, salt and pepper, and continue to cook for 5 minutes. Add the herbs and remaining oil, and allow simply to warm in the pan over a low heat for a further 5–6 minutes. Remove from the stove and leave to stand and cool.

Transfer to a clean bowl, cover and leave to infuse in a cool place (the refrigerator if necessary) for 24 hours. The oil can now be strained to release all the flavours from the peppers. It is important not to overpress or you will create a purée. The red pepper oil is ready, seasoning again when needed. If refrigerated this oil can last for several months.

● *The oil and peppers can be liquidized before straining. This will create a puréed oil, holding a thicker consistency, but with a much shorter shelf life and needing to be refrigerated.*

Pastries

Shortcrust and sweet shortcrust pastry

A straightforward plain flour will always work well here. Self-raising is sometimes used but this can create too cakey a texture.

For plain shortcrust, the fat content can be split between butter and lard; the two work well together, giving a good flavour, and the lard really shortens the dough. Sweet shortcrust is best made with butter alone, as lard doesn't help the finished taste. The fats should be cool before using, but not necessarily refrigerated, as this can make crumbing hard work.

Always rest the finished dough for 20–30 minutes. The gluten content in the flour reacts with the liquid (water or milk), giving a better texture to roll and work with. Always roll pastry out on a cool and lightly floured surface. Pastry must remain cold, and the flour will prevent the pastry from sticking.

Makes about 400g (14oz) shortcrust pastry and about 450g (1lb) sweet shortcrust pastry

- 225g (8oz) plain flour
- pinch of salt
- 50g (2oz) butter (100g/4oz if the lard is omitted), diced
- 50g (2oz) lard, diced (optional)
- 1 small egg (optional) or an extra 2–3 tablespoons water or milk
- 2 tablespoons water or milk
- 50–75g (2–3oz) caster or icing sugar (for sweet shortcrust only)

Method Sift the flour with the salt. Rub the butter and lard, if using, into the flour until a breadcrumb texture is achieved. Beat the egg, if using, with the water or milk and work gently into the crumbs to form a smooth dough (if excess crumbs are left in the bowl, add an extra tablespoon of water or milk). Wrap in cling film and allow to relax in the fridge for 20–30 minutes before using.

When needed, remove from the fridge and allow to come to a cool room temperature before rolling.

For the sweet shortcrust pastry, simply add the caster or icing sugar once the breadcrumb stage has been reached, omit the lard and use all butter.

● *The pinch of salt can be omitted from the sweet pastry. The scraped seeds from a vanilla pod added to the pastry mix at its crumb stage will add another flavour, which enhances the taste of many fillings.*

● *Another flavour that works very well in the sweet version is the finely grated zest of 1 lemon.*

● *When lining a flan case or mould, it's best to leave excess pastry hanging over the edge during the cooking time to prevent it from shrinking into the case. Once removed from the oven, gently trim the excess pastry away leaving a neat finish.*

Puff pastry

This is the recipe for puff pastry which uses the classic method. It is more time-consuming than the simple, quicker version (see right), but it rises more evenly and has a good finish.

Makes about 450g (1lb)
- 225g (8oz) butter
- 225g (8oz) plain flour
- pinch of salt
- 150ml (5fl oz) cold water
- few drops of lemon juice

Method Cut off 50g (2oz) of the butter, melt it, then leave it to cool. Leave the rest out to soften.

Sift the flour and salt together into a large bowl and make a well in the centre. Pour the water, lemon juice and cooled melted butter into the well and fold in the flour to make a pliable dough. Wrap in cling film and allow to rest in the fridge for 20 minutes.

On a lightly floured board, roll out the dough on four sides, leaving a lump in the centre. The dough should look like a cross-roads. The remaining butter should have softened to a similar texture to the dough; it should then be easy to roll it without it melting, but not so hard that it will break the pastry. Sit the butter on the centre lump of the dough and fold over each pastry flap. Pat the pastry into a 30 × 15cm (12 × 6in) rectangle and leave this to rest in the fridge for 10–15 minutes.

Roll out the pastry lengthwise to make it double in length to about 60cm (24in), but the same width. Fold in both ends to the centre and then fold once more. This is called a double turn and should be completed a further three times, but each time you roll you need to turn the pastry 90° to maintain an even rising (put the folded edge on the left before rolling and you can't go wrong!). Always roll the pastry out to the same length before making your double turn. It is also important to rest the pastry for a minimum of 30 minutes in the fridge before each rolling. After its final turn the pastry will need a 1-hour refrigerated rest before using.

Simple puff pastry

Making puff pastry in the traditional way cannot be beaten. This recipe, however, is a lot quicker and does bring you very close to it. The resulting pastry can be used in any recipe needing puff pastry. Any not used will freeze very well. Good puff pastry can also be bought.

Makes about 750g (1¾lb)
- 300g (11oz) butter, chilled
- 450g (1lb) plain flour
- 1 teaspoon salt
- 200–225ml (7–8fl oz) cold water

Method Cut the chilled butter into small cubes. Sieve the flour with the salt. Add the butter, gently rubbing into the flour but not totally breaking down. Add the water, mixing to a pliable dough, still with pieces of butter showing. Turn onto a floured surface and roll into a rectangle approximately 45 × 15cm (18 × 6in). Fold the top edge over by one-third and then fold the bottom edge up over it. Leave to rest for 20 minutes. Turn the pastry by 90° and repeat the rolling, folding and resting sequence three times, resting for 1 hour once complete. The pastry is now ready to use.

● *A lemony pastry can be made with the grated zest and juice from a lemon. Follow the recipe, adding only 175–210ml (6–7½fl oz) of liquid, comprised of three parts water to one part juice and zest.*

Extras

Mashed potatoes

These potatoes eat beautifully with almost any dish.

Serves 4–6
- 900g (2lb) large floury potatoes, preferably Maris Piper, peeled and quartered
- salt and pepper
- 75–100g (3–4oz) butter
- 100ml (3½fl oz) milk, or single cream for a richer finish
- freshly grated nutmeg

Method Boil the potatoes in salted water until tender, approximately 20–25 minutes, depending on size. Drain off all the water and replace the lid. Shake the pan vigorously, which will start to break up the boiled potatoes. Add the butter and milk or cream, a little at a time, while mashing the potatoes. Season with salt and pepper and some freshly grated nutmeg, according to taste. The mashed potatoes are now ready to eat.

● *For an even softer creamier finish, the milk or cream quantity can be increased to 150ml (¼pint). Pushing the boiled potatoes through a drum sieve or potato ricer will also create a smoother finish. If using one of these utensils, it is important that the potatoes are sieved while still hot, and mashed while still warm. If left to cool before being mashed, the potatoes can become granular in texture.*

Poached eggs

There are one or two dishes in this book that require poached eggs. I love their consistency, with the soft yolks, once cut, spilling into the other flavours. But there are also one or two secrets concerning the perfect poached egg, and I'm going to share those with you.

A fairly generous quantity of vinegar, up to one-third of the water content, can be added. This helps set the protein of the whites almost instantly around the yolks, without tainting their fresh flavour. It's also very important that the water is deep. This means that the egg will be poaching before reaching the base of the pan and spreading.

Serves 4
- 4 eggs
- malt or white wine vinegar

Method Fill a saucepan with two-thirds water and one-third vinegar; at the very least add a generous quantity of vinegar. Bring to a rapid simmer and whisk vigorously. Crack an egg into the centre and poach for 3–3½ minutes. As the liquid turns, it pulls and sets the white around the yolks, leaving a wonderful round shape. Serve straight away or plunge into iced water to stop the cooking process. Once all the eggs have been poached and cooled, trim off any excess whites to leave perfectly shaped eggs. To reheat, plunge into rapidly simmering water for 1 minute: the eggs are now ready.

● *All four eggs can be poached together, placing one after the other in the centre of the rotating liquid. However, if cooking beforehand and keeping refrigerated in iced water until needed, poach each separately for perfect cooking times.*

Greengage and walnut chutney

It is such a shame that greengages have a short season of just a couple of months. One thing is for sure, it's during mid-August into September that we should take full advantage of this green plum. Jams are an obvious choice, with this recipe following not too far behind.

Fruit chutneys, a sweet-and-sour combination that is found somewhere between jam and pickle, offer a real service to many of our British summer buffets. Cheese is also a very good pal that welcomes these flavours with open arms. The *Baked cheese puffs* (page 94), once broken to reveal their Gruyère-flavoured steam and crust, are more than happy to be helped along with a sharp little kick from this particular chutney.

Makes about 600ml (1pint)
- 150g (5oz) granulated sugar
- 150ml (¼pint) cider vinegar
- ½ onion, finely chopped
- zest and juice of 1 orange
- 1 teaspoon mixed spice
- pinch of salt
- 450g (1lb) greengages, halved and stoned
- 2 apples, peeled and cut into small dice
- 50g (2oz) walnuts, chopped

Method Warm the sugar and vinegar together in a saucepan. Add the chopped onion, orange juice and zest, mixed spice and pinch of salt. Bring to the boil and simmer for 5 minutes. Quarter each greengage half then add them to the saucepan along with the diced apple. Bring back to a simmer and cook for a further 15–20 minutes until the fruits have become tender. Strain the chutney in a large sieve or colander, collecting all of the juices. The liquor can now be returned to the saucepan, and boiled and reduced to a syrupy consistency. Once at this stage the syrup can be mixed through the fruits, adding the walnuts, and the chutney is ready to be placed in sterilized jars (page 11), or simply kept covered and refrigerated until needed. For maximum flavour the chutney is best served at room temperature.

Stock syrup

This recipe can be used for sorbets, poaching fruits and as a base for sweet-flavoured syrups. The quantities listed here will yield approximately 450ml (¾pint) of finished syrup. The recipe can also be halved, providing just enough for a soft sorbet, such as the *Raspberry sorbet* (page 171).

The syrup can be simmered and reduced by a quarter to a third when it's to be used with highly acidic fruits.

Makes 450ml (¾pint)
- 300ml (½pint) water
- 225g (8oz) caster sugar

Method Bring the water and the sugar to the boil. Simmer for 10–15 minutes until the sugar has completely dissolved and thickened the syrup. Allow to cool, and keep refrigerated in an airtight jar, so it does not pick up any other flavours.

Creams and sweet things

Crème Anglaise (custard sauce)

This recipe will give you the tastiest of custard flavours.

Makes 450ml (¾pint)
- 4 egg yolks
- 50g (2oz) caster sugar
- 1 vanilla pod, split (optional)
- 150ml (¼pint) milk
- 150ml (¼pint) double cream

Method Beat the egg yolks and sugar together in a bowl until well blended. Scrape the seeds from inside the vanilla pod, if using, into the milk and cream in a saucepan, add the pod too and bring to the boil. Sit the bowl of egg yolks and sugar over a pan of hot water and whisk, pouring the hot milk and cream slowly into the mixture. As the egg yolks cook, the custard will thicken. Keep stirring until it starts to coat the back of a spoon, then remove the bowl from the heat and the vanilla pod from the custard. Serve warm or cold.

To prevent a skin forming while cooling, cover the custard with greaseproof paper or cling film while it cools, or stir it occasionally.

The custard can be brought back up to heat over a pan of hot water, but it must never boil. If that happens, the sauce will separate.

Pastry cream

This pastry cream is the perfect base for endless fruit tarts: simply blind-bake sweet shortcrust or puff pastry, then spoon in the cream and top with the fruits. The addition of the finely grated zest from 1–2 lemons or oranges gives it a citrus finish. The zest from one of each also works very well, particularly if topping with soft summer fruits.

Kept refrigerated, the pastry cream will maintain its fresh flavour for up to 2–3 days. Once refrigerated it will set very firm, needing to be well beaten before use, particularly if adding extra cream. For a looser consistency, add just 15g (½oz) flour. There is a choice of three flours to choose from when making this recipe. The most classic is plain flour with cornflour close behind. The custard powder creates its own custard and, when used with this recipe, can help provide a richer colour without interfering with the natural flavour.

Makes about 300ml (½pint)
- 300ml (½pint) milk
- 1 vanilla pod, split and seeds scraped out
- 3 large egg yolks
- 75g (3oz) caster sugar
- 25g (1oz) plain flour, cornflour or custard powder (15g/ ½oz for a looser consistency)
- icing sugar, for dusting

Method Heat the milk to a rapid simmer with the vanilla pod and seeds. Whisk together the egg yolks and sugar to a light ribbon consistency. Sieve the flour or custard powder over the egg and stir in well. When boiling, pour the milk into the egg mixture and whisk until completely incorporated. Return the cream to the saucepan, stirring frequently, and bring to a rapid simmer. Cook at this temperature for 2–3 minutes then strain through a sieve into a clean bowl. Dust with icing sugar to prevent the cream from forming a skin. Once cold, the cream is ready to use, or cover with cling film and refrigerate until needed.

● *Before straining the pastry cream, you could add 25g (1oz) of butter along with 3 tablespoons of double cream. The two lift and enrich the finished cream.*

● *If vanilla pods are unavailable, vanilla essence can be used.*

Vanilla whipped pastry cream

This recipe works very well as an accompaniment to any desserts, including fruit-based sweets and tarts, particularly the *Cointreau champagne raspberries* (page 172). The quantities required are quite easy to remember, just whip one part cream to two parts of the chilled pastry cream.

Makes 300–350ml (½pint–12fl oz)
- 200ml (7 fl oz) *Pastry cream* (see opposite)
- ½ vanilla pod, seeds scraped out
- 100ml (3½fl oz) double or whipping cream

Method Beat the pastry cream to a soft creamy consistency. Add the vanilla seeds to the cream and whip to soft peaks. Fold into the pastry cream and serve.

● *A teaspoon of icing sugar can be added to the cream before whisking for a sweeter finish. If vanilla pods are unavailable, vanilla essence can be used.*

Tuile biscuits

These little curved biscuits ('tiles' is the literal translation of the French word *tuile*) can be used to accompany so many desserts, whether as baskets to hold fruits or ice-creams and sorbets, or simply shaped to offer as an extra crispy bite. The best way to shape the tuile paste is to cut a square, circle, triangle, tear drop, leaf or whichever shape you're looking for from the centre of an ice-cream tub lid. It's the remaining space left in the lid that creates the template once the shape has been cut out and discarded. The excess plastic of the template can be trimmed away leaving a 1–1½cm (½–¾in) border. For large biscuits, a 10–12cm (4–5in) diameter lid will be needed. For the smaller, almost petit-four size, 6–8cm (2½–3in) will be plenty. The finished mix will last up to 10 days, if kept refrigerated.

Makes 16–18 large or 30–34 small biscuits
- 2 egg whites
- 75g (3oz) icing sugar
- 50g (2oz) plain flour, sieved
- 50g (2oz) butter, melted

Method Preheat the oven to 200°C/400°F/Gas 6 and line a baking sheet with parchment. Place the egg whites and icing sugar together in a bowl and whisk for 30 seconds, then add the flour. Once well mixed together, stir in

the melted butter to form a paste.

Using a palette knife, spread the mix evenly across the shape in the template, on parchment paper. Now lift the template, leaving the paste shape in place. Repeat the process until the baking sheet is covered. Bake in the preheated oven for 6–8 minutes (10 minutes maximum) until the tuiles are golden brown. Remove the tuiles from the oven and, while still hot, press them to your desired shape.

To shape a tuile into a cup, place the warm biscuit in, or over the outside of, a cup. For a curved shape, lay the biscuits over a rolling pin, or you can split the cardboard centre of a cling-film or kitchen-foil roll lengthwise, line it with parchment paper and lay the tuile inside, presentation-side down. (You can always return the tuiles to the oven for a few seconds to rewarm and resoften them.) Tuiles will keep for up to 48 hours if kept in an airtight container.

● *For a nutty finish, nibbed or flaked almonds, or chopped pistachio nuts, can be sprinkled over the tuiles before cooking.*

● *Lemon or orange zest, from just one fruit, can be added to the mix for a citrusy touch.*

Chocolate shavings and pencils

Chocolate is such a versatile ingredient and one that adapts so well to different textures, consistencies, shapes and sizes. Creating visual garnishes is not a path that I often, if ever, venture down. However, chocolate is an exception! Making large chocolate shavings, perhaps milk or white, to garnish a dark mousse really is not difficult. Not only does it provide a great visual effect, but it also gives another texture and strength of flavour. Chocolate pencils require a little practice but, once mastered, make a spectacular garnish.

For the shavings
These are the simpler of the two.

● 225g (8oz) chocolate block (minimum), to achieve the best scroll effect

Method Remove the chocolate from its packaging and leave it to come to room temperature. If too cold, the chocolate's texture will splinter rather than scroll. Hold a small metal pastry scraper, palette knife or 5cm (2in) diameter cutter at a 30–45° angle on the chocolate. Pull it across the chocolate, not too violently, and the shavings will appear. Continue until all of the chocolate is used. The shavings, as cut, are best placed on a tray or plate as they are made. Once the job is complete, these can be frozen until needed.

For the pencils
To create the best chocolate pencils, a metal pastry scraper will be needed, preferably 10cm (4in) wide to provide the best pencil-like results. It's the undersides of the baking sheets that are going to be used, so it's important that these are well cleaned.

● 2 clean, flat, firm baking sheets
● 100g (4oz) chocolate block

Method Preheat the oven to 50°C/120°F/Gas¼–½ and heat the baking sheets. The chocolate block can now be run slowly up and down the undersides of the baking sheets in even lines. In contact with the warm tray, the chocolate will melt, leaving a thin, even coat covering the tray. Once both trays are coated leave them to cool to set. The refrigerator will obviously be the first and quickest choice, but it's important the chocolate is allowed to return to room temperature before you attempt to pencil it. If the chocolate is too hard, it will crumble rather than roll.

Push the scraper between the chocolate and tray, using a short rapid movement. This will produce a long thin pencil shape. Leave the pencil on the tray, and move 1–2cm (½–¾in) down the chocolate before starting the next.

Once all the chocolate on the trays has been scrolled, refrigerate to set before lifting and placing the pencils in a suitable container and freezing. Because they are so thin they are best used directly from the freezer, defrosting very quickly once placed on the dessert. One or two per portion will be plenty.